FOR BETTER... FOREVER!

FOR BETTER... FOREVER!

A Catholic Guide to Lifelong Marriage

GREGORY K. POPCAK, MSW, LCSW

Our Sunday Visitor Publishing Division
Our Sunday Visitor, Inc.
Huntington, Indiana 46750

ISBN: 0-87973-688-7
LCCCN: 98-67325

Cover design by Tyler Ottinger
PRINTED IN THE UNITED STATES OF AMERICA

688

For Isaiah, whose short life helped me become a better man. And for my children who remain with me. May God grant them many blessed years, may they live in health and happiness, and may they find the love He has for them.

Table of Contents

Acknowledgments

Although it has been my privilege to put these words to paper, I would not have been able to credibly write a single sentence if this book had not already been "written" in the daily life of my marriage. In this all-important sense, I wish to credit my wife as a true coauthor. She has allowed our marriage to be the laboratory for everything in *For Better . . . Forever!* In addition to being a truly good woman, an enviable mother, and a generous lover, she is my best critic, my most astute adviser, and a patient editor. When I look at her, I can only imagine feeling something close to what Joseph must have felt for his wife. To me, she is everything God created woman to be, and I am daily blessed by her loving presence.

I also wish to thank Mike Aquilina, my dear friend, editor of *New Covenant* magazine and de facto agent for this book, who provided me with support, good counsel, excellent resources, and whose writing assignments allowed me to write *For Better . . . Forever!* "on the installment plan."

Likewise, I offer my gratitude to Our Sunday Visitor, Inc., in particular Greg Erlandson, editor in chief, for supporting this project before it was a project, to Jackie Lindsey, acquisitions editor, for her enthusiastic reception, and to Henry O'Brien, managing editor, who did such a fabulous job fine-tuning the text of this book.

Finally, I wish to thank God for every chapter of my life that has been, and those yet to come; the Blessed Mother for her constant intercession; the Church, who nursed me in my youth and continues to be a source of joy, nourishment, and challenge in my adulthood; and my parents, who lovingly led me to all of these.

For better . . . *forever!*

Gregory K. Popcak, MSW, LCSW

Preface

❖ ❖ ❖

Gregory Popcak's *For Better . . . Forever!* is a book about married love. In many concrete ways it helps us to realize what love really is: how dear it is, and how much it costs.

Becoming a great lover — and building with the person dearest to you a love that lasts forever — is no small task.

But love can be made to last, and hearts can become great enough to love generously. What everyone wishes to have from love can be attained. Those who really want to have great lives and a great love, and are willing to do the things that they obviously must do to achieve lasting love, can take possession of what they want.

It is not easy. But every other way of living is tougher. Giving everything to grow in generous love seems demanding, but there is no other way of becoming what every person wants to be.

This is an important book. It will help many couples find the ways to make married love wonderful, and to make it grow with the years.

Mr. Popcak has drawn the advice he gives from many kinds of sources. He knows well the most creative psychologists and sociologists of our time, who have had the courage to tell people what really is needed to make married love last and grow.

He writes also out of the personal experiences in his own life, and the experiences he has shared with a great host of couples in the adventures of marriage counseling. From such experiences he has come to sketch wonderfully well-defined and encouraging ways in which lovers learn how to mount up to the generosity and greatness of heart marriage demands.

He speaks a precious earthly wisdom, and helps us to see how ordinary wisdom is enriched by the sublime but also earthly wisdom of faith.

He also helps us to realize the many ways in which Christ is the great teacher of life and of love. Christ not only shows us, sometimes in astonishingly luminous ways, things we might not have realized about love. But he also gives us the power to live and love without finding it burdensome to give more than we thought we could.

None of us can really be happy unless we find love, and learn to live love generously. Couples everywhere can find in these pages insightful and inspiring helps to live in the ways they most need to live.

Rev. Ronald Lawler, O.F.M. Cap.

Part 1

What Are We Doing Here Anyway?

CHAPTER 1

What's in It for You?

Every married couple wants to live "happily ever after."

The problem is, not too many people know what it takes. This book will show you. *For Better . . . Forever!* integrates cutting-edge psychology with orthodox Christianity in a way that I believe will surprise you, challenge you, and revitalize your marriage.

"Are happily-ever-after marriages even possible?" Much to everyone's surprise, they are, even in the Digital Age. Recent psychological research has identified a group of married couples I call the *Exceptional Seven Percent.* These are couples in first-and-forever marriages (or *Exceptional Marriages*) who report significantly greater-than-average happiness, fulfillment, and longevity. These couples have very different ideas from their less satisfied counterparts toward everything from what they build their marriages around to how they handle conflict, from how they keep love alive to how they maintain the vitality of their marriage though the years. "Well," you're thinking, "bully for them. They were probably born that way."

Survey said *(insert obnoxious buzzer noise here):* "Wrong!" Studies suggest that only two factors set these remarkable couples apart: relationship skills and life experience. This finding is supported by the fact that another seven to eight percent of *second* marriages fall into the *Exceptional* category, bringing the *Exceptional* couples' tally to approximately fifteen percent of all marriages. If these *Exceptional* couples were born to have uncommonly rewarding marriages, then half of them wouldn't have had to get divorced to learn how to do it! The good news is, even if you were not born a "collaborative genius," as Drs. William J.

Lederer and Don D. Jackson of the Palo Alto Mental Research Institute called such a person, you can learn how to become one. And, thanks to this book, you won't have to get divorced to do it. Better still, all of the attitudes and habits practiced by these couples are completely consistent with solid Christian teaching.

For Better . . . Forever! is divided into two main parts to help you achieve a truly fulfilling, long-lasting, Christ-centered marriage.

In the first part of this book (Chapters 1-5), we will be trying to answer the question "What are we doing here anyway?"

What is the one reason for marrying that guarantees the lifelong relevance and success of a marriage? Where does your marriage fall on *The Relationship Pathway* and what do you need to do to become part of the *Exceptional Seven Percent*? How does your Christianity increase your chances of reaching the top of the marital food chain? How can you make sure your love lasts forever? Part 1 answers these questions and more.

Part 2, which covers Chapters 6-11, will show us the "Road to Intimacy."

All of us claim we want intimacy. Do you know what it takes to get it? This section of *For Better . . . Forever!* examines the four qualities that make up marital intimacy and helps you make certain that you have enough of each. Here you will discover how the *Exceptional Seven Percent* are drawn closer together because of their arguments instead of in spite of them. Plus, *For Better . . . Forever!* will expose the real secrets behind a completely *toe-curling, eye-popping, mind-blowing* (and yes, *profoundly* spiritual) *sexuality.* Go figure!

Perhaps you, dear reader, have started to ask yourself: "Who is this guy, anyway?"

My name is Gregory K. Popcak (pronounced POP-chak), MSW, LCSW. I am a Roman Catholic Christian, a marriage and family counselor in private practice, and most importantly to me, I try to live by one motto: "Love God. Love my family. Lead others to do the same." I am not always successful in the pursuit of this ideal, but I seek to live it every day. To this end, I have spent years researching what it takes to have a rewarding marriage and family life, and I am pleased to say that God has blessed me with one of those "exceptional marriages" (not to mention some exceptional children as well). Imagine my relief to find that all that dry psychology stuff I read through the years actually works!

But fortunately, this book is not about me. My goal is to deliver the results of practical research on good marriages by such luminaries in the field as Dr. Judith Wallerstein and Sandra Blakeslee *(The Good Marriage: How and Why Love Lasts)*, Dr. Pepper Schwartz *(Peer Marriage)*, Dr. John

Gottman *(Why Marriages Succeed or Fail: And How You Can Make Yours Last)*, Drs. William J. Lederer and Don D. Jackson *(The Mirages of Marriage)*, Dr. Aaron T. Beck *(Love Is Never Enough: How Couples Can Overcome Misunderstandings, Resolve Conflicts, and Solve Relationship Problems Through Cognitive Therapy)*, and Michele Weiner-Davis *(Divorce Busting: A Revolutionary and Rapid Program for "Staying Together")*.

Moreover, it is my attempt to show you how to integrate such research into the spiritual framework of your Christian life. I mentioned earlier that *For Better . . . Forever!* would combine cutting-edge research with orthodox Christian theology. Although I am a therapist, and I have a theology degree as well, I am not a theologian. To bring you the best of both psychological and theological worlds, I have relied heavily on the writings of such prominent and respected Christian thinkers as John Paul II, William May, Janet Smith, Rev. Richard Hogan, Rev. John LeVoir, John Crosby, Very Rev. Cormac Burke, Rev. Ronald Lawler, and C. S. Lewis, to name but a few.

I have tried to the best of my ability to translate the writings of these great Christian scholars into simple, practical terms. I will leave it to you to decide how well I fulfill my task and, most importantly, I respectfully defer all final judgment of my success to the greater wisdom and teaching authority to our Mother, the Church. With all this in mind, it is my sincerest hope that the information contained within these pages will help both you and your marriage become what God created them to be.

An Impossible Dream

When my wife and I underwent preparation for our marriage, the pastor guiding our experience said a remarkable thing: "I've never lost one of my couples [to divorce]. If you make it past me, I know you'll do just fine."

I would like to make a similar promise to you. It is my prayer that as you read these pages, your life, your faith, and your marriage will be transformed; made meaningful in ways you never thought possible. I know that sounds like a tall order, and it is. Ultimately, you will need to be the judge of how well I fulfill my mission; but from the very beginning I want to let you know that God created you with all the qualities necessary to have a wonderful marriage. This is even more true if you are baptized, confirmed, married, and active in the life of the Church. Why? Because while pagans have to figure love out for themselves, *Christians* are constantly being given the grace to discover what God infused into us at our baptism: traits that predispose us both to perfect love and enviable marriages. I've heard it said that Jesus Christ is "the ultimate meaning of an interpersonal relationship [marriage]." Well, of course he is. He created marriage! If we who follow his example can't have powerful, profoundly loving marriages, then no one can.

Ready to Begin?

You have undoubtedly heard that every Christian is called to evangelize, but what occurs to most of us who hear this is, "If you think I'm gonna stand on some street corner thumpin' a Bible and draggin' people into church by their ears, then you got another think comin'." Frankly, I agree with you, but true Christian evangelization isn't about Bible-thumping; it is about *relationship*. "Look at those Christians. See how they love."

It is my hope that reading this book will in some way help you achieve the kind of marriage that makes people — biased against Christianity in general, and bigoted against the Church in particular — stop and say, "Y'know, I'm not sure I agree with everything I hear about that Church, but if it makes marriages like that . . ."

So, are you ready to shake things up?

Do you want to wake up every morning thrilled to start a new day with your mate?

Do you want to have the kind of marriage that will make the neighbors sick with jealousy? (Of course you do, admit it.)

Do you want to know what God *really* intended when he created marriage?

C
H
A
P
T
E
R

The Secret of Marital Bliss — Revealed!

Why do people get married?

Why do Christians, in particular, get married?

For that matter, why are you married? (Or, if not already married, why are you planning to get married?)

The most common answers are: "For love," "For companionship," or even "For security," and these are fine — to a point. Still, it may surprise you to know that love, companionship, and security are not enough to guarantee the lifelong success and happiness of any marriage, especially a Christian marriage. For example, what holds such a relationship together when a husband goes through an extended period of stress and wakes up morning after morning not feeling particularly loving — or in love? What about the wife who, at a vulnerable point in her marriage, wonders if she hasn't found a "better" companion at work, the gym, or even church? Alternatively, what happens to a marriage built around maintaining security when the couple is tired of settling for "just the basics" of life and longs for more intimacy, more excitement, more joy, or just plain "more"?

The Secret of a Divorce-Proof Marriage

There is only *one reason for marrying* that guarantees the lifelong happiness and relevance of a marriage, only one reason that even comes close to addressing the true meaning of a Christian marriage. More than love and companionship, the real function of a Christian marriage is *for a husband and wife to help each other become the people God created them to be.*

God didn't go to all the trouble of instituting the sacrament of matrimony just so that he could bless your guaranteed date for bowling night. The real dignity of your Christian marriage comes from promising to spend every single day of your lives discovering and fulfilling your identities in Christ. In other words, marriage is a partnership in actualizing your Christian destiny.

Scripture tells us that "whether we live or whether we die, we are the Lord's" (Rom 14:8). Through marriage, God gives each one of us a sacred trust; to prepare our mate to spend eternity in heaven with *him*. This is what that nice-sounding phrase exhorting husbands and wives to be Christ to one another means. In essence, God says to every person who marries in the Church, "*I am choosing you* to play a central role in your partner's sanctification. He or she may not make it without you. Be sure that your spouse makes it with you."

This responsibility should not come as a huge surprise to you; after all, sanctification is the chief work of any sacrament. When you marry in the Church, you are not simply saying, "We love each other." Or, "We're best friends." Or even, "We are really hot for each other." *Of course* all of these should be true. But even more importantly, when you marry in the Church, you are acknowledging that from now until the day you die, *God has made you responsible*, second only to the saving work of Jesus Christ and your partner's free will, to see that your husband or wife becomes the person God created him or her to be. And, you are acknowledging that you sincerely believe you have a better chance, with your partner than without him,* of becoming all God intends *you* to be. As one Protestant minister's wife said to me, "Jesus saved me, but my husband has everything to do with what shape I'm in when I get there." Amen, sister.

In His Image

So, what did God create you to be? How do you know what your identity in Christ is? I think the answer lies in the Scripture that tells us we are created in God's image and likeness. We might not be able to identify God in a lineup. We don't know the color of his skin and hair, or his weight, or the size of his nose; but we do know what he looks like. We "see" God every day in his compassion, mercy, justice, truth, love, creativity, wisdom, and so on. I believe that being created in his image refers to those aspects of himself, those virtues (love, truth, wisdom, justice,

---

*To avoid using "him or her" and similar constructions for the most part, I will be switching occasionally and arbitrarily between the masculine and feminine genders throughout this work.

compassion, etc.), which he encoded in our DNA at conception (metaphorically speaking). As C. S. Lewis writes, "[God] lends us a little of His reasoning powers and that is how we think: He puts a little of His love into us and that is how we love one another" *(Mere Christianity)*.

Baptism is the foundation of our Christian identity. When we were baptized, God gave us some incredible gifts. In addition to washing our souls clean of original sin, he infused us with sanctifying grace, gave us the three theological virtues of faith, hope, and charity, bestowed upon us the seven gifts of the Holy Spirit (wisdom, understanding, counsel, fortitude, knowledge, piety, fear of the Lord), granted us moral virtues (e.g., prudence, justice, temperance), and empowered us to bear the twelve fruits of the Holy Spirit (charity, joy, peace, patience, kindness, goodness, generosity, gentleness, faithfulness, modesty, self-control, chastity). To have an identity in Christ is to live out these freely given virtues and qualities in the unique way the circumstances of our lives demand. To have an identity in Christ is also to know and pursue the reason God put us on this earth. What are we here to do? What is our mission? The more our daily choices and behaviors reflect these God-given values, virtues, dreams, and goals, the more solid our Christian identity. While each one of us is individually responsible to God for living out this identity, it is the job of a sacramental marriage to support, nurture, and encourage us in this pursuit.

"Pretty words, Greg," you may comment. "But what do they mean in real life?"

Practically speaking, being partners in Christian identity means that when your spouse asks for more from you, you are obliged to give it, not necessarily because your spouse deserves such generosity (we so seldom deserve to be loved), but because you have a responsibility to God to demonstrate that generosity. You may not *feel* like doing more romantic things for your mate, but through these gestures you participate in God's plan for letting your partner know how special she is to God. You may fear the vulnerability you feel in lovemaking, but that vulnerability is the very thing you and your partner must learn to enjoy if you want to become open to God's eternal love. Whenever you hold back in your married life, you prevent God from loving your mate the way he wants to love him — the way your mate needs to be loved. Remember, God requires you to be Christ to your spouse. When was the last time Christ refused you a sign of his affection? When did he ever refuse to share the comfort of his precious body with you? You may not have deserved it, and God may or may not have felt like doing it, but, oddly, these issues never came up.

And this is just the beginning. Do you encourage the creativity of your mate — as God does — or do you say, "Why would you want to do something silly like that?" Do you affirm the beauty of your husband or wife — as God does — or do you criticize your wife and/or treat her with benign neglect? Do you seek to fulfill your partner's dreams, goals, and needs — as God does — or do you cling to your own comfort, asking your spouse to limit herself to what you deem acceptable or "reasonable"? Do you hide out behind that "Men are rational, women are emotional" nonsense, or do you seek to exhibit the *whole, rational, and emotive personhood* that God himself does?

For the Christian, being a master of marital skills has little to do with being a good earthbound companion and everything to do with being a collaborator in God's plan of salvation for you and your mate. If your spouse isn't even worth a couple of flowers, a card, some good conversation, or some physical affection from you, how will your mate ever learn to accept the immense bounty of love that God has prepared for her in his heavenly kingdom?

Helping your mate get to heaven involves a great deal more than getting to church on Sunday and praying your Rosary. It involves all that — *plus* being the loving, attentive, generous spouse Christ would be if he were married to your partner. Have you ever really appreciated the importance of your role as a husband or wife in God's plan? Grasping this importance is the essential first step of answering the call of the Church, "Families, become what you are" *(Familiaris Consortio)*.

Up until now we have been discussing the sanctifying role of marriage — that is, marriage's role in making us more complete and godly people. But while every sacrament is in some way concerned with our sanctification, every sacrament also gives us special kinds of grace (graces of state) that enable us to successfully do a particular job in the Christian life. For example, through our baptism in water and the Spirit, we are sanctified by having the stain of original sin washed clean, and we are sanctified by being given the grace to resist future temptation to sin. But baptism also imparts other graces (graces of state) that enable us to do three jobs. They are: (1) to be *priests* (to give personal sacrifice, praise, and worship to God); (2) to be *prophets* (to proclaim the truth of God's word and deeds); and (3) to be *kings* (to conduct ourselves in a manner that is becoming of a son or daughter of the Most High God). Likewise, in addition to sanctifying us, God, through the sacrament of matrimony, gives us special graces to complete particular tasks. These tasks are: (1) to restore the original unity that existed between man and woman (in Adam and Eve) and (2) to bring forth new life.

22

The Unitive End of Marriage

Lately, it has become popular to say, as the title of one book tells us, that "men are from Mars and women are from Venus." Supposedly, women are communicative, sensitive, emotive, relational, nurturing, loving, and supportive. Men, on the other hand, like football.

And never the twain shall meet.

If this is true of our experience today — and sadly, for many, it is — then we need to remember that this is not the way God intended, or intends, it to be. When God created woman, Adam said, "This at last is bone of my bones and flesh of my flesh" (Gen 2:23). Adam did not — to paraphrase Professor Henry Higgins — say, "Why can't this woman be more like a man?"

The estrangement and confusion present-day men and women experience around one another is a direct result of original sin. Clearly, it is not the way things ought to be. The "regrettable apple incident" was to men and women what the Tower of Babel was to the world.

The good news is that for *at least* a few million years before John Gray (of *Venus and Mars* fame) came along, God, through marriage, has been giving us the grace we need to restore the true partnership Adam and Eve experienced with each other, and to overcome the false differences that keep men and women at odds. Theologically speaking, this is the grace underlying what is known as the "unitive end" of marriage. When a man and woman freely and completely give themselves to each other, the permanence of their bond — among other things — enables them to spend a lifetime becoming fluent in each other's "languages." By doing this, men and women, in the end, become fully human. "And the two shall become one" (Mt 19:5).

Of course, saying that God gives us the grace to overcome false, or invalid, differences between men and women is not to deny that there are real differences between the sexes. But the differences are much more subtle and profound than the polarized, overly simplistic definitions to which many in our society cling (e.g., "Men are rational. Women are emotional"; "Men don't do housework and don't take care of small children. Women shouldn't work out of the home"; etc.). As moral theologian William May explains in his book *Marriage: The Rock on which the Family Is Built,* gender differences are supposed to be differences in *"emphasis."*

What does this mean? In the beginning, God shared the *same* aspects of himself (i.e., the same sets of characteristics and virtues) with both male and female *human beings.* As John Paul II demonstrates in *The Original Unity of Men and Women,* the fact that Adam said of Eve,

"This at last is bone of my bones and flesh of my flesh" (Gen 2:23), dramatically shows that Eve — body, mind, and soul — was a being to whom Adam could relate completely. Our first parents were made of the same essential biological, psychological, emotional, and spiritual stuff.

At the dawn of creation, both men *and* women were given the ability to reason, emote, love, communicate, produce, set goals, nurture, and so on. Likewise, both men *and* women were called to live out *all* of these qualities to the fullest. However, based on how God created their bodies, Adam and Eve had different *styles* of applying these qualities to everyday life (see the entry "Theology of the Body" in *Our Sunday Visitor's Encyclopedia of Catholic Doctrine*; also John Paul II's *The Original Unity of Man and Woman*). So, for example, while both Adam and Eve were given the responsibility to nurture, emote, communicate, etc., God created Eve's body to *emphasize* such qualities in her life, and this emphasis was what God called "femininity." Likewise, while both Adam and Eve were given the responsibility to make plans, set goals, provide for their needs, solve problems, and so forth, God created Adam's body to *emphasize* such qualities in his life, and this emphasis is what the Lord called "masculinity."

A good example of these emphases at work is how men and women practice their call to nurture young children. God ordained a woman's body to nurse her young. But even though men cannot lactate, God still requires them to be abundantly present and active in the lives of their children, just as God, our Father, is present and active in our lives. God gave both men and women the ability to be *fully* nurturing and loving, but he ordained the sexes to express this fullness in equally valuable yet different and complementary ways. As John Paul II teaches us, men and women must prayerfully contemplate and emphasize their *bodies' unique capabilities* to first understand true masculinity and femininity. Then, we must use our masculinity and femininity as the prism through which we express our *full humanity*.

As you read above, the pre-fallen Adam and Eve fully exhibited all the qualities God gave them, although they tended to emphasize these qualities differently. But after the fall of humankind, masculine and feminine "emphases" stopped being that, and became whole other languages. Men and women staked out separate domains and forbade their mates from ever crossing the line — as if their mates ever would want to. This tragic estrangement continued throughout history, worsening and worsening until men and women began to feel as if they were born on two completely different planets (Mars and Venus, so to speak).

But God never intended for masculinity and femininity to be different languages. Rather, he intended that they should be complementary expressions of a shared *humanity*. Through marriage, God gives husbands and wives the grace necessary to restore the original unity experienced by our first parents. God does not give us an insufficient grace, allowing us to merely coexist in some Martian/Venusian truce. Instead, God gives husbands and wives all the grace they need to transcend false differences, discover that they were really earthlings all along, and speak one language again: a language of joyful, mutual love and service, a language created by the Father, exemplified by the Son, and sustained by the Holy Spirit.

Become What You Are

God gives us unitive grace, but we must be willing to do the work that grace empowers us to do. Earlier in this chapter, I wrote that a Christian marriage must be founded on the belief that you have a better chance, with your mate than without him, of becoming the person God created you to be. But too many Christian husbands and wives do not have *complementary* roles; instead, they have *compensatory* roles that inhibit their growth as human beings and as Christians. For example, certain wives never learn to do or become *A*, *B*, or *C*, because, as they put it, "That's what my husband is for." Similarly, certain husbands never learn to do or become *X*, *Y*, or *Z*, because "That's what my wife is for." What such individuals forget is that they are passing up the chance God gives them to become the people he created them to be: competent, fully formed, human beings eager to challenge the limitations original sin placed upon their bodies, minds, spirits, and relationships. Sanctification is not just about overcoming spiritual obstacles, it is about overcoming physical, emotional, and psychological ones as well. Are you taking advantage of the marital grace God gives you to become fully human? Or are you hiding behind the pathetic excuse "That's just not what women *[or men]* are supposed to be"?

Such a statement is a cop-out unworthy of your Christian dignity. Men must be men like Jesus Christ is a man. And women must be women like the Virgin Mary or the Proverbs 31 wife is a woman. Only then will Christian husbands and wives be able to experience the truth of complementarity and the fullness of marital grace.

If you are a Christian married person, God is giving you the grace to do the work. In order to understand the *specific* work you must do, consider the following and answer the accompanying questions.

Your Specific Work
Step One: Embrace Your Masculinity or Femininity

Prayerfully contemplate your body. What can you do with your body that your spouse simply cannot do, or do as well, with his or hers? This is God's definition of masculinity and femininity. Emphasize these things in your life.

Step Two: Embrace Your Humanity

What domestic jobs (e.g., cooking and housekeeping, taking care of the finances, nurturing and playing with the children, etc.) are you *physically capable* of doing, but don't do (or do extremely rarely) simply because you lack practice or don't like doing them? What tasks do you require your mate to do for you, simply because you lack practice or don't like doing them?

What qualities (e.g., emotionality, rationality, communicativeness, affection, etc.) do you lack in your life, or excuse yourself for not having because "That's not how women *[or men]* are supposed to be"?

The tasks, domestic responsibilities, and personal qualities you listed above are exactly the areas you must develop in your life in order to become the human being God created you to be; in order to have a marriage based on complementarity and sanctification, instead of simple compensation or spiritual enabling. To develop these aspects of yourself is to participate fully in the grace God gives you through the unitive end of marriage. Do you have the guts to become the new Adam and new Eve on your block? As a Christian married couple, you are being called to nothing less by God. Will you accept his call?

While you think about this, let's examine one final benefit and function of a Christian marriage.

The Procreative End of Marriage

You just read about building unity in your marriage. Now we are going to take it a step further. A true, unified love is life-giving, not just metaphorically, in the sense of emotionally energizing a couple, but literally, in the procreative sense. Children represent the miraculous unity between a husband and wife like nothing else.

In his *Letter to Families*, Pope John Paul II tells us that "rather than closing [spouses] up in themselves, [a couple's unity] opens them up towards new life, towards a new person. As parents, they will be capable of giving life to a being like themselves, not only bone of their bones and flesh of their flesh . . . , but an image and likeness of God — a person."

As Mother Teresa was fond of reminding us, Jesus said, "Anyone who welcomes a little child, welcomes me" (cf. Mt 18:5, Mk 9:37, and Lk 9:48). Spouses who truly love each other and love our Lord will welcome the children he wants to give them.

Over the last several years, certain people have taken a lot of swings at what they think is "the Church's position" on procreation. Unfortunately, these people are often too blinded by their own self-righteous, prejudiced ignorance to see that what they are swinging at isn't the Church's teaching at all, but rather a Monty Pythonized (see *The Meaning of Life*) pop-culture bastardization of Church teaching. (Thank you for letting me get that off my chest. I feel much better now.) So, if you what to know the truth, read on.

"Because God is a lover, he is also a creator" (*OSV's Encyclopedia of Catholic Doctrine*). God loves loving. Love is what God does best, but a lover isn't much good without a beloved. This is why God seems to be endlessly fascinated with creating new things. It gives him more to love.

God especially loves to create people. As the Church tells us in the Vatican Council II document *Gaudium et Spes*, the human being is "the only creature on earth whom God willed for its own sake." Why? Because we are the only creatures he gets to spend an eternity loving. We are the only earthly beings built to last — so to speak. One can only guess that for God it is a joy beyond words to create creatures whom he can love *eternally*. This same God, who generously longs to share all of his joy with us, gives husbands and wives a taste of the particular joy that comprises creating and loving the creation, by inviting us to bring his children into the world through the act of procreation.

God gives many benefits and responsibilities to those husbands and wives who welcome his invitation to create life with him. Each of these benefits manifests another way "the two become one" (cf. Mt 19:5). I'll hit the top four here.

1. Really Great Sex ∽ One of the most amazing benefits that comes from being open to life is that it makes lovemaking a powerful, spiritual, earth-shattering, even redemptive, event. My wife and I regularly share a truly wonderful sex life, but I must tell you that the times we conceived our three children were the most amazing, loving experiences I have ever encountered. All of the books in the popular press about "spiritual sex" and "tantric lovemaking" have nothing on the sheer joy, vulnerability, spirituality, and total self-gift that accompany knowing that "tonight

27

we are making a baby." Likewise there are many books that proclaim the virtues of "simultaneous orgasm" and, to be honest, they speak a truth. But nothing, absolutely nothing, compares to the profound joy that occurs when *a husband, a wife, and God climax together* — and a life is created. How sad it is that our sexuality has been so perverted by the pagans and misrepresented by the media that a statement such as the one I just made might actually be shocking to many of you reading this book. But the fact remains: Sex is a good that God gave to the godly. The pagans stole it from us when we weren't looking, and it's time we take it back (see Chapter 9). Through the procreative work of marriage, God gives us the grace to do just that. To paraphrase Scott Hahn, God empowers us to experience a love so profound that in nine months it has to be given its own name.

2. Really Great Sex — Part II ∽ Even when a couple has valid reasons for delaying or postponing pregnancy (see third item, *Responsible Parenthood*, facing page), the joy of continuing to be open to life brings a more profound dimension to lovemaking. This is made possible by practicing "natural family planning," or NFP.

NFP and artificial contraception exemplify radically different mindsets about sexuality. On the one hand, contraception is always one spouse's responsibility (usually the woman's). Contraception treats pregnancy as a disease that should be prevented — an optional by-product of pleasure. Various forms of artificial contraception (the Pill, for instance) often have harmful side effects; they are prone to failure; they make sex habitual rather than special; they present physical barriers to intimacy; and they can make conceiving extremely difficult even after one stops using them. On the other hand, NFP is the shared responsibility of a husband and wife. NFP facilitates communication between them about each other's bodies (added bonus: the husband will never be surprised by PMS); it requires a husband and wife to continually talk and pray about their priorities and becoming or being parents; it is completely natural with no side effects; it is 99.9 percent effective; it keeps lovemaking fresh and exciting due to periodic abstinence; it requires the couple to focus on relationship and romance rather than just habitual sex; and it is as effective for helping couples conceive as well as avoid pregnancy (in fact, ob-gyns use modified forms of it as a first-line treatment of infertility.) Couples who practice NFP constantly seek after God's will for their lives in a way no contracepting couple ever does. They experience a sharing of one another and a level of communication that no contracepting couple ever could. NFP couples practice "Sex for Real" and this kind of sex has it all over every other kind there is. No less a spiritual authority than comedian Paul Reiser (of television's *Mad About You*) agrees with me.

> Once sex is for real and not just for entertainment purposes, it's a much scarier proposition. . . . [But] to our pleasant surprise, this Sex for Real was really something. Without those spontaneity-killing trips to the medicine cabinet, there was suddenly . . . a certain devil-may-care flair that put an extra smile on everybody's face. Sometimes you just have to say, "God bless God — He knows what He's doing."
>
> — COMEDIAN PAUL REISER
> *Babyhood*

But if a spiritual heavyweight like Mr. Reiser can't convince you, I guess I'll just have to rely on the pope. John Paul II himself noted that the spouses who work together to prayerfully discern *each month* whether or not God is calling them to have a child, unlike contracepting couples, accept what John Paul II says in his *Letter to Families:* "Both [spouses] are responsible for their potential and later actual fatherhood and motherhood. The husband cannot fail to acknowledge and accept the result of a decision that has also been his own. He cannot hide behind such expressions as: 'I don't know,' 'I didn't want it,' or 'You're the one who wanted it.' "

The sexuality an NFP couple gives to each other is beautiful, creative, passionate, intentional, responsible, mutually caring, mutually consented to, and prayerfully discerned. Because NFP allows couples to achieve such a high level of communication, prayer, and cooperation, it is little wonder that the divorce rate of NFP couples averages around five percent compared to between forty and fifty percent in the general public.

3. Responsible Parenthood ∼ Of course the true joy of Catholic procreation (and this is the part you'll *never* hear about in the media) is that it doesn't stop at conception. When we Catholics say "yes" to the gift of a child, the Church teaches that we must also be in a position to say "yes" to the forming of that child's body, mind, and soul. Procreation is *a continuous event that extends from the moment of conception to the time our children are returned to God.* Procreation is the act by which Christians cooperate with God to form minds and souls, not just bodies. Or, as John Paul II puts it, "Fatherhood and motherhood represent a *responsibility which is not simply physical but spiritual in nature*" (*Letter to Families;* emphasis in original).

The Church recognizes that the joy of conception can become so intoxicating that some Christians will pursue that joy as an end in itself, without regard to their responsibility for properly nourishing the *bodies, minds, and souls* of children entrusted to their care. To counter this potentially harmful tendency, the Church teaches "responsible parenthood" (see, for instance, *Humanae Vitae, Familiaris Consortio, Letter to Families,* and *OSV's Encyclopedia of Catholic Doctrine*). That is, in discerning God's will for the size of our families, we are obliged to consider the resources (or lack thereof) he has given us to provide for the physical, emotional, and spiritual needs of a child. The following quote from Our Sunday Visitor's adult catechism, *The Teaching of Christ,* explains responsible parenthood better than I ever could.

> For while a child is a great blessing, it is sometimes very important for parents to give careful thought to the size of their families. Husband and wife "will thoughtfully take into account both their own welfare and that of their children, those already born and those which may be foreseen. For this accounting they will reckon with both the material and the spiritual conditions of the times as well as of their state of life. Finally, they will consult the interests of the family group, of temporal society, and of the Church herself. The married partners should make this judgment, in the sight of God" (GS 50).
>
> — D. WUERL, R. LAWLER, AND T. LAWLER
> The Teaching of Christ, quoting the Vatican II
> document Pastoral Constitution on the
> Church in the Modern World (Gaudium et
> Spes)

When parents' physical, economic, emotional, or psychological resources are lacking to the degree that they cannot adequately provide for a child's body, mind, or soul, the Church invites the husband and wife to pursue another kind of joy, the joy that accompanies mastering one's drives and perfecting one's sexuality. Which brings me to the last point.

4. Spiritual Sexuality ～ Aristotle, who lived some four centuries before Christ, tells us: "The man who abstains from bodily pleasures and delights in this very fact is temperate, while the man who is annoyed at it is self-indulgent" *(Nicomachean Ethics).*

In my counseling practice, I have never met a person who likes himself *because* he drinks too much, eats too much, plays too much, sleeps too much, or otherwise abuses himself. Caving in to every whim of our bodies is one of the quickest ways to destroy self-esteem. That's why people who eat, drink, play, and sleep in moderation are happier and healthier than people who don't do enough of those things, or do them too much. The same is true about sex.

I hardly think that any sane person would argue the point that there are about a million ways we can use our sexuality to abuse ourselves and others. Most commonly, we treat our sexuality as if it were a street drug we take to make us happy. Or, we use it to inflate a pathetic self-image ("Hey! I can't be all bad. I got some!"). Not only does this reduce oneself to his or her least common denominator (insects "get some" too, after all), it hurts others because it turns them into things to be used (or things to be resented when they refuse to be used).

Any abuse of self or others decreases our chances of being happy with God in heaven. Because of this, husbands and wives are encouraged by the Church to make use of periodic abstinence (as practiced in NFP) as a *spiritual exercise* to help one another master, purify, and perfect their sexuality. By the way, this is not a Catholic phenomenon. Hinduism, Buddhism, and several popular Eastern texts on spiritual sexuality all speak of the benefits of sexual abstinence in various forms. In fact, I believe virtually every major spiritual system on earth (except, of course, American pop psych) values some form of abstinence as a means of purifying both sexuality and the human person.

God always returns more than we give him, and the choice to practice periodic abstinence as a spiritual exercise is no exception. In addition to the fruit it will bear in our marital communication and self-esteem, there is a considerable amount of anecdotal evidence suggesting that men who abstain periodically are more able to postpone ejaculation in intercourse. Likewise, men and women who practice periodic abstinence have reported more intense and frequent orgasms than other couples. God always rewards his faithful.

Look, I'll say it again: NFP is a wonderful gift, and if you don't practice it, you are missing out, big time. In fact, you cannot experience the fullness of your sexuality without it. Call the Couple-to-Couple League today at 513-471-2000 to learn more about the treasures of responsible parenthood, natural family planning, and loving guidance as a way of life for you and your children. Call today. Not because I told you to or because "the Pope says you should" but because you are a thinking, praying, rational human being who can only make decisions about accepting or rejecting something if you truly know what it is that you are accepting or rejecting. Neither Christ nor the Church wants anyone to rot in his or her own ignorance. Challenge yours. Get the information you need to properly form your own conscience and make your own decision. But I warn you: Once you find out what Catholic sexuality is really all about, you'll be hooked.

The true beauty of all the marital graces (sanctifying grace, the grace to restore the original unity of men and women, and the grace to perfect our sexuality and share in the joy of creating and loving new children of God) is that they work off of one another and amplify each other in a continuous and ever-widening circle of redemption. The sanctifying grace of marriage propels us to become all that God created us to be, which empowers us to bridge the gap that exists between men and women; it entitles us to share in the joy of creating and loving; it helps us become more of what God created us to be, and so on, until we are made "perfect, as our heavenly Father is perfect" (Mt 5:48).

Clearly, in the hands of someone who knows what he or she is doing, marriage is an awe-inspiring thing. It is one of the best tools we have for perfecting each other in love.

Obstacles to Partnership

> Love is . . . the fundamental and innate vocation of every
> human being.
>
> — POPE JOHN PAUL II
> Familiaris Consortio

As you can see, a good marriage is truly a powerful tool that God can use to help us become the ideal creatures he intended us to be. But in both my personal and professional experience, I have encountered two major obstacles to living out this ideal: an addiction to comfort and a game I call *Marital Chicken*.

Addiction to Comfort ∼ Too many people view marriage as an institution of convenience. Nothing exemplifies this better than the statement "Thank God I'm married, because that means I will never have to do any of that romantic stuff *[or change the oil, wash dishes, earn a living]* ever again." This sentiment is a great tragedy because it completely misses the point of a Christian marriage. For the Christian — especially the Catholic Christian — a marriage license is not a "sloth permit"; rather, it is a call to work even harder on the most important task in the world: the actualization of your personhood and the sanctification of you and your spouse. But even when we are not so pathetically addicted to our own convenience as this, we can still fall prey to a love of comfort. We *could* be more present, more romantic, more sexual, a better listener, or a more attentive mate; but, to be perfectly honest, we're tired and just a little too comfy in our own corner of the house. It happens to all of us, men *and* women. We are called to be Christ to our mate, but too often "Christ" is sacked out on the sofa, hiding out in a hobby or job, or out saving the rest of the world instead of actively searching for the hundred or so ways he or she could *literally* be a savior right at home.

Marital Chicken ⟿ The second insidious obstacle to love is the game of *Marital Chicken*. When a couple plays *Marital Chicken*, two grown-ups sit around whining, "If you were more romantic *[or sexual, helpful, complimentary, emotional, rational, etc.]*, maybe I *would* be more romantic *[or sexual, helpful, complimentary, emotional, rational, etc.]*. But I know *you*. You'll never change!"

Playing this game allows us to avoid confronting our own fears of intimacy while getting to feel self-righteous at the same time. As you can imagine, the game is fairly addicting. What couples playing *Marital Chicken* forget is that they are not really responsible to their partners for living out those loving qualities. Rather, such couples must become more affectionate (or sexual, helpful, complimentary, emotional, rational, etc.) because that is the person *they* want to be — because that is the person *God is calling the couples to be.* When I die and God asks me if I lived out my vocation to love, I really don't think the Almighty is going to accept an excuse such as "Well, Lord, I *would* have, if only *my spouse* had been more *[fill in the blank].*"

Part of being Christ to one another involves being loving not because our mates deserve such generosity (we so seldom deserve to be loved) but because our Christian dignity requires this of us. As C. S. Lewis writes in *The Four Loves*, "All who have good parents, wives, husbands, or children may be sure that at some times . . . [they] are loved not because they are lovable but because Love Himself is in those who love them."

Loving our mates the way Christ would love them — whether they "deserve" it or not — is absolutely essential to our own growth as Christians. To reject this responsibility is to reject God's call in our lives and injure our relationship with him. "As you did it to one of the least of these . . . you did it to me" (Mt 25:40).

By refusing to respond to our call to love, too many of us offend our own dignity, destroy our own self-esteem, and foster alienation in our marriages. We are constantly being tempted to play manipulative games with our mates, valuing our own convenience and comfort above all else. When we do this, husbands and wives slowly turn each other into "bitches," "avoiders," or — at best — shriveled-up, bitter, emotional scorekeepers. What we need to be doing is turning each other into saints and, thank God, by learning how to use the graces of marriage, we can. Nothing can come between those couples who believe the fulfillment of their identities in Christ is inextricably tied to the success of their marital partnership. Nothing can embitter those couples who understand their role in preparing one another to share the joy of God's heavenly kingdom. When a husband and wife respond to their innate call to love and work to fulfill each other's Christian destinies, they open the door to a truly vital, loving, spiritual, *sacramental* marriage. They guarantee that they will remain both faithful and joyful together through good times and bad, wealth and poverty, sickness and health, loving and cherishing each other until they deliver their mate to the heavenly Father, who will smile upon them and say, "Well done, [my] good and faithful servant" (Mt 25:21).

Renew Your Vows

As the years go by, sometimes couples forget why they got married. Sometimes they wonder if they ever knew. I want to prevent that from happening to you, or if it has begun to happen in your marriage, I want to get you started on the way back.

The following exercise is intended to serve two needs. First, it will help you to clarify both your identity in Christ and what you must do to live out that identity more consistently in your life and marriage. Next, it will help you identify how to make your marriage a partnership in fulfilling that Christian destiny. In essence, by the end of this chapter, you will have developed a "mission statement" around which to build your life and marriage. Don't expect to fulfill every part of that mission statement today. Rather, view it as a plan of action, an itinerary for what you will be working toward over the next fifty years of your life.

෨ᔆᔆ

Partners in Christ Exercise
Part One: Your Christian Identity

Directions: Take some time to prayerfully meditate on the questions below. Do not share your answers with your mate at this time. This first part is about *your* identity in Christ, the identity that you would be responsible for living out, whether or not you were ever married.

1. Most of the virtues listed below were given to you freely and automatically at your baptism. Of them all, which virtues do you believe God has made dearest to your heart? Identify a few virtues that are *most important* to you. Use the list below, or write your own in the space pro-

vided. (If you have a hard time answering, try thinking of the qualities you wish to be *most* known for at the end of your life.)

___Love ___Faith ___Hope ___Wisdom
___Understanding ___Fortitude ___Integrity ___Counsel
___Holiness ___Fear of the Lord ___Prudence ___Knowledge
___Justice ___Moderation ___Charity ___Joy
___Peace ___Patience ___Kindness ___Goodness
___Generosity ___Gentleness ___Faithfulness ___Modesty
___Self-control ___Chastity ___Service ___Hospitality
___Compassion ___Creativity

Others: _____

_____

2. Write the virtues you indicated in the form of a personal motto. For example:

"With God's help, I will spend my life pursuing the following virtues: love, wisdom, and service."

Now it's your turn.

"With God's help, I will spend my life pursuing: _____

_____."

3a. Recall the things that irritate you most about your spouse. Annoying habits, traits, infuriating opinions or behaviors, etc. Write one or two of the most trying examples here: _____

_____

3b. When your spouse does these annoying things, how, specifically, will you change your behavior to more adequately reflect your chosen motto? (For example: "How can I respond more lovingly when my wife is late?")

4. We all hold back from our mates. What do you hold back? How will God's grace and the virtues you identified help you overcome this selfishness? How will you motivate yourself to give more generously to your mate?

5. What steps must you take so that your work life, parenting life, and personal life can more adequately reflect your personal motto? (For example: take a parenting class, go on a couples' retreat, do more spiritual reading, go to daily Mass, get additional job training, etc.)

6a. What goals or accomplishments do you believe God is asking you to achieve in your lifetime? (Think of those most heartfelt desires that you have dismissed as silly but somehow won't go away.)

6b. Do you have all the resources you need to accomplish these goals? If not, what do you need (e.g., more schooling, counseling, a different job, particular life experiences, etc.)? Write these things down.

Part Two: Your Partnership

Directions: You and your mate should now share and discuss your answers to Part One. During this discussion keep in mind that your mate has arrived at her answers to Part One through prayerful discernment. Her answers reflect her genuine beliefs about the identity God is making her responsible for fulfilling. This identity may involve things you don't appreciate, think are silly, or don't like; but God didn't ask your opinion when he gave your mate this mission. He only demands that you be faithful to the promises you made in your marriage and help your partner fulfill her identity. Remember, your mate may not make it without you, but you are responsible to God to make certain she makes it with you.

Discuss: In order to become the partner God asks you to be to your mate, what specific actions must you take, what skills must you develop, or what choices must you make in your daily life? What must you do to increase your mate's chances of fulfilling his identity in Christ?

Part Three: A Promise

Take turns pledging the following.

(If you are reading this book as part of the *For Better . . . Forever!* parish-based marriage enrichment program, you will make this promise with the other couples in your group at a Mass before your next meeting.)

(Say your partner's name:) I genuinely respect the person you are, and the person God wants you to be. To that end, I promise that I will work to see the good in the things you value, especially when I don't understand. I will never say that the dreams, goals, or values God has placed in your heart are silly, or unworthy of my time and attention. I promise to be the most important influence in your life, second only to our Savior, Jesus Christ, because I love and honor who you are and who God is calling you to become. I promise that I will love you and support you with all of my life, all the days of my life. And I promise that with the Lord's help, I will be your best hope for arriving, properly attired, at the heavenly banquet.

_____ / _____
Husband's Signature   / Wife's Signature

Summary

You have just encountered a great many tough questions. If you weren't sure how to answer some of them, the next chapter will clarify some things for you. For now, it is good enough for you to keep asking yourself the following questions:

What does God want from my life?

What does God want from my mate's life?

What must we do to help each other come closer to fulfilling this mission every day?

Pursuing the answers to these three questions throughout one's life is the secret to a long-lasting, exceptionally joyful *Christian* marriage.

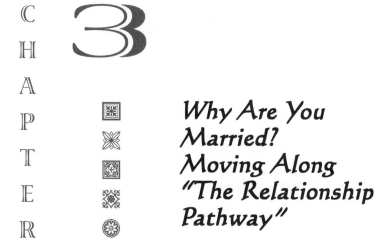

CHAPTER 3

Why Are You Married? Moving Along "The Relationship Pathway"

The preceding chapter set the standard for which we all must strive. Virtually every marriage — especially yours — has the potential to achieve the ideals I just described. That being said, it is also true that some couples have more work to do than others in order to achieve the fullness of their marriage. This chapter will help you identify the specific work you will have to do.

The Relationship Pathway

Other authors have identified different marital types. The problem is that until recently, no one has identified any meaningful connection between them. So, for example, Dr. Sigmund Q. Psychologist might be able to tell you that you have a "Green Marriage" (whatever that means) and that it is distinctly different from, and perhaps inferior to, a "Blue Marriage" (whatever that means). But the good doctor would probably not be able to tell you what predisposes you to your "Green Marriage" or how to move yourself into a "Blue Marriage" (except, maybe, by suggesting that you "take more time together" or "marry someone else").

To organize the different marital categories in a meaningful way, and show couples how to move from one stage to the next in a logical fashion, I developed *The Relationship Pathway*. *The Relationship Pathway* orders the different categories of marriage along a continuum of identity strength. "Huh?" you say. Let me explain it this way.

If you've ever read a pop-psych book, or for that matter, watched *Oprah*, you know that it is important to have an "identity" before you enter into a marriage. In the last chapter, I explained what having an "identity in Christ" means. This time, I'm talking mostly about "psychological identity." Simply put:

1. You know you have at least the *seeds* of an identity if you can identify, without having to think too hard about it, the dreams, goals, virtues, and values that are important to you.

2. You know the *strength* of your identity by the degree to which your daily life, choices, and relationships *reflect* those dreams, goals, virtues, and values.

For the Christian, an identity in Christ and psychological identity are supposed to be the same thing. In fact, a strong, personal commitment to our God-given baptismal virtues almost always guarantees a solid psychological identity.

But as the work of many developmental psychologists (especially Abraham "Hierarchy of Needs" Maslow) shows us, not everyone builds his or her identity around the same things. Some people build their identities around escape, their sole concern being to numb themselves with enough drugs, alcohol, sex, or chaos to get through the day. Other people center themselves around the basic needs of life — pursuing a "guarantee" of financial or emotional security and/or the acceptance of others. Still others build their lives around pursuing "success" as defined by the society and/or institutions to which they belong. And finally, the highest-functioning group build their identities around a clear, internalized value system. This system may incorporate either the values espoused by the women's movement or more traditional, religious values; but either way, their lives are a clear reflection of their deeply held beliefs.

What you build *your* life around is directly related to the type of marriage you have, as well as the happiness and longevity you can expect from that marriage. For you, as a Christian, what you build your identity around is also directly related to the degree of sacramental grace to which you are currently opening yourself in your marriage. If it is true that the purpose of marriage is to "*help each other become all God created you to be*" (and it is), then every married couple — especially the Christian married couple — is capable of and responsible for spending married life moving up *The Relationship Pathway.*

The Relationship Pathway: Step by Step

As you can see by looking at the following figure, there are five major types of marriages (each of these comes in different varieties, but we'll deal with that later). These five types of marriage are organized — left to right — from least to most desirable, from least to greatest longevity, from least to greatest participation in marital grace.

The Relationship Pathway

Every relationship travels left to right from its starting point on The Relationship Pathway.
As couples meet new challenges and learn new skills, both their identity strength and marital satisfaction increase.

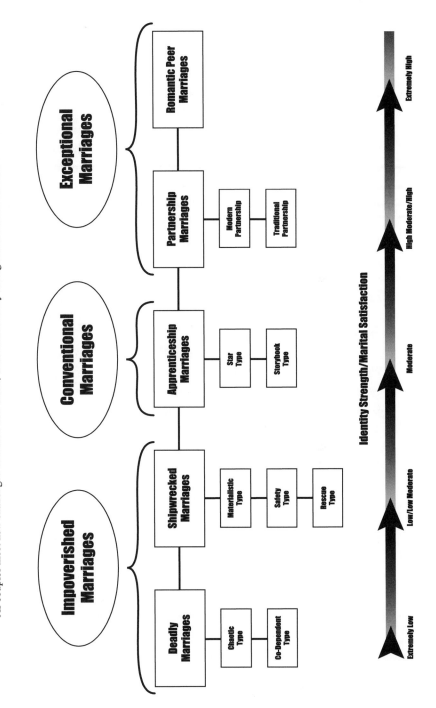

Though every couple starts out at a different point on *The Relationship Pathway*, we all move along *The Pathway* one stage at a time. No skipping grades. Each stage represents the mastery of different skills and presents new challenges. Likewise, each stage does not merely reflect a change in attitude about relationships, but rather a change in attitude about the way you view your whole life. As such, it often takes a major crisis of the kind that makes us say, "I don't know anything, anymore," to motivate us to make the personal changes necessary to move from one relationship stage to the next. A person can move up *The Relationship Pathway* without going through such a crisis, but he would have to be seriously and consistently attentive to his psychological and spiritual growth. Frankly, most of us are too lazy and distracted or not sufficiently motivated to do this, and so God has to occasionally resort to less subtle means — like allowing our lives to fall apart — in order to get our attention and facilitate a move toward greater identity strength and deeper intimacy with him and our mates.

Read the following pages with an eye toward picking out your type of marriage. Here are some tips:

1. Resist the urge to overestimate or underestimate your marital strengths.

Try to be as honest as possible. Nobody's keeping score on you. Pay close attention to the recommendations given at the end of each marital type. If they apply to you, start working on them, even if all the descriptions in a particular category don't apply to you.

2. Don't demonize your mate and canonize yourself.

Some people I know try to place themselves at the top of *The Relationship Pathway* and their mates at the bottom. This is not the way it works. We all marry people whose identities are built around similar things to our own. In fact, your entire circle of friends probably does not include people more than one whole stage up or down from you. To repeat: Don't try to canonize yourself by demonizing your mate. Chances are, if you married a rotten apple, you're not so shiny yourself.

3. You might be stuck in the middle.

Because it takes so much energy to move from one stage to the next, and because these stages are organized along a continuum, don't be surprised if you find yourself between two stages. Simply choose the stage you think you lean more toward and start working on the recommendations listed in that section first.

4. Relax.

Some people have a tendency to feel a little overwhelmed at the amount of information presented over the next few pages. Relax. No one is going to test you and you can read it over as often as you like. Plus, for your convenience, there is a summary I call "The Relationship Pathway at a Glance" comparing the major characteristics of each relationship type near the end of this chapter. I work hard so you don't have to!

In order to help you understand the progression from one stage to the next, we'll start at the bottom and work our way up. Ready?

1. Impoverished Marriages

People in *Impoverished Marriages* (see figure on following page) build their lives around one or the other of two themes: escaping reality (which they deem too difficult or uninteresting to deal with) or acquiring and accumulating the basic needs of life (food, clothing, shelter, money, safety). Whichever theme more accurately describes a couple's life will determine whether they have a *Deadly Marriage* or a *Shipwrecked Marriage* — respectively. Both are fairly common marital types. Let's examine the *Deadly Marriage* relationships first.

Deadly Marriages

People in *Deadly Marriages* build their lives around escaping reality either through the serious abuse of drugs or alcohol, or by surrounding themselves with people who have so many problems that they never have to deal with their own. These marriages exhibit both extremely low longevity (often under five years) and extremely low satisfaction. Individuals who are attracted to "bad boy/bad girl" types usually find themselves in one kind or another of *Deadly Marriage*.

The couples in *Deadly Marriages* are not huge goal setters and, as a general rule, they try not to think too hard. Personally meaningful work is out of the question. Jobs — if they exist at all — are usually menial, occasional, and poorly attended. Most of the time, the individuals in this category are happy to have enough cash to get through the day. Drugs, alcohol, sex, and violence are major players. In fact, if these relationships survive at all, it is usually because of some threat of violence. *Deadly Marriages* come in two varieties: *Chaotic* and *Co-dependent*.

Chaotic Marriages occur when two people, equally committed to their own self-destruction (through substance abuse and other high-risk behaviors) use each other as drinking buddies, sex partners, and often, punching bags. The only way to have a worse relationship is to marry a serial killer. On the bright side, you can really only go up from here.

Co-dependent Marriages occur when one person — whose life is a

43

The Relationship Pathway

Every relationship travels left to right from its starting point on The Relationship Pathway.
As couples meet new challenges and learn new skills, both their identity strength and marital satisfaction increase.

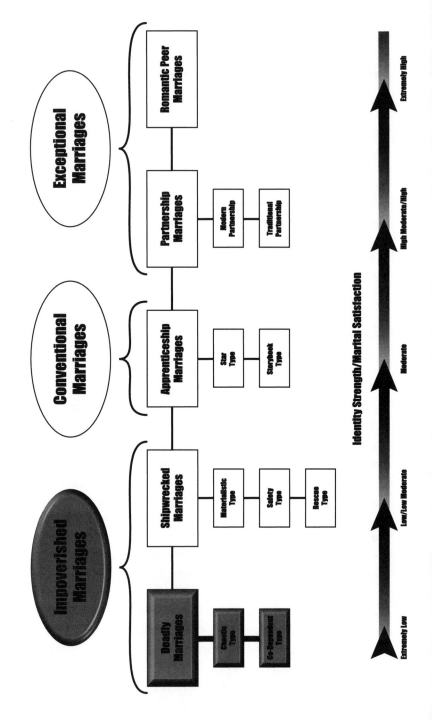

wreck — builds her life around saving another person from his chaotic, self-destructive tendencies. *Co-dependents* usually are not addicted to any chemicals themselves but are escapists just the same. Let me give you an analogy. Some people tell me they like to watch soap operas because the actors' problems are so convoluted that, for an hour or so, viewers can forget their own. *Co-dependent* people live their whole lives like this. They put off solving any of their own laundry list of dysfunctions by escaping into someone else's even more hopeless life. The *Co-dependent* logic goes like this: "I can't save myself so I will try to save this unsavable person, after which they can save me." It never works, which, for many *Co-dependents* is just fine. They have produced their own never-ending, wonderfully mind-numbing soap opera.

Prognosis and Recommendations for Deadly Marriages

These are the only two marriages that research unquestionably and consistently says are better off dissolved. In fact, these are the two types of marriages that most clearly meet the psychological impairment criterion for an annulment. For Catholics, decisions such as the latter are up to marriage tribunals, of course; but from my experience, you wouldn't get much argument from them. The sad truth is, in couples such as the ones I have just described, there are barely two *people* present, much less a marriage.

If you are in either type of *Deadly* relationship (i.e., *Chaotic* or *Co-dependent*), I recommend that you and/or your mate begin participating in as many of the following as you can — immediately if not sooner: Alcoholics Anonymous, Narcotics Anonymous, Al-Anon (a group for overcoming co-dependency), drug and/or alcohol rehabilitation, and individual counseling. Your focus on escape has prevented you from expecting even the basics from life. Things like food, income, shelter, and safety are not luxuries. In order to move to the next stage in your life, you must at least develop enough strength to acquire these for yourself. Get help today.

Having viewed the worst, let's take a look at the next stage up, the second category of *Impoverished Marriages: Shipwrecked Marriages.*

Shipwrecked Marriages

This category (see figure, next page) is a serious step up from the last, and yet, there remain major struggles for couples in this group. Historically, these were the couples who "learned to love each other" through a great deal of strong family support, fierce cultural identity, and socially supported, compulsory church attendance. With the demise or devaluation of all of these social supports, marriages in this category

The Relationship Pathway

Every relationship travels left to right from its starting point on The Relationship Pathway. As couples meet new challenges and learn new skills, both their identity strength and marital satisfaction increase.

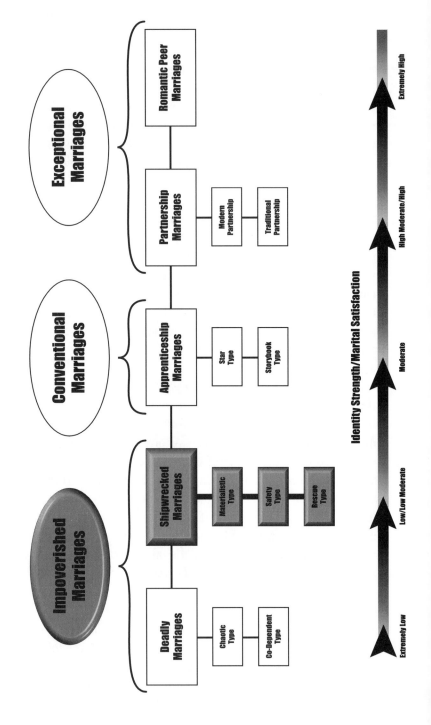

are the highest-risk, quasi-healthy relationships on *The Relationship Pathway*. They can — and do — evolve into genuinely happy marriages. But due to both a lack of personal conviction on the couple's part and the lack of social pressure and/or support to work it out, a huge number of these marriages don't make it past ten years or thereabouts. In my opinion, it is this group that needs the most education and support from families and the Church. Far too many of these couples are unidentified and unhelped. In my seminars, I teach pastors and other professionals how to identify and support these couples. For more information, contact the Pastoral Solutions Institute at 740-266-6461 (see Appendix 2).

The *Shipwrecked Marriage* is built around achieving the basics in life (food, clothing, shelter, money, safety), and this is fine to a point. The problem comes from the fact that this is all these marriages are about. After the initial honeymoon warmth wears off, the couple quickly deteriorates into a functional, brother/sister relationship that focuses on guaranteeing security and companionship at the cost of any real intimacy, passion, or growth. In fact, if at any point one member of this couple ever asks for more intimacy, friendship, passion, or depth from her partner, she is often soundly dismissed, verbally abused, or effectively ignored until the "threat" passes. Growth for many *Shipwrecked* couples is a dangerous thing. It requires shaking things up, and they have already been shaken enough in their lives.

The best way I could describe the challenges facing these marriages, as well as the marriages themselves, is to ask you to imagine two couples who went on a sailing trip only to be thrown overboard during a terrible storm. The first couple survived in a life raft but had no supplies. They starved for three days until they found an island overflowing with coconuts and breadfruit. At first, they were very happy; but ten years later, when the hope of rescue was long extinguished, they had their fill of "that damn stuff" and were even more sick of each other. The wife and the husband often thought about leaving the island, alone or together; but both feared that they would be eaten by the sharks that they occasionally spotted offshore. Still, the questions turned around and around in their heads: Should they try to leave the island together? Should they go it alone? Or, should they just sit there in silence, and eat their breadfruit and coconuts?

The second couple were thrown overboard as well, but they barely survived by hanging on to a piece of the ship's wreckage. They floated for three days before they washed ashore on a different island than the other couple. Unfortunately, it was an island inhabited by cannibals. Narrowly escaping with their lives, they were forced to swim five miles offshore to the next island and were almost eaten by sharks in the process. Unfortunately, this island was an active volcano that began erupting one day after they arrived. Forced to float for three more days on the open sea, they finally found a resting place. The island they ended up on afforded them little to eat and even less to do, but they felt lucky to be alive and safe. Ten years later, when all hope of rescue had passed, they were perfectly content to sit on that impoverished little island. Sometimes they would dream of a miracle, but frankly, they were just as happy to stay put. Knowing how dangerous the world could be kept them from ever wanting to leave the island on their own power and, in some strange way, it kept them happy with their truly meager lives.

Shipwrecked couples are identified by four major traits: (1) There is an emphasis on acquiring and/or accumulating the basics of life. (2) The estrangement between men and women is greatly felt. (3) Sex is often used as a substitute for real intimacy. (4) There is either no belief system or a wide chasm exists between professed beliefs and actual life.

Let's look at these one at a time.

1. A Priority on Meeting the Basics of Life ∽ Couples in *Shipwrecked Marriages* either marry too young to know that they can and should expect more than the basics from life, or they have spent most of their childhoods in *Chaotic* or *Co-dependent* homes (their stormy sea), where the basics were never guaranteed. Their identities revolve around the pursuit of "security," defined as either all the money they can hoard or all the safety they can provide for themselves. While no person could be faulted for wanting security, there is little more to these marriages than this. As one *Shipwrecked* wife told me, "I don't know if I could say I ever really loved him. But he doesn't beat me, he doesn't drink too much, he doesn't sleep around — well, not anymore — and he makes a good living. What do I have to complain about?"

Their desperate need for security causes a mutual dependence to develop between husband and wife: She needs to be provided for; he needs her presence to prop up his self-esteem. Each member brings half of an identity to the marriage, and each uses the other to fill in the void. If ever one or the other tried to leave the marriage, the one leaving would usually encounter threats of suicide or homicide from his or her mate: "You're killing me. I might as well end it. Maybe I'll take you with me."

This intense dependency leads to an understandable fear of conflict. "Life is too short to fight" is the most quoted motto of these couples. As such, many of their own needs go unmet "for the sake of the marriage," and resentment builds as a result. Superficially, these couples look like fine salt-of-the-earth types. But the collective pull of all their unmet — and sometimes unidentified — personal needs often cause them to develop a host of hidden compulsive behaviors that include functional alcoholism and/or substance abuse (i.e., serious chemical abuse that does not affect work behavior), compulsive shopping, compulsive gambling (yes, lotto and bingo count), prescribed substance abuse, hypochondria, and sexual addictions. Depression, anxiety disorders, and other stress-induced physical disorders are also extremely common here.

As you learned in the preceding chapter, marriage is supposed to feed the psychological and spiritual growth of the husband and wife. But in the worst-case scenario, *Shipwrecked* couples treat marriage as if it were the blood-sucking plant in *Little Shop of Horrors*. Every day the marriage screams, *"Feed me!"* and the spouses sacrifice more and more of their dreams, goals, virtues, and values to it until they are nothing but bloodless shells. All the while they keep saying, "This is what husbands and wives are supposed to do."

Challenging and changing the inverted structure of their marriage is the major challenge that stands between *Shipwrecked* couples and the next stage. This job is never easy, but it is easier for some than others.

2. Male and Female Estrangement Most Deeply Felt Here ∼ There is probably greater estrangement between men and women in *Deadly Marriages*, but they really don't care about it. This is the first category of couples healthy enough to notice the world that separates men and women at their most basic, post-fallen levels. Unfortunately, they are not initially knowledgeable enough to do anything about these differences except assume that "that's just the way things are."

As a result, couples in *Shipwrecked Marriages* live out a rigid, legalistic, completely polarized view of male and female roles. Men *are* men *because* they *do A, B, C.* Women *are* women *because* they *do X, Y, Z.* Husbands and wives in this category constantly complain about how their mates don't understand their world and couldn't survive without them. Though they would never admit it to you, this is exactly how they want it. Where there is helplessness, there is hope for the future of the marriage.

Learning how to understand the way men and women communicate and relate at their most basic level is the second challenge *Shipwrecked* couples must overcome to achieve the next level of their marriage.

3. A Tendency to Use Sex as a Substitute for Real Intimacy ∼ *Shipwrecked* couples are at once love-starved and fairly unknowledgeable about how to get love. Sex serves as a good substitute. *Shipwrecked* men and women tend to use sex as a way to prove their relationship is stable. While this is not universally true, it is more the rule than the exception. It is not uncommon for these couples to come to counseling complaining of a genuine distaste for each other, vicious — even physically violent — arguments, and assorted hurtful experiences, and then go on to tell me how either they have sex every day, or that the biggest problem they encounter is that their mates won't sleep with them (as many women complain about this as do men). Many of the *Shipwrecked* couples I have seen truly hated each other at the beginning of counseling, but as long as the sex was "good" or plentiful, the husband, wife, or both considered the core of their marriage to be solid.

4. A Nominal Connection to Their Dreams, Values, and Goals ～ Couples in this category have some vague idea about what they wish their lives could be like. They also have some idea about how the world *should* work, but any personal aspirations or beliefs are secondary to "making a living" or "keeping the peace."

Shipwrecked couples fall into three categories when it comes to their attitudes toward "values groups" (i.e., churches, the women's movement, personal growth groups, etc.).

a. The Escapists ～ At the very bottom of the *Shipwrecked* pile are those who have an almost paranoid fear of religion *or* use their faith as just one more compulsive behavior/escape from reality. If individuals in the escapist category do belong to a belief group, their membership has little to do with living out a set of values and everything to do with escaping the "evil world." They are overly concerned with outward appearances of specialness or "holiness" and would often be perfectly happy to run over anybody — including their own spouses or children — who stood between them and attending another meeting to support "the cause." They tend to be boorish, isolationist, argumentative, and paranoid in their dealings with others. Christians in this category seem to be very interested in whom God is going to strike dead next. Other examples include radical feminists, militia members, and people who salivate over the end times.

b. Goin' Through the Motions ～ These individuals usually fall at about the middle of the *Shipwrecked* category. They are often active members of values groups but not so much because they really believe anything the group teaches or even enjoy attending. Mostly they go because they don't want everybody looking at them and saying, "Why don't you go?" They tend to be somewhat rigid and legalistic. Their faith and service is not a joy; it is an obligation.

c. The "Open-minded" Person ∽ Folks here tend to be at the higher end of the *Shipwrecked* category. Individuals in this category pride themselves on being open-minded, but this is a polite and ennobling way of saying that they really don't stand for anything. Their motto is, "Do what you want as long as you aren't hurting me." They tend to be highly suspicious of values groups and avoid them, saying, "They're all a bunch of hypocrites. I don't need anyone telling me how to run my life." Or, "All those people want is your money." Such individuals forget that it's easy not to be a hypocrite when you don't really stand for anything.

Others in this category tend to gravitate toward cheap spiritualities, like New Age ideas, horoscopes, fortune-telling, or even an *overemphasis* on the otherworldly, overly emotional aspects of some Christian spiritualities, all of which — taken on their own — can seem to promise secret knowledge and immeasurable joy without asking much of them in return.

Shipwrecked Marriages: The Two Major Types

As you can see, while *Shipwrecked* couples may have some vague idea about their dreams, goals, values, and virtues, all of these take a backseat to securing a comfortable, safe life. The set of "the basics" such individuals value more will determine if they gravitate toward a *Materialistic Marriage* or a *Safety Marriage.*

THE SHIPWRECKED MATERIALISTIC MARRIAGE

Couples in this category tend to define success as "economic security." As children, many *Shipwrecked* husbands and wives often had to do without the most basic essentials. As adults, they are going to make certain they never have to do without again. The great temptation here is not knowing when enough is enough. The more they have, the more they have to lose, so the harder they must work to keep it.

The husbands in this category reign supreme. They are usually workaholics and are often high-functioning alcoholics as well. They are often known throughout the community as generous and likable. They are the kind of men who seem to know everybody but, when you really think about it, have no close friends. Their wives were initially attracted to their gregarious nature, but the charm wears off after marriage. These men are simply awful when it comes to relationship skills. When their wives ask for more time, affection, or intimacy, the men respond either by handing over the credit card or screaming, "I can never do enough for you!" and punishing them in some way. If their wives persist in asking for more closeness, these men can become more abrasive or outright abusive.

The wives, for their part, tend to be very dutiful and very lonely. They are often mothers by default — that is, they were not qualified to do anything else and so the job of motherhood fell to them. Homemaking is usually considered unskilled labor. Though *Shipwrecked* moms say they love their children, love runs neck and neck with resentment. They feel trapped both by their own inability to meet their needs and by the level of financial security to which they are accustomed. They tend to take the anger they feel toward their husbands out on their children, either by overpunishing for tiny infractions or setting up the children in constant opposition to their father, all the while undermining the father's authority and framing it as "protecting the children from their dad's temper." Often, the women are "shop-a-holics" who rationalize, "If all he's good for is money, then . . ." Anxiety disorders, prescribed substance abuse, and long-term bouts of depression are common.

Of course, as I mentioned earlier, the husband is just as dependent on his wife. At the very least, she is his trophy and serves to prop up his fragile ego. "I can't be all bad," he tells himself. "After all, I am married." The husband tends to be extremely jealous and often accuses his wife of having affairs, even in the absence of any evidence. This jealousy sometimes is an attempt to mask the guilt he has over his own philandering. Alternatively, his jealousy may eventually motivate the wife to have an affair ("If I'm going to get the punishment, I might as well commit the crime"). The wife learns fairly early on that threatening to leave her husband is the most efficient way to have her requests granted, but any ground gained is quickly lost (about three months, max) once order is restored.

There are other characteristics, but these are the most common examples. Let's take a look at the second type of *Shipwrecked Marriage*.

THE SHIPWRECKED SAFETY MARRIAGE

This is the marriage that occurs when a woman, perhaps determined to have a safer, less chaotic adulthood than childhood, marries a man to whom she is emotionally and relationally superior. He is often a man who was seriously ill as a child, or was severely coddled for one reason or another. He may be a "nice man," but not much more can be said about him.

The marriage is built around avoiding conflict. By her choice of a husband, the wife makes fairly certain that any arguments will be had on her terms, in her time. Though, typically, she is content to remain quiet as well. "Life is too short to argue" could very well be her motto.

Other than having chronic financial troubles (they are hardly the corporate killer types), those in the *Safety Marriage* category coexist pretty much as you would expect until the wife decides she has had her fill of safety and wants more intimacy and passion from her marriage. At this point, she usually discovers that the man who was unable to threaten her also lacks the ability to love her as well as she would like. At best, he is a painfully slow learner. The wife will probably begin pushing her husband to go to therapy, participate in encounter groups, read self-help books, or anything else in the hope that the good example of more passionate — or at least motivated — men will rub off on him. For his part, he is content to sit on the couch. From this point forward, there will be tension in the marriage, though it may not be voiced. Instead, they live like brother and sister, and the wife attempts to get her intimacy needs met through an enmeshed relationship with her children. Because of the woman's influence, couples in *Safety Marriages* are more likely to be religiously involved than their *Materialistic* counterparts.

The marriage faces a major crisis when the children leave the nest. But it is interesting to note how many of these children do not leave — or leave extremely late. The mother will usually make a big fuss about how irresponsible an adult child is, but she often enables the child's irresponsibility, thereby postponing being stuck in an empty house with no one to talk to.

There is a third type of *Shipwrecked Marriage:* the *Rescue Marriage,* which we will now discuss.

THE RESCUE MARRIAGE

This type was identified by Dr. Judith Wallerstein and Sandra Blakeslee in their book *The Good Marriage*. It represents a less severe version or some combination of the two types of *Shipwrecked Marriage* we've already examined. The couples in this third category have been wounded in such a way that they are simply content with the basics and never learn to want more. To repeat the sailing analogy that began this section, I would like to point out that these couples are like the second couple who encountered cannibals, volcanoes, and all manner of horrible threats and are just happy to be alive. This is not really a marriage that those with a normal history aspire to, but it works for them. They tend to exhibit high longevity and moderate satisfaction.

There is an important qualifier to add here. Having a traumatic history is not sufficient in itself to send couples to this relatively functional version of *Shipwrecked Marriage.* Just as many people have traumatic pasts and simply reinvent this past in their marriage. *That* people who build their lives around personal comfort and achieving the basics will have some version of the *Shipwrecked Marriage* is not a question. However, determining which of these people will end up in the more functional version of this marriage is, at best, a crapshoot. More research is required to settle this question.

Prognosis and Recommendations for Shipwrecked Marriages

Historically, *Shipwrecked Marriages* lasted forever, though they were less than happy. In contemporary times, these marriages don't last as they used to. The increased social outlets for women, combined with the decreased social pressure to keep marriages together, often provide a deadly one-two punch to the *Shipwrecked Marriage*. Around the ten-year mark, the wife asserts either her independence or greater expectations for life. This causes a major upheaval — usually in the form of divorce — that few couples in *Shipwrecked Marriages* survive. Because the mutual neediness is so high, these divorces tend to be extremely messy (think Vietnam, but with lawyers).

Pastorally speaking, these couples are the ones whose attempts to get annulments cause the greatest controversy. On the one hand, while they *are* emotionally, socially, and psychologically immature, many (I'm guesstimating, but let's say all but the lowest functioning twenty to thirty percent) lack the serious psychological or characterological flaws that would enable them to meet the psychological impairment requirements for annulment. On the other hand, most of these couples have no clue what their marriages are really supposed to be about.

Because these couples are the highest risk on the quasi-healthy scale, pastors — and the Church in general — need to be more careful about identifying and counseling these couples before marriage. One-day "marriage-preparation" programs conducted in the parish are questionably effective in general and completely useless for couples in this group. While the Church cannot be expected to hand out declarations of nullity like candy, no mother who is good and loving holds her children responsible for breaking rules she did not teach them well. In her failure to properly identify, educate, and counsel engaged couples in this category, the Church sets herself up for the public scandal that currently surrounds the issue of annulments. It is a tragedy that is eminently preventable in most cases. Those pastors and Family Life office coordinators interested in learning more about this should contact my office.

For you married couples who think you might be in a *Shipwrecked Marriage*, you might be surprised to know that I believe your marriage is *absolutely worth saving*. It is my contention that marital grace is *meant* for you because you have the most to gain by participating more fully in it. Additionally, research indicates that the problems resulting from divorce outweigh the benefits for most *Shipwrecked Marriages*. Many *Shipwrecked* couples in crisis say, "How can all our arguing be good for the kids? Why should we stay in a loveless marriage?" In the first place, arguing is perfectly fine for kids to witness as long as it is productive. If your arguments aren't productive, then the answer isn't to divorce; rather, the answer is to get some counseling to learn how to have productive arguments (also, see Chapter 8). In the second place, a marriage is only loveless if the two people in the marriage have stopped being loving. In this sense, you are absolutely right. Kids should *not* be forced to have their self-esteem run over by lazy, immature parents who simply refuse to do the work necessary to give their children loving homes. Of course these children will be stuck with lazy, immature parents even after a divorce. The solution to a "loveless" marriage is for a husband and wife to grow up, to learn the skills they need to be loving, and to fulfill their promises to God, their mate, and their children even if they don't *feel* like doing any of these. Whether your marriage is loveless or not is completely up to you (see Chapter 4). This work is hard, but if it were not possible, I would not have an eighty-percent success rate in my marriage counseling practice. More than any other couple, you have the potential to take your bare-bones marriage and make something truly beautiful out of it. You may doubt me. You may lack the energy; but if you can find the motivation, you will, with God's help, create something beautiful. The following four tips, as well as many other chapters in this book, will be helpful to you.

1. Expect more from life.

You have learned that it was either foolish or selfish to want more than "security" from life. To a large degree, this is what has caused you to build your marriage upside-down. Marriage is not supposed to suck the life out of you to sustain itself; sacramental marriage is supposed to be a life-giving thing that empowers you to be what God created you to be. The first step in turning your marriage around is to stop thinking of your dreams, goals, virtues, and values as some sort of "lovely fantasy" that you'll take up one day after you win the lottery. You must prayerfully identify those things God has placed in your heart as important to your fulfillment *and* you must begin making plans to fulfill them. Finding meaningful — as opposed to merely practical or even important — work and roles is essential to entering the next stage of your marriage. You don't need to leave your marriage to do this. In fact, you can probably accomplish these things more efficiently in the context of the security of your marriage. It is always easier to blame a spouse for being "controlling" than it is to admit that you are in the miserable place you are because you have no plans and no backbone. Stop thinking of yourself as selfish and make your spouse be responsible for helping you. You may require counseling to do this. You may even need to live apart from your mate for a time, but you must find a way to balance your God-given mission and the unbreakable promise you made to serve God by remaining with your mate. The Church's position on marriages like yours is quite clear. As John Paul II wrote in *Love and Responsibility*, some couples "may cease to feel that there is any subjective justification for this union [marriage], and gradually fall into a state of mind which is psychologically and physiologically incompatible with it. Such a condition warrants separation from 'bed and table,' but cannot annul the fact that they are objectively united and united in wedlock."

The Holy Father's comments refer especially to those *Shipwrecked* couples in the middle of the crisis that comes before graduating to the next stage on *The Relationship Pathway* (i.e., *Conventional Marriages*). The transition to a better marriage is a difficult one. Your pastor, supportive groups like Promise Keepers, Marriage Encounter, and Retrouvailles, plus a good counselor can help. Don't let your pride stop you from making use of these resources.

2. Learn to meet your own needs.

In order for love to blossom in your marriage, you have to rout out your dependency. What do you rely on your mate to do for you that, at this point, you are unable to do for yourself? Earn a living? Clean house? Cook? Feel good about yourself? Learn to do these things as best you can. If you need more schooling, get it. If you need counseling, get it. If you need practice, practice. Need chokes off love. If you want love, you must stop being so needy.

3. Relate to your mate.

Shipwrecked spouses spend far too much time standing around wondering what their mates want from them. You have no excuse for this. Books like Christian counselor Gary Smalley's *Hidden Keys of a Loving, Lasting Marriage* or John Gray's *Mars and Venus* series and programs like Promise Keepers, PAIRS (an acronym for Practical Application of Intimate Relationship Skills), or Retrouvailles were meant for you (see Appendix 3). Take advantage of them today. Also, seek individual and/or marriage counseling to help you be accountable for the changes you want to make.

4. Get over your addiction to comfort.

Because of your chaotic past, you may tend to feel like you've earned a bit of peace and quiet. Unfortunately, this is going to make you obstinately unwilling to give any more to your mate than you decide is necessary. You will have a tendency to be blatantly dismissive toward, or passively ignoring of, your spouse's requests for more time, more attention, more anything. This is a recipe for disaster. If you wanted comfort, you should have bought an easy chair, not a marriage license. Get to work on fulfilling your and your mate's identities in Christ. Get to work on it now.

Closing Comments on Shipwrecked Marriages

We have covered the toughest ground first. The next stage represents the lion's share of marriages and what *Shipwrecked* couples will graduate to if they complete the work I outlined above. Let's take a look.

2. Conventional Marriages

Most marriages fall into this category (see figure on following page). Yours is very probably one. The good news is that these *Conventional Marriages* are basically happy, "good enough" marriages with a potential for greatness if the couple is willing to do the work. Because many couples consider these to be the "we have arrived" marriages, I want you to pay special attention to the following pages. There are still a few traps the unsuspecting couple can fall into. I call the marriages in this category *Apprenticeship Marriages* because even though they exhibit many of the skills necessary for a good marriage, the couples in them have not mastered these skills to the level that couples higher up on *The Relationship Pathway* have. *Apprenticeship Marriages* consist of two people who are more or less confident in their ability to meet their own basic needs (financial and emotional). Individuals in this category know who they are by what they do (their work, preferences, or roles they play in society). This is the first relationship on the continuum that is primarily centered on love (as opposed to mere companionship), although the couple tends to define love as "making each other happy." As long as a husband or wife feels "taken care of" by the other, all will go well. However, if one person drops the ball, things can go downhill rather quickly, as this upsets the quid pro quo arrangement, and taps into the couple's fears of being taken advantage of (or taken for granted). You will see how this plays out as you read this section.

In addition to these qualities, there are three "entrance requirements" to the *Conventional/Apprenticeship* category: (1) Meaningful work and roles. (2) Negotiating basic gender differences. (3) Beginnings of an organized value system.

1. Both men and women fulfill meaningful work and roles.

The Relationship Pathway

Every relationship travels left to right from its starting point on The Relationship Pathway.
As couples meet new challenges and learn new skills, both their identity strength and marital satisfaction increase.

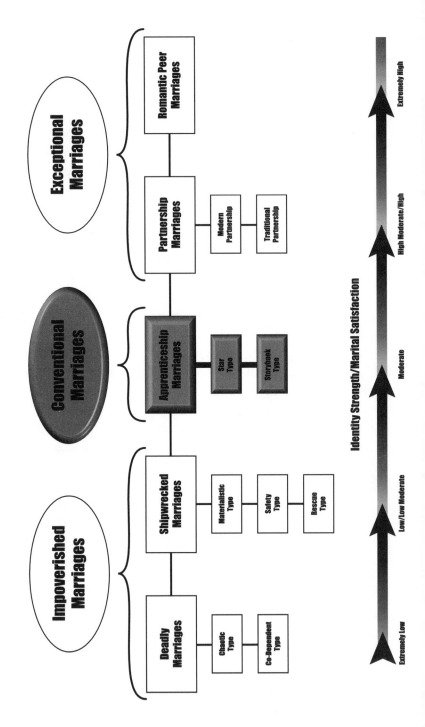

Pursuing work — or another social role (for example, parenthood) — that is viewed as meaningful for its own sake is the single most important distinction of the *Apprenticeship* couple. Whereas *Shipwrecked* couples work (a) to meet basic needs and/or (b) to win the approval and esteem of those around them, *Apprenticeship* couples work because they have found something they truly enjoy doing. This is the difference, for instance, between a physician who practices medicine for the money, power, and glamour, and the physician who loves the art of medicine. For that matter, it is the difference between the mother who stays at home because she is not qualified for anything else and the mother who stays at home because she genuinely values the work of mothering. The tendency of *Apprenticeship* couples to identify with their work has the potential to be either the saving grace of the marriage (it gives them something interesting to talk about) or, if they aren't careful, its downfall (it takes too much time away from the relationship). If you have found either a career that you love, or another social role — like parenting — with which you closely identify (not just by default), then chances are your relationship is at least a *Conventional/Apprenticeship Marriage*.

2. They have negotiated the basic differences between men and women.

Unlike their *Shipwrecked* counterparts, individuals in this category no longer relate to the opposite sex as creatures from another planet. They may occasionally feel that they do not completely understand where their spouses are coming from because they are women (or men), but this is the exception, not the rule. While not as accomplished at this as higher functioning couples on *The Relationship Pathway*, both men and women in this group are better at expressing their emotions, communicating, and meeting their own needs than are their *Shipwrecked* counterparts. They tend to hide out less behind pathetic sayings like "It's a guy thing," or "You're not a woman so you wouldn't understand." *Apprenticeship* men and women genuinely try to understand and be sensitive to the experiences of the opposite sex. They are beginning to be in touch with both their masculine and feminine sides.

3. They have begun an organized value system.

Remember, *Shipwrecked* couples will tell you that they have "values," but they are hard-pressed to name them. Likewise, there is a wide disparity between their professed beliefs and their actual lives. For example, *Shipwrecked* women may talk about "equality and independence," but then they will let their husbands treat them like dirt. *Shipwrecked* men talk about marriage being "fifty-fifty" but wouldn't get off the couch to change the channel much less dust the furniture.

Alternatively, *Apprenticeship* couples' lives tend to reflect — more or less — a loose conglomeration of values generally espoused by polite civilization and the organizations to which they belong. This is the "good enough" marriage of the "good enough" Christian.

Apprenticeship couples are good at setting personal limits ("Don't speak to me that way!") and are also very concerned with the division of household labor (arguments about this are common, but at least the couple is arguing on the same page). Likewise, individuals in this category will have some sense of social consciousness that may center on "equality" or "family values." In middle and later phases of the *Apprenticeship* stage of the couple's relationship, the spouses will tend to spend a great deal of time out in the community furthering their social agenda. The tragedy is that these individuals who can be very generous to their work and community tend to be less giving at home.

As the spouses mature and their value system develops, they will probably seek a group of like-minded believers. At first, such groups will be professional associations or community organizations (Rotary, Lions, the Chamber of Commerce, etc.), but ultimately couples in *Apprenticeship Marriages* will be drawn to more developed values groups that may profess either secular values (i.e., women's movement or "men's groups") or more traditional, religious ones (churches). Regardless, *Apprenticeship* couples tend to have an important but shallow connection to the beliefs professed by the groups to which they belong. They tend to view their involvement as important but are cautious against being taken in by something, and don't like "being told what to do." As one Catholic *Apprentice* I know told me: "I don't know that I agree with a lot of the Church's teachings. I don't even know if what the Church says [about God] is true, but I go because I draw comfort from the rituals."

The primary value of faith and religion for couples in *Apprenticeship Marriages* is their ability to provide stable social roles and values. They are especially concerned with their group's views on gender roles, sexuality, and politics. However, the *Apprentice* is always quick to point out that he thinks for himself — as if that were a question.

If you have at least a social membership in a "values group" (because it is important to you, not because you are afraid of disappointing someone), then chances are good you are squarely in the *Apprenticeship* category.

Apprenticeship Couples: Through the Years

Couples in this category genuinely love each other, and their marriages are often envied by their less socially established friends. But as the name implies, *Apprenticeship* couples will need to develop their skills a bit before they can master the intimacy that people in the *Exceptional Marriages* have achieved.

Perhaps the best way to describe the course of these relationships is to relate the experience my wife and I had of living in our first apartment. It was a cozy place. Small — but filled with love. Even though it was tiny, it suited us perfectly, since we didn't have much back then. We just enjoyed having a home to call our own, and it was a great place to start a life.

As time went by, however, we began to outgrow our tiny nest. We acquired more stuff and needed more space to work on our "projects." One day, it seemed to us that the rooms were getting smaller. The same home that used to feel cozy started making us feel a bit claustrophobic. We needed more space. Our hopes and dreams would no longer fit into such a small package. It was time to remodel — or move on.

I am telling you about our "starter home" because *Apprenticeship Marriages* are kind of like "starter marriages." They are warm relationships with a solid, basic structure; but after a certain amount of time they are going to need some remodeling to accommodate the couple's growth. There are three phases of life to each relationship on *The Relationship Pathway*. I will not address them for the other types of marriages because we simply don't have the space here, but I will address them for the *Apprenticeship Marriage,* since it is such a common first-marriage type.

Phase-One Apprentice: The Early Phase ∼ This is often the phase of the "warm-fuzzy marriage." At this point couples are still in the early stages of their career/social roles and though their futures look promising, they are not yet actualized. To make up for the lack of challenge in the other parts of their lives, *Apprenticeship* couples pour themselves into their role of husband and wife. They make a point of doing romantic things for each other, supporting each other's interests and, in general, being best friends.

Phase Two: The Middle Phase ∼ Things are starting to take off now. Careers are cooking, kids are being cranked out, and the community-at-large is callin' your name. This is a very heady time of life for *Apprenticeship* couples, who are finally getting to harvest the fruit they have been cultivating for so long now. The problem is that instead of enjoying each other's glory, the spouses often spend so much time taking care of business — as it were — that they forget their primary obligation to each other. Often, one mate's attempts to ask the other to spend more time concentrating on the marriage are rebuffed by such comments as, "Can't you see how busy I am? You should know I love you. Why are you being so needy *[or controlling or demanding]* just when everything is starting to take off for me?"

In my opinion, too many couples let the resulting crisis of neglect be the beginning of the end of their marriages. They fail to realize that it is a normal part of their relationship's evolution. Rather than doing the work they need to do in order to become more intimate partners, each spouse delays *his or her own* growth by hiding out behind *Pathetic Excuse for a Divorce No. 1:* "We grew apart."

Phase Three: The Late Phase ∼ Assuming the spouses in an *Apprenticeship Marriage* survive the middle-phase crisis of balancing personal success with intimacy, they enter a phase of questioning. They look at all their accomplishments, possessions, awards, and titles and say, "Is this all there is to life?" At this point, *Apprenticeship* couples will choose one of three options in their marriage.

1. They decide that they, as spouses, have nothing in common and will divorce.

2. They decide that while they have grown apart, this is as it should be at their stage of life. They accept the estrangement, and having achieved a comfortable marital holding pattern, continue to concentrate on career and community success.

3. They start looking for deeper answers. They may read philosophy, study the theology of their church, or seek to discover the spirituality of work and parenthood. It is this pursuit of a personal commitment to a value system that will motivate them to give more of themselves than they are initially comfortable giving to their mate. This self-gift will change the dynamic of the marriage and raise it to a new level of intimacy (the *Partnership Marriages*).

True intimacy requires a willingness to be loving even when doing so makes you uncomfortable — even when your partner doesn't deserve such generosity. This is difficult for many *Apprenticeship* couples because they are afraid of losing themselves in a marriage or being taken advantage of. It isn't that they *really* think their partners are going to use them as boot scrapers; it's just that "you can never be too sure." What these couples must eventually come to learn is that a person with solid identity cannot get lost in a relationship, no matter how close. The real issue is that while *Apprenticeship* couples are on their way to finding their identities, they haven't quite arrived yet. A person whose identity is in its toddlerhood experiences a constant struggle between the desire to be close to someone and the fear of getting too close and losing oneself. As you read through both types of marriages in this category, you will see how this dynamic plays itself out in many different ways.

As I've already suggested, a major theme of *Apprenticeship Marriages* is establishing the couple's identities — and young, growing, identities need plenty of nourishment. Approval and accomplishments provide that. *Apprentices* hungrily seek out opportunities to prove themselves and "get involved." They are the very active members of professional associations, church clubs, political groups, and community organizations. These people don't just belong to organizations — often they *are* the organization. If they have careers, they tend to err on the workaholic side not so much for the money (as with *Shipwrecked* spouses) as for the joy of being "the best" at something. They may be fairly self-critical (experienced as feeling "driven") and have a hard time saying "no" to people. In fact, *Apprenticeship* couples sometimes become so busy pleasing the rest of the world that they don't have much time or energy left for each other. Taking time for each other will be one of the first skills *Apprenticeship* couples will need to master.

Since the pursuit of a more solid identity is a central theme of these marriages, whether a person believes the best way to further his identity is to work himself silly for it, or to marry for it, will determine whether he prefers a *Star Marriage*, a *Storybook Marriage,* or some combination of the two. First, let's take a look at *Star Marriages*.

Star Marriages

Star couples lean toward the basic values espoused by the women's movement. They tend to be fairly liberal in their politics and sexual attitudes, and *Star* wives seem inclined to favor hyphenated last names. Mixed with Christianity, the *Stars'* more liberal politics tend to endear them to social-justice issues, and righting perceived wrongs in the Church like "exclusive" language, a male-only clergy, and the Church's position on sexual issues in general and artificial birth control in particular. People in *Star Marriages* (also known as "near-peer" marriages) are very committed to their careers (whether high-paying and glamorous, or not) and tend to draw most of their sense of self from the work that they do. *Star Marriages* exhibit moderate longevity and moderate satisfaction. What attracts *Stars* to each other is often that they are the most attractive, talented, intelligent, and/or creative people in their respective circles. They are excited by each other's ambitions, and both husband and wife are — or have strong ambitions to be — *Stars* in their own right.

While there is genuine love at the heart of this marriage, it is often constrained by a mutual understanding that careers come first. *Star* husbands and wives may border on workaholism; but unlike *Shipwrecked Materialistic* couples who do it for the money, *Star* couples work for the thrill of being "the best" at something. At first, this mutual drive is exciting. It can be a thrill to be around a talented, creative, ambitious, competent, and interesting person. But if the spouses aren't careful to take time for each other, their marriage can become a collective monologue, consisting of two people who talk, do projects, and live in the same house but rarely *really* relate to each other. Intimacy would come with an investment of time, but time is the most precious commodity for *Star* couples, who sometimes have some difficulty choosing their marriage over their work, even when it is necessary. Again, they are afraid of losing their identity, or perhaps of becoming a *Shipwrecked* couple like their parents may have been. Choosing to come home early from work or deciding to turn down a project or promotion for the sake of spending more time together may seem just a little too much like passing up a golden opportunity to shine. As one *Star* wife put it, "I love him, but I have to stay busy. He knows I can't turn away work just so we can sit at home and stare at each other."

It is not that *Stars* don't *want* to be available to their mates, it's simply that their identities require them to be elsewhere most of the time. This tends to put a damper on their sex life. Though *Star* couples tend to be more sexually liberal than their *Storybook* counterparts, they are often just too tired to be physically intimate. Both types of *Apprenticeship* couples view sex not so much as something that flows from a good relationship and gives life to the couple, but rather as "one more thing to do at the end of the day" (albeit a moderately pleasant thing). As such, when a couple is busy, lovemaking is the first thing that goes out the window.

Combining all of these factors means that *Star* couples are at moderate risk for affairs. Considering that such couples spend so much time at work or the gym, or are involved in other interests — and not with their mates — it should not come as a surprise that they often find attractive, more relevant (and available) companions in those places. Even if affairs do not occur, without proper maintenance the *Star* couple runs an extremely high risk of growing apart.

A second, major threat to *Star Marriages* is childbirth. Because *Stars* fear losing themselves in a marriage, they tend to be ambivalent about the "parent trap" in general. *Star* couples may want children, but they are perhaps slightly more concerned with maintaining the balance of power in the relationship.

If the couple does not achieve a certain intimacy before the birth of a child, the *Star Marriage* may suffer an affair or other life-threatening crisis after the child is born. The risk of such a crisis increases exponentially if the *Star* wife wants to stay home with the child. Since "balance of power" is synonymous with "economic equality" in a *Star Marriage*, stay-at-home moms upset the equation. Stay-at-home moms, for all they contribute, don't earn much. For all his stated high-mindedness about women needing to have the freedom to make their own choices, the *Star* husband often starts to resent all the financial burden being placed upon him. He feels guilty about this resentment — of course. But that doesn't necessarily stop him from treating his wife with mild contempt, or running to the arms of another *Star* woman he meets at the office.

Even if the *Star* wife doesn't stay home, the couple will have some issues to work out. Research shows that women in this category tend to work two shifts, the first at the office and the second at home. The husband has his heart in the right place but doesn't always stand behind his words. He often leaves too much of the parenting and housework to his wife. This will be a major source of conflict for this couple.

The turmoil that follows the above crises often ends the relationship, but it doesn't have to. In my opinion, it mustn't. There is a great deal that is good about these couples: specifically their creativity, intelligence, mutual respect, and love. A crisis is not a sign that the marriage is bad; rather, it is a sign that *Star* couples have been holding back from each other and didn't know how to reach out for a long time. If these couples would simply take some of their ambition and apply it to having the best marriage on the block, they could create something truly incredible. I will offer specific recommendations for *Star* couples in a moment; but right now let's explore *The Storybook Marriage,* the second type of *Apprenticeship Couple.*

The Storybook Marriage

Storybook Marriages, like their *Star* counterparts, exhibit moderate longevity and moderate satisfaction. They are built around the roles supported by a devotion to "family values." These marriages tend to happen when both husband and wife *could* support themselves. But truth be told, the woman drawn to this marriage views any job she may have as a way to pass the time until she can achieve her primary objective — landing "Mr. Right." Perhaps the following is the best way to explain *Storybook Marriages.* "Once upon a time, there was a Princess who wanted to be a *Star;* but she, for one reason or another, thought it was unlikely or inappropriate to become a *Star* in her own right. So, she found herself a Prince who exhibited stardom through his promising future, or even better, his membership in a prominent family (i.e., your neighborhood's version of the Kennedys). At the very least, he was viewed as a 'catch' and she hitched her coach to him. They had a beautiful wedding and lived happily ever after — basically." That's fine as far as it goes, but as you may have guessed, there's more to the story.

Storybook Marriages tend to be viewed as a way to advance the career of the husband and the social standing of both. Both Prince and Princess are joiners — like their *Star* counterparts; but the organizations they join will revolve around his or his family's interests: their church, their club, or their civic organizations (although she quickly learns to maintain the social calendars of these groups). Again, like the *Stars*, these people don't just join organizations — most often they *are* the organization.

The Princess in this fairy tale tends to be more physically attractive than average. She learned early on that her appearance was her best asset for getting what she wanted in life. Although she may resent this fact, she has most likely used it to her advantage at one time or another. She also tends to pride herself on being outwardly deferential. Early in the marriage, when she does state her preferences, she tends to back down at the earliest signs of husbandly disagreement, "I guess you know what's best. *Really,* honey, that's fine" *(stoop, sigh, sulk).* But this meekness dissipates as the years go by. In fact, the Princess definitely comes to see herself as "the great woman behind the great man." She is willing and able to push her Prince to achieve his potential when necessary. Conflict may arise if his career performance and choices fail to meet her expectations.

The Princess is exceptionally devoted to her home and children, whom she loves dearly; but because she really never found her own place in society at large, she may struggle with feelings of worthlessness when she compares herself to *Star* wives. Her conflicted feelings are not helped by the husband who — though he esteems "family values" in general — tends to resent her dependence on him to be breadwinner and "man of the house." He often expresses his resentment either by constantly saying, "You need to get out of the house and do something," or by passively taking her, and her work, for granted.

Withholding sex, treating it like a job, or being sexually timid because passion isn't "ladylike" are some of the ways the Princess tries to prove her worth. She often can overcome this if the husband would work on his romantic skills; but, then again, the husband says he would be more romantic if she were more sexual (remember *Marital Chicken?*). Another way the Princess asserts her independence is to stage petty rebellions (for example, buying items and lying to her husband about their cost). Or, she works out of the home but sees her money as "her money" and his money as "our money."

The Prince, for his part, tends to see himself as the head of the household. However, unlike the *Shipwrecked* husband, the Prince is a benevolent dictator. For instance, he is always careful to explain to his wife why his way is the "right way." He doesn't intend to come off as Supreme Commander in Chief of the domestic front. He is basically a decent person. His main faults are that he likes to be comfortable, tends not to ask for an opinion twice, and comes into the relationship believing that someone would actually *want* to devote her whole life to taking care of him. After all, *his* mom did, and the Princess led him to believe she would *before* the wedding. In other words, he is both old-fashioned *and* naïve.

The Prince's other struggle is that because so much of his identity may be tied up in "being a *[insert profession, cultural heritage, or his family name here]*," he has a very hard time standing up to bosses or Mummy and Daddy, even when his marriage depends on it. The *Storybook* partners love each other well enough; but like their counterparts in *Star Marriages,* they find that their love tends to be limited to what each spouse can give without stretching himself or herself too much. There is a great deal of lip service paid to requests for the husband to come home from work early, or the wife to be more sexual, or for the couple to go out on more dates, or any other such thing; but "unforeseen circumstances" always seem to prevent the requests from actually being fulfilled. Such circumstances (like the proverbial "last-minute meeting" or desire-killing "headache") serve the function of letting yourself off the hook with your spouse, while still keeping her approval. People aren't stupid though, and, after a while, these lame excuses wear thin. Eventually the couple begins to play *Marital Chicken* (see Chapter 2), saying, "Why do *I* always have to be the one who gives in first?" or "I would be more sexual *[or romantic, communicative, complimentary]* if you would be more sexual *[or romantic, communicative, complimentary]*, but I know you. You'll never change!" *Star* couples play this game too, usually around negotiating work schedules.

This relationship goes along fine — by all appearances — until a few years after the birth of the first child. Then one of two things often happens. The first possibility is that the Princess gets caught up in her role of mother and begins doting on the child. The husband's neediness flares up and he becomes resentful, even jealous of the child (or children). He sometimes acts out this resentment by whining, "When are you going to make time for me?" — which makes her want to be around him less, which makes him whine more (there's that *Marital Chicken* again). If this cycle is not broken, it will most likely result in the husband's having an affair, or being seriously tempted. As a result of this crisis, the spouses will either divorce or finally begin to do the work they need to do to move their marriage to a more intimate, open place.

The second possible crisis that occurs after children are born to the *Storybook* couple is that one day the wife can't stand staying in "her place" anymore. Seemingly out of the blue, she announces to a completely shocked Prince that he is a controlling bastard, screaming: "This whole marriage is about *you*! *Your* job, *your* family, *your* kids, *your* money! When do I get what I want?" (Sometimes this announcement is accompanied by the news that she is having an affair with someone who really appreciates her.)

If the Prince responds with some version of, "You're nuts! Shut up, will you?" the marriage is doomed. She will do everything short of burning down the house to prove that, in fact, she is not crazy — thank you very much.

If, on the other hand, the Prince overcomes his shock and responds with a sincere, "Oh my God, I never wanted you to feel that way. Everything we have is at your disposal. You decide what you want and do whatever you need to get it. In fact I'll help you!" — the couple will go on to have a very fulfilling partnership.

Recommendations for Star and Storybook Marriages

Many *Apprenticeship* couples get divorced, mostly because they "grew apart." But it is important for any Catholic *Apprenticeship* couple to know that except in perhaps the rarest cases, *Apprenticeship Marriage*s most likely do not meet the basic criteria for psychological or characterological incapacity used by marriage tribunals to decide declarations of nullity (annulments). Moreover, research definitely demonstrates that the emotional and psychological costs of *Apprenticeship* divorces far outweigh any short-term benefits.

This being the case, *Apprenticeship* couples would benefit from a clearer understanding of the points I explained in Chapter 2. When I have the opportunity to counsel Christian *Apprenticeship* couples, I explain the concept of marriage as a partnership in fulfilling Christian identities. They are absolutely shocked. "I never heard that before!" is the most common comment. How sad. At any rate, once they have heard it, you would be amazed to see how quickly these couples are able to turn their marriages around. About ninety-five percent of the Christian *Appren-*

ticeship couples I explain this to stay together and, better still, build stronger, more fulfilling marriages. Modern-day *Apprentices* tend to be very psychologically savvy and are very interested in "personal growth and fulfillment." Explaining marriage to them in these terms suddenly makes everything come together. Almost immediately, the couple seated before me with the "I dare you to make me love my spouse" look on their faces become a couple who are interested in what I have to say and motivated to make things work. I would like to offer a charitable challenge to all those in charge of preparing couples for marriage: "Don't just teach couples the theology of marriage; teach them what the theology means to their daily life." Saying that the two become one in Christ, or that husbands and wives are supposed to be Christ to one another, or even that the husband and wife's relationship is supposed to mirror Christ's relationship with the Church — all this is well and good. It is certainly orthodox, scriptural, and poetic enough. But we need to take it to the next level. We need to say, in practical, specific terms, what all this means. Otherwise it's just Theospeak — psychobabble's distant, more religious cousin. I once heard someone say that it should be required of all seminary graduates to be able to explain the greatest mysteries of the Catholic faith to a kindergarten class. Would that this were so.

As I stated earlier, *Star* and *Storybook Marriages* are not bad; they are just a teeny bit shallow and lacking in intimacy. If *Star* and *Storybook* couples spent as much energy making intimacy work as they did playing roles, such couples would be set for life. If you find yourself in a *Storybook* or *Star Marriage*, you will benefit from the following six suggestions.

1. Take time for each other.

Whether *Star* or *Storybook*, both kinds of *Apprenticeship Marriages* can get very lonely if you aren't careful. So, be careful. The world will not stop revolving if you turn down a project, or stand up to certain members of your family (Mom or Dad, for instance). Make decisions with your marriage in mind. This applies to *Apprenticeship* stay-at-home moms as well, who may tend to ignore their marriages and get lost in their mothering and housekeeping roles. Take time to be with your spouse. One author suggests that to have a good marriage, you must spend at least fifteen hours per week one-on-one with your partner (sleeping hours don't count — you cheater). Are you ready to do this? You need to be if you want your marriage to survive and thrive.

Perhaps the most important thing you need to know that will empower you to make this choice is the Church's teaching on the value of work. In John Paul II's *Laborem Exercens* (the encyclical "on human work"), he explains that work is for people, not the other way around. In other words, if you are a married person, your primary obligation — that is, what you give the majority of your energy and time to — must be loving your family. Your "fundamental and innate call" is to love. Not work. Work is important. Work is fulfilling, but work must play a supportive role in family life. Work must nourish the family, not destroy it or compete with it. As Fathers Hogan and LeVoir say in their analysis of John Paul II's teaching on family life, "The familial bond was established by God prior to the invitation to share in his creative act through work. Further, the family is more closely associated with God since it is in the family that new life is brought forth" *(Covenant of Love)*.

If the work you do draws your family closer together, then that is one thing. If the work you do competes with your family or even threatens it, then you have some rethinking to do. This applies to parenting as well. *Apprenticeship* couples are so concerned with their children's socialization that they involve them in fourteen thousand activities — on Wednesday. The most important key to good socialization is spending time with one's parents. Think about it. From whom are your kids more likely to learn good manners, confidence, and values (the goals of socialization)? You? Or the other kids at the Lord of the Flies Day Camp?

2. Develop your own intimacy skills.

You need to work on your intimacy skills. What's that you say? Your intimacy skills are just fine? Well, OK. But how about taking this pop quiz just to be sure: "Can you offer opinions when asked without getting defensive? Can you listen to other people's very different opinions without getting angry or feeling threatened? Are you afraid of losing yourself in your marriage? Are you afraid of loving your mate more than she loves you? Do you play *Marital Chicken*? Do you have a hard time saying 'no' to everyone except your mate? Do you have roles based on compensation rather than complementarity?"

If you answered "yes" to one or more of the last five questions above, you may indeed have some work to do (see Part 2 of this book for help and more information).

You could also use some "partnership lessons." Specifically you need to learn how to help meet your partner's needs while remaining true to your own (see Chapter 8). This is a major challenge that stands between you and a truly *Exceptional Marriage*. For example, how can you balance your mate's need for you to spend more time with her and your need to complete certain projects? How can you balance your need to communicate more with your mate's need for more physical intimacy? How can you balance your desire for career advancement with your mate's own desire for career advancement and still have a family life? A good counselor can help you if you get stuck, or just want to know more. Chapter 8 of this book will also be a good resource for you.

3. Never, never, never accept the "I don't know" or "Whatever you want, honey" answer. (This is an especially big concern for early-stage *Storybook Marriages*.)

"I don't know" isn't an answer. It is capitulation. Eventually such responses will infect your marriage with resentment. This is one infection you don't want to have to clean.

Make the point early that you value and expect your partner's input (this applies to both men and women). Don't be afraid to be ridiculous about this. You may starve for three days waiting for your spouse to tell you at what restaurant he or she would prefer to have dinner, but you will have saved yourself a big mess in the end.

4. You must learn to be loving even when doing so makes you uncomfortable.

Conventional/Apprenticeship spouses often work very hard at loving their partners the way they themselves want to be loved, but they tend to ignore the things their partners really want them to do. For example, a *Conventional* wife may kill herself redecorating the house for her husband only to be greeted with minimal thanks because it just isn't that meaningful to him. Now, *he* would just fall in love with her all over again if she would cook chicken wings and watch *Monday Night Football* with him, but she would never do that because "You know I hate football." What happens over time is the husband becomes resentful because "She never does anything to show me she loves me," and the wife becomes resentful because "He never appreciates the things I do to show him I love him." *Apprenticeship* husbands act in similar ways toward their wives. There are a million examples of this in every *Apprenticeship Marriage.* The problem is — to put it in management terms — the couple is working hard but not working smart. If you want a successful marriage, you need to love your mate in a way that is meaningful *to her*, not simply in a way that you think *should* be meaningful (see Chapter 7). You are going to need to do this even when it makes you uncomfortable, not because your spouse necessarily *deserves* such generosity (it is so rare that people deserve to be loved), but because that is the kind of loving, generous, self-giving person *you* want to be at the end of your life. People always say to me, "But what if I do all these loving things for her and she doesn't do anything for me? That would make me look pathetic."

Look, do you *really* think your mate is such a putz that she would not lovingly respond to your loving efforts? More likely, you are simply using this statement as an excuse to avoid dealing with your *own* fears of intimacy, of upsetting the balance of power in your marriage and becoming a victim. Well, it's time to grow up a little. Admittedly, this can be a big step. Ask God for help; certainly he knows what it's like to give more love than he gets. If you can't do it on your own, a good counselor can help you.

5. Learn some advanced techniques.

Though you have negotiated most of the basic differences between men and women, you could benefit from some more advanced marital techniques. These will be explained in Chapter 7. But for now it will be enough for you to know that because you get so much of your identity from what you do, you have a tendency to confuse preferences with identity. For example, you might say things like, "My husband *[wife]* and I are completely different people. He *[she]* is a person who likes football *[shopping, classical music, country music, yellow, red, etc.]*. That's just not me."

Let's get this straight. Those may be things you like or enjoy; but unless you are a remarkably shallow person — and I am sure you are not — those things are not who you *are*. Who are you, really? You *are* a person who values love, wisdom, generosity, etc., who might be willing to challenge your *dislike* of football, shopping, classical music, country music, yellow, red, etc., if it meant giving you an opportunity to *become* more loving, wise, generous, and so on. This is how the *Exceptional Seven Percent* treat such differences between partners. We would be wise to imitate them.

Earlier, I said *Conventional* couples' identities are in their toddlerhood, and the above is a perfect example of this. Two-year-olds know who they *are* because of their preferences and the things they do. A two-year-old may, for example, identify himself as "the boy who only eats sandwiches with the peanut butter on *top* of the jelly and the crust cut off." If you mess with this order, he will act as if you have destroyed his whole world. *Conventional* husbands and wives do the same thing. "I would *never* be caught dead eating *X*, watching *Y*, shopping at *A*, doing *Z*. That's just not me!" This attitude is genuinely obnoxious and woefully immature. It limits a person's growth, and plants the seeds of estrangement in a marriage. Start identifying with your values, not your preferences. Go back over Chapter 2. Chapters 4, 6, and 7 will also help you sort this out.

6. Bring your values home.

This is the *single, most important challenge* that confronts you. It will enable you overcome all of the challenges I have described thus far. To move to the next stage, you are going to have to treat your value system as more than a nice social agenda, an important thing to do, a good way to meet people, or an upstanding way to spend Sunday mornings. You are going to have to learn more about your faith (and/or beliefs) and start practicing it even when it stretches you, even if that means you can no longer be a "smorgasbord Christian," picking and choosing among the various beliefs held by your church (or other "values group"). Why must you do this? Two reasons.

The first is accountability. Your comfortable value system isn't enough to motivate you to be loving and faithful to your mate even when you are angry with her — even when she doesn't "deserve" this generosity. Right now, you tend to be loving to her when she is loving to you. You can be giving to her as long as she is equally giving to you. But to get to the next level, one of you is going to have to start giving more of yourself than would seem reasonable at first. The only way to do this and maintain your integrity is if you see this self-gift as an exercise in spiritual growth, an opportunity to become a better example of the values you claim to hold, more of the person you believe God created you to be. If you do not make yourself truly accountable to the values held by your church, you will be unable to give more of yourself than your mate has earned without feeling like a sucker.

The second reason is fidelity. When your marriage goes through the normal crisis that accompanies the transition to the next stage of married life, you may feel for a time that you and your mate have nothing in common. Like the roles you and your mate play in society have evolved into two separate worlds that you may have little interest in bringing together. This is a normal crisis, but it is a crisis nonetheless. The only thing that will keep you from running to the arms of someone who "understands you" better than your mate is clinging to the values taught by your church. If you do the work necessary to carry your marriage through this phase, your relationship will be counted among the top fifteen to twenty percent of all marriages and you will be that much closer to becoming the person God created you to be. But if you only have the easy values of polite society to hold on to, you're going to blow it. You already have meaningful work. Now it is time to develop a value system that is meaningful beyond the meetings you attend, the boards on which you serve, and the good social values you uphold. This is especially true if you are a Christian. Christianity is more than a way of leading a good, upstanding life. Christianity is primarily concerned with sanctifying everything you do: from the way you work to the way you love, from the way you treat others to the way you make love to your spouse. More than anything else it is about surrendering your life to the Divine Truth that will set you free to spend eternity with the loving God who made you. Christianity is more than a social agenda. It is time to bring your life into closer communion with your spirituality and values — even the parts you don't like. I know you resent being preached at, and so do I; but complaining that your pride is offended doesn't make the sermon any less true.

Conclusion to Apprenticeship Marriages

Exceptional Marriages — the next stop on *The Relationship Pathway* —will show how all the principles I described above work in real life. But before we go there, I'd like you to read the following passage from *The Velveteen Rabbit.* It is the story of a toy rabbit that very desperately wants to become real. I like to refer to it when I'm tempted to choose my own comfort over intimacy. In this excerpt, the Velveteen Rabbit seeks advice from the oldest toy in the nursery: a shabby leather-covered rocking horse.

> "Real isn't how you are made," said the Skin Horse. "It's a thing that happens to you. When a child loves you for a long, long time not just to play with, but *really* loves you, then you become Real."
>
> Does it hurt?" asked the Rabbit.
>
> "Sometimes," said the Skin Horse, for he was always truthful. "When you are Real you don't mind being hurt."
>
> "Does it happen all at once, . . . or bit by bit?"
>
> "It doesn't happen all at once," said the Skin Horse. "You become. It takes a long time. *That's why it doesn't often happen to people who break easily, or have sharp edges, or who have to be carefully kept"* [italics mine].

A good marriage happens about the time we stop carefully keeping ourselves. Let's take a look at some of those marriages that have been, as the Skin Horse in *The Velveteen Rabbit* would say, "loved into Real."

3. Exceptional Marriages

These are the marriages *Apprenticeship* couples are trying to emulate. The relationships in this category (see figure, facing page) are primarily concerned with pursuing intimacy. Once you can meet your basic needs and have a solid sense of your own place in the world, you are ready

The Relationship Pathway

Every relationship travels left to right from its starting point on The Relationship Pathway.
As couples meet new challenges and learn new skills, both their identity strength and marital satisfaction increase.

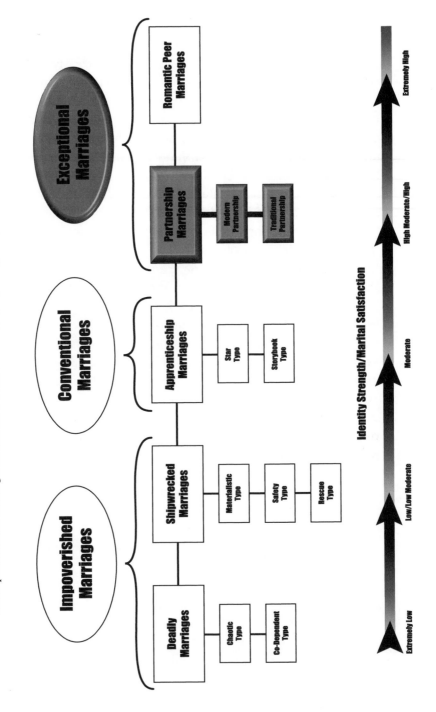

to begin building something larger than yourself: an *Exceptional Marriage* (also referred to in the literature as a *Romantic Peer Marriage*). Besides the high value they place on intimacy, couples in *Exceptional Marriages* have another quality that sets them apart. In an *Exceptional Marriage*, husbands and wives are *equally skilled* at communicating and respectfully expressing their emotions. Research clearly shows that you can't have a good marriage unless you are peers in these areas (see Chapters 7 and 8 for more information and help). In fact, one of the main reasons couples in less-good marriages have best friends and lovers who are not their spouses is that they are searching for someone who will understand them. Couples in *Exceptional Marriages* do not struggle with this problem.

There are two major categories of *Exceptional Marriages: Partnership Marriages* and *Romantic Peer Marriages*. While they are different from each other in important ways they do share some common ground. Couples in both marriages make decisions on their time, energy, and work by considering their marriage and family first. They are comfortable turning down projects, invitations to social functions, or even certain friendships and career moves that would take too much time away from their marriage. To varying degrees, what allows these couples to make such bold decisions is their own *deeply personal commitment to a value system*. They rely on this set of beliefs for guidance in making all major decisions. An *Exceptional Marriage* might be based on qualities esteemed by the women's movement, or a more theologically oriented system. Either way, the values will include egalitarianism and mutual respect, and if the spouses belong to an organization supporting their beliefs, the couple's commitment will be more than a superficial one (this is opposed to *Apprenticeship* couples who view their memberships as "important roles" they play). In addition to making decisions with their marriage in mind, the spouses' adherence to a value system allows them to do the following.

✔ *They are loving even when it requires them to grow or it seems "unfair."*

Couples in *Exceptional Marriages* are secure enough to know they will not allow themselves to be walked over. They would be financially and emotionally capable of leaving a marriage today if they decided it was necessary. Because they are secure in themselves, they do not keep a running tally of offenses like couples in less-good marriages do. Likewise, they are willing to challenge their own preferences, weaknesses, and ways of doing things. This commitment to a value system frees up people in *Exceptional Marriages* to act in loving ways not because their

76

spouses always deserve it, but because they see themselves as individuals who value intimacy, compassion, love, and commitment. Not to live up to those values is to disappoint themselves.

✔ *They see their mates as essential partners in helping them live up to all of their values and goals in life.*

Research on *Exceptional Marriages* attests to their uncommon longevity and happiness. What makes them so special? As I suggested early in the chapter, it is the goals these couples have built their marriages around.

Most marriages enter a crisis when couples run out of goals. That's why so many relationships end after medical or graduate school, when children are born, when children leave the nest, or even when couples retire. All of these milestones are goals on which people base their less-good marriages. When the goal is completed, couples experience a major shake-up as they scramble to figure out, "Now what?"

In *Exceptional Marriages*, the primary goal in life — more than having a nice home, raising kids, or traveling after retirement — is *being a loving person* (among other qualities). This goal lasts a lifetime. Marriages built around such a goal will always be relevant.

How do you know if you are building your marriage around such a value system? A more *Conventional* couple will read the above statement about being a loving person and think, "Oh, yeah, well, I want that too." But a person in an *Exceptional Marriage* will think, "Yes. That's what I want more than anything else. And I would be willing to get off the fast track in my career, reduce the number of friends I have, and decrease my involvement in other activities to get it."

Just as important as having a value system is viewing your mate as an essential partner in helping you live up to those values. Couples in *Exceptional Marriages* believe that their partners are instrumental in helping them achieve their goal of being a more loving and/or secure, confident, creative, fun, open, intimate person. Let me give you an example. My wife and I are best friends, close confidants, passionate lovers, and each other's dearest companions. But even if all these things failed one day (and for many couples they do at one point or another), I would never seek a divorce because there is one thing that I admire about her more than anything else: I know that there is not a single person in the world who can call me on (i.e., lead me to Christ), or call me up short, the way she can. I need her feedback, and I work very hard to give her good feedback as well. There are times when we argue or become frustrated with each other as we struggle to solve problems together. But divorce is never an option because no matter how upset we feel in the heat of the moment, we know that we would not be the people we are today without each other. Moreover, we are confident that we will be better people tomorrow because of each other's influence. Even in our angriest, most frustrating times, we would rather cut out our own hearts than go through a divorce. We know any tension experienced during a heated argument is simply a growing pain that accompanies becoming more loving, wise, intimate, open people.

I share my own story simply because my marriage is a ready example, but my wife and I are not alone in this experience. If you doubt me, take a look at books like Dr. Judith Wallerstein and Sandra Blakeslee's *The Good Marriage* or Dr. Pepper Schwartz's *Peer Marriage;* I believe such books will make a believer out of you. Both are based on major studies of *Exceptional Marriages* and provide much of the evidence to back up my statements here.

There are a few other items that make *Exceptional Marriages* unique, but you will read about those as we explore the two major categories of *Exceptional Marriages*. Because the central theme of an *Exceptional Marriage* is living out and mastering a particular value system, whether the spouses are still learning that value system or have internalized it (own it) will determine whether they have a *Partnership Marriage* or a *Romantic Peer Marriage.*

Partnership Marriages

Partnership Marriages exhibit high longevity and high satisfaction. The couples in *Partnership Marriages* construct their intimacy within a framework of fairness. Each partner contributes equally to the marriage (financially and emotionally) from his or her own pool of resources. There are two main differences between a *Partnership* couple and an *Apprenticeship* couple.

First, where *Apprentices* tend to view church (or other values group) as something they do, *Partners* are beginning to see church (or other values group) as something they are. In other words, where *Apprentices* believed they were faithful members of "Values Group X" because they attended meetings faithfully, raised money for X's causes, and chaired various committees, *Partners* may do much of this plus bring their values home. They are beginning to ask hard questions about how their lives and roles as husbands and wives actually measure up to the values espoused by their group, and they are working to make changes in their lives and marriages accordingly.

Second, where *Apprentices* view marriage as a way to *compensate* for individual weaknesses (see *The Unitive End of Marriage* in Chapter 2),

Partners view marriage as an opportunity to *overcome* individual weaknesses. *Partners* seek to grow in competence in areas that they might otherwise find uninteresting. For example, a traditional *Apprenticeship* husband might cook if he *had* to, or the traditional *Apprenticeship* wife might put gas in the car if she *had* to; but the *Partnership* husband would be taking cooking classes while his wife was learning to change the oil. Not because they had to, but because they saw a personal limitation and wanted to overcome it so that they could be better *Partners* to one another. "Why should I make my mate take all the responsibility for car maintenance *[or cooking, cleaning, paying bills, etc.]*. I'm perfectly capable of learning, and that would free us up for more important things."

Because of their more personalized value system and their mutual pursuit of competence, a *Partnership* couple's definition of equality is more flexible than the *Apprenticeship* couple's. Whereas *Apprenticeship* couples base their definition of equality on what society tells them is equal, *Partnership* couples determine equality on the basis of what they themselves consider to be equal. What the partners decide is an equal contribution will determine whether they have a *Modern Partnership* or a *Traditional Partnership*.

Modern Partnership spouses usually define equality in terms of "splitting most tasks down the middle." Both partners work out of the home (thus splitting the financial responsibilities) and both do their best to divide domestic chores and child-rearing equally, although, as George Orwell might put it, the woman is slightly "more equal" on the domestic front. With the home and kids, the *Partnership* husband is more like an eager "assistant general manager" who stands at the ready to do whatever is necessary. He doesn't have to be told twice — but sometimes he still has to be told. Both *Partners* are very concerned with "pulling their weight" to help the marriage function well and have no problems letting the other know what is needed at any time. They are good friends, and good problem solvers.

The major difficulty that *Modern Partners* face is that they constantly feel pulled in every direction. Both husband *and* wife feel guilty about not being at home when they are at work and feel stressed about work when they are at home; but even though this is uncomfortable, it is a shared experience. Everything is fair, and that makes it OK.

Traditional Partners also divide responsibilities equally. But instead of having two people split every task down the middle, like their *Modern* counterparts, *Traditional Partners* attempt to divide all the tasks into two equal categories. The man usually assumes the breadwinner role, but does not restrict himself to this as a husband in a less-good marriage would. He is expected, and expects himself, to be an active father, cook, and housekeeper. The wife generally supervises the domestic front; but her input on financial matters is expected and respected, unlike the patronizing attitude and "womanly deference" that mark many less-good marriages. Further, whereas the domestic and child-rearing responsibilities in *Shipwrecked Marriages* are poorly regarded as servitude (falling to the woman because she has little else going for her), and whereas stay-at-home moms in *Storybook Marriages* constantly vacillate between feeling their motherhood is "important" and feeling it is "not fulfilling," wives in *Traditional Partnerships* choose motherhood and homemaking as a genuine profession. Women in *Traditional Partnerships* often leave interesting and personally relevant careers because their value system places importance on being home to take care of the children. They concentrate on the spirituality of parenthood. This understanding of the spirituality of their role prevents them from ever doubting their worth.

An analogy might help illustrate this point. If a *Storybook* wife met a *Star* wife for lunch, the *Storybook* wife would go home to her husband and say, "Why do you love me? I'm not very interesting. I don't do anything glamorous or important like so-and-so does." Meanwhile, the *Star* wife would go home to her husband and say, "I'm making all the wrong choices in my life. I'm not here for you and the kids like so-and-so is. Why do you love me?" Now if a *Traditional Partnership* wife met a *Modern Partnership* wife for lunch they would have a lovely time, note at some point, "Isn't it wonderful how God is so present in our lives even though the choices we make are different?" — and that would be that. No anguish. No guilt. Just satisfaction with the fact that they have made the right choices for themselves.

In addition to the spiritual confidence felt by *Traditional Partnership* wives, they also believe they can make a greater financial contribution to the family by staying home. *Traditional Partners* cite the statistic that couples with children often keep less than ten to fifteen percent of a second spouse's income after subtracting expenses such as day care. Wives in *Traditional Partnerships* also have the right to delegate any responsibilities that they deem to be more than their fair share to husbands or hired help.

Recently, there has been an upswing in *Traditional Partnerships* because of "attachment parenting" and the home-schooling movement's gain in popularity. Wives who are *Traditional Partners* struggle for a name that denotes the esteem in which they hold their profession. They dislike names like "housewife" or even "homemaker," preferring titles like "family manager" or "professional parent." These alternative titles are respected by both husband and wife and are meant to convey the professional attitude they have toward running a home and actively raising children.

Prognosis and Recommendations for Modern and Traditional Partnerships

Couples in *Partnership Marriages* of both types are generally very stable. Whether or not they can explicitly state the points I expressed in Chapter 2, their lives reflect these attitudes. Furthermore, in both types of *Partnerships*, the husband and wife are quite capable of taking care of themselves and like it that way. They see their marriage neither as a "partnership in comfort" nor as a way to establish their place in the world, but rather as a genuine partnership in which they are working toward goals of intimacy, equality, and mutual service and respect.

Both types of *Partnership Marriages* are busy. But unlike their counterparts in *Apprenticeship Marriages*, the spouses are not only willing to take time for each other, but actively schedule that time. Sometimes this means turning down work or other obligations that conflict with their *rendezvous*. "Unforeseen circumstances" that prevent couples from having their scheduled time are extremely rare. Likewise, in both *Modern* and *Traditional Partnerships*, the husband and wife see each other as co-parents. This is in contrast to couples in less-good marriages who refer to a father caring for his child as "baby-sitting."

Partners are very well-skilled when it comes to negotiating conflict (see Chapter 8). There are very few problems, big or small, that this couple cannot resolve to the satisfaction of both. Despite this fact, two issues may eventually bring some partners to counseling. The first is that, ironically, their deep friendship can have a dampening effect on their sex life. For many people, even so-called "evolved" people, sex still has overtones of being something "bad," "naughty, " or "rebellious." At the very least, sex is often used as a way to prove one's desirability to a mate. Since so little in *Partnership Marriages* is lacking, and the couple's mutual respect leaves little left to prove, *Partners* often experience what Dr. Pepper Schwartz calls "an incest taboo." As one *Partnership* wife put it, "I love sex and I really don't have any hang-ups about it; it's just that I have a hard time 'getting nasty' with someone I respect so much."

What helps *Partnership* spouses through this phase is redeeming their idea of what it is to be sexual. *Partnership* couples with happy sex lives view lovemaking as a spiritual act, a celebration and logical outcome of all that is good in their marriage. Chapter 9 of this book will help you understand this transition better, but it will do for now to know that one of the major tasks for *Partnership* couples is to change their understanding of sex as "getting nasty" to sex as a "free and open celebration of our love." (This is different from *Storybook* couples who sometimes pretend to have redeemed their sexuality by thinking of it the same way they think of Aunt McGillicuddy's antique urn: They regard it with respect, esteem it from a distance, and once a month they dust it. "But for God's sake, don't fuss with it too much!")

The only other issue that tends to plague *Partners* is a constant sense of being pulled in separate directions. Husbands in *Traditional Partnerships* often want to be home with the children as much as their wives, and both *Modern Partners* would probably rather be home with the children; but they all still value financial security and success a little too much to make this possible. There is nothing wrong with this, except that it contributes to their sense of "torn-ness." The couple who accepts this "torn-ness" as a fact of life will not be able to do better than a *Partnership Marriage* — but frankly, most of us should be so lucky. Couples who choose to pursue their values even if it means risking financial success will go on to become *Romantic Peers*.

Romantic Peer Marriages

As far as current research goes, this is the top of the marital food chain. Whereas *Partnership Marriages* focus on intimacy in the context of fairness, *Romantic Peers* (see figure, facing page) focus on intimacy in the context of self-actualization and sanctification. To this couple, nothing is more important than helping each other live out a deeply held set of values. Other couples have values; but what makes *Romantic Peers* different from *Partners* is that while *Partners* still look to a church or other social group to clarify their value system, *Romantic Peers* have almost completely internalized — or "own" — their values. Christian *Peers* will remain active in their churches because Christianity values fellowship and community so much. But for the most part, Christian *Peers* have incorporated the tenets of the group into their lives and no longer have to check with anyone else to see if they are "doing it right." They do what they do, not because they are *supposed* to, or to fit in, but because they have a deep, personal understanding of what living by a certain set of values means *in their unique set of circumstances*. Even so, these individuals are sensitive to the possibility of falling victim to pride ("Look at how wonderfully I'm living out all my Christian values!"). As such, many Christian *Peers* seek regular, individual spiritual direction. Typically, this stage of marriage coincides with the stages of spiritual growth that Father Benedict Groeschel calls the "Illuminative Way," or even the "Unitive Way," in his book *Spiritual Passages*.

The Relationship Pathway

Every relationship travels left to right from its starting point on The Relationship Pathway.
As couples meet new challenges and learn new skills, both their identity strength and marital satisfaction increase.

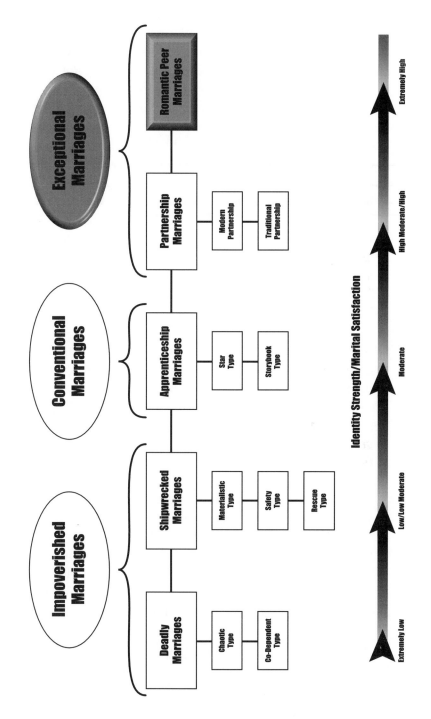

Three qualities are the hallmarks of these marriages: simplification, competence, and egalitarianism.

First, let's look at simplification. Both husband and wife are definitely off the fast track. They *could* work more, but they have come to the conclusion that the time and money isn't worth the cost to their pursuit of intimacy and other values. Don't get me wrong: *Romantic Peers* aren't deadbeats — they just have more important things to do. In particular, I mean loving each other and their children. *Romantic Peers* are not martyrs. They don't give up anything they really need; but they know how to give up everything that is not valuable, like approval, or more money than their needs and most important wants require.

Second, both husband and wife are competent at all aspects of family life. Who dusts the table? Whoever bumps into it first. He is equally good at household chores and does them without being asked, almost without thinking about it. Who works outside the home? Whoever feels his or her values calling him or her to do so at this time. Who takes care of the kids? They both do. *Romantic Peers* are co-parents in the extreme. They love each other and their children more than anything in the world. This is not some saying that simply rolls off the tongue. Their lives genuinely reflect this devotion.

Third, they value egalitarianism over equality. What does this mean? Basically, people who value equality know they are equal because they *do* the same things or the same amount of things as someone else. People who value egalitarianism know they *are* equal, and don't feel the need to prove it by dividing jobs up into nice even piles or by declaring certain tasks to be beneath them. I'll give you a practical, albeit somewhat silly example of how a couple going up *The Relationship Pathway* grows in egalitarianism. The *Shipwrecked* wife might rather die a slow, torturous death than change a lightbulb if she considered it her husband's job; but she would exhaust three hundred times as much energy nagging him to do it. The *Apprenticeship* wife would change the bulb if her husband didn't get to it when she asked, but she would secretly resent his dereliction of duty for the rest of her life. The *Partnership* wife changes the bulb without a second thought. The *Peer* wife would not only change the bulb without thinking about it, but also might have the whole house rewired — to code — by the time her husband came home.

Likewise, the *Shipwrecked* husband would consider watching his children akin to "baby-sitting," something beneath his dignity. He is loath to do it and looks for the earliest opportunity to sack out on the sofa. The *Apprenticeship* husband knows that he *should* want to watch his kids, but it would only be a matter of time before he got bored and sent them to play in the basement so he could get some work done. The *Partnership* husband would eagerly play with the children and would be happy to give his wife a break whenever she asked for it. And the *Peer* husband would be begging his wife to go out so that he could get some time alone with his kids (and the house would be immaculate when she got back).

Egalitarianism means that spouses do not quibble over who does what and how much. They both do whatever needs to be done when it needs to be done and respect each other's ability to do it. To them, masculinity and femininity is not a matter of the jobs a person does; it is a matter of emphasis of certain qualities (see *The Unitive End of Marriage* in Chapter 2).

Some Christians have a difficult time understanding how this is an acceptable way for husbands and wives to behave. How can husbands and wives be so independently competent and still be faithful to both their "male and female roles" and the exhortation found in the Letter to the Ephesians: "Be subject to one another out of reverence for Christ. Wives, be subject to your husbands, as to the Lord. For the husband is the head of the wife. . ." (5:21-23).

As for the question concerning male and female roles, I refer you back to Chapter 2 (under the subhead *The Unitive End of Marriage*), in which I explained the Church's teaching that the real God-given differences between men and women are differences in *emphasis*. As for the passage from Ephesians, I will defer to the writings of the Church and theologians like Pope John Paul II (especially in his *Mulieris Dignitatem,* an apostolic letter "on the dignity and vocation of women"), Germaine Grisez, and William May, to name but a few. Essentially, in any human structure there is a naturally occurring authority, somebody who, whether he admits it or not, is the person looked to for a final decision in emergencies or when there is a deadlock. This kind of authority is a simple sociological fact and is *distinctly different from power or domination,* both of which are unacceptable qualities for any Christian to exhibit. Considering this, all decisions that affect the family should be made with the full cooperation of both husband and wife (and possibly the children). Further, decisions must *not* be made on the basis of who has more power, or whose turn it is to "win"; rather, they should be made on the basis of whose idea more clearly benefits the general good of the family. Therefore, in most instances, the husband and wife will be just as willing to defer to each other, just as Christ demands (cf. Eph 5:21). However, there will be times when either emergencies occur, or when consultation among the family members yields no clear winning answer. In these times, assuming the man is deferring to Christ (cf. Eph 5:21) and has the good of the family foremost in his heart and mind, the man would cast the deciding ballot. This designation is a result of the qualities God ordained Adam to emphasize, qualities that, assuming he is acting in deference to Christ and truly has the good of the family as his foremost thought, make him more likely to be able to discern God's will for his family.

Equality can be at odds with this notion of headship because it values distribution of power over everything else. When equality is the highest value, *the good of the family* often falls victim to the "whoever got his or her way last time must lose this time" mentality. Egalitarianism is not at odds with this model of headship, however, because decisions are never made on the basis of power. The reason for a decision should never come down to: "Because I can." When egalitarianism is valued over either simple "equality" or oversimplified "gender roles," every decision is made with the genuine welfare and happiness of all concerned as the first and only consideration.

The level of competence couples in this category have attained has other benefits. *Romantic Peers* are so good at taking care of themselves and each other that to outsiders their marriages just seem to happen magically. They are what Drs. Lederer and Jackson of the Palo Alto Mental Research Center described as "collaborative geniuses." Of course a great deal of very hard work goes into making these marriages , but it is most definitely a labor of love. *Romantic Peers* are each other's best friends, have virtually no secrets from each other, and have achieved a level of spiritual sexuality that is truly enviable. Unlike couples in less-good marriages that go through periods of boredom with each other, *Romantic Peers'* relationships actually become more vital, exciting, fun, and fulfilling as the years go by.

If they struggle with anything, it is their relative social isolation. *Romantic Peers* are too busy loving each other and living their own lives to have the energy for the *Sturm und Drang* that comes with having too many acquaintances. This is in contrast to *Shipwrecked* couples who avoid others because they fear them, and *Apprenticeship* couples who gorge themselves on a frenzy of acquaintances.

Abraham Maslow, developer of the "Hierarchy of Needs," did some early work researching self-actualizing people. His findings apply to *Romantic Peers* as well. They are at peace in times of uncertainty, are good at accepting themselves and others, can be both spontaneous and creative, have a good sense of humor, value their privacy, can take care of themselves, are capable of deeply intimate relationships, and have an open, positive attitude about life.

Whether or not you think you will ever arrive at such a place in

86

your life, you could learn a lot from such people. The rest of this book concerns itself with teaching you how both *Partners* and *Romantic Peers* solve problems, keep love alive, and maintain the relevance of their marriage throughout the years.

The Relationship Pathway at a Glance

It would be easy to write an entire book on the nuances and traits of each type of marriage I have mentioned in this chapter. I hope that by covering the main points of each marriage, you have a better idea where you come from, where you are at this point in your marriage, and where you will be going from here. We have covered a lot of ground. If you find yourself a bit confused about the various types of marriages, don't worry, the following will provide a ready reference of all the points you need to remember.

The Relationship Pathway at a Glance
Category of relationship:
Deadly • Shipwrecked • Conventional • Exceptional

Types of relationship in the category:
Deadly • Chaotic or *Co-dependent* Relationships.
Shipwrecked • Materialistic or *Safety Marriages.*
Conventional • Star or *Storybook Marriages.*
Exceptional • Modern/Traditional Partnership Marriage or *Romantic Peer Marriage.*

These relationships are primarily concerned with:
Deadly • Escaping reality. Either by losing oneself in chemicals and other high-risk behaviors or by placing more importance on having someone to "love" than acquiring the basics in life (i.e., meeting basic expenses or safety needs).

Shipwrecked • Accumulating the basics of life, that is, safety and/ or money to buy food, clothing, shelter. In *Materialistic Marriages*, money is also used to gain respect. "I am what I have." *Safety Marriages* have "avoiding conflict" as a central theme.

Conventional • Establishing the couple's place in the world. *Star* couples identify with work; *Storybook* couples identify with "traditional social roles." In both cases, the relationship takes a back seat to pursuing acceptance in society at large. Couples act out roles without understanding the values underlying the roles.

Exceptional • Pursuing intimacy. Couples have established themselves and now are ready to make decisions with their marriages in mind. They are committed not just to a social role but have begun to internalize the values that accompany that social role.

Longevity rating:

Deadly • Low.

Shipwrecked • High to moderate, major crises at ten and twenty years.

Conventional • Moderate.

Exceptional • High moderate — high.

Satisfaction rating:

Deadly • When it's good, it's very, very good; and when it's bad, it's awful, with no in-between.

Shipwrecked • Low to moderate.

Conventional • Moderate.

Exceptional • High moderate — high.

How common are affairs?

Deadly • Extremely common.

Shipwrecked • Very common.

Conventional • Somewhat common around childbirth and midlife.

Exceptional • Uncommon to very uncommon.

Capacity for love:

Deadly • Extremely low. Relationship is mostly about neediness and dependency. For these couples, "love" and "needy desperation" are indistinguishable.

Shipwrecked • Low to moderate. Relationship is more about companionship and meeting basic needs than about love. Couples lack maturity to do the work love requires. *Materialistic Marriages* add "spouse as trophy" to this mix.

Conventional • Moderate. There is love here, but it is a "comfortable" kind of love, limited by the self-protective nature of both spouses. Both are afraid of losing themselves. Careers and others often come first. Though couples may say they regret this, they do little to change it, pointing out that "everyone needs his or her space."

Exceptional • High. Relationship is primarily concerned with the pursuit of love and intimacy. To varying degrees, the partners are willing to make concessions in their work life, friendships, and community involvement for the sake of the marriage and the family as well as the goal of "being a loving person."

Major problems this relationship encounters:
Deadly • Addictions, abuse, dependency of all kinds. Problems meeting needs in all areas of life.

Shipwrecked • High-functioning alcoholism. Addictions to gambling and sex. Many are workaholics and "shop-a-holics." Women lead lives of "quiet desperation." Men and women don't understand each other.

Conventional • Spouses love each other but maintain some emotional distance. Become defensive when this distance is threatened. Fairly high risk for growing apart if couple is not careful to share interests and time, and to bring separate worlds together.

Exceptional • Couple's friendship may spawn "incest taboo" to sex. Couple also may feel somewhat conflicted about leaving career fast track or experiencing social isolation that comes with not having a marriage like everyone else has.

Decision that allows couple to begin to move to next stage:
Deadly • The decision to pursue the basic needs of life.

Shipwrecked • The decision to pursue an identity beyond the marriage.

Conventional • The decision to value love and/or intimacy over involvement in career, community organizations, and approval of friends. The decision to pursue a deeper commitment to one's value system.

Exceptional • The decision to internalize the couple's value system and pursue self-actualization.

Skills that couple must develop in order to move to next stage:
Deadly • Must learn how to meet basic needs for self.

Shipwrecked • Must go beyond "the basics." Must stop selling themselves out for "security." Must learn to overcome the basic differences between male and female communication styles. Must find a way to contribute to the community at large. Must accept accountability to "values group" essential for growth.

Conventional • Most overcome fear of "losing self." Must confront the shallowness of role-playing and pursue a greater meaning of life. Must learn to love even when it is uncomfortable to do so.

Exceptional • *Partnership* couples must learn to view sex as the "free and logical expression of all that is good in a relationship" instead of

89

a performance, an energy-draining activity, or "bad" thing. Must face challenges to value system from careers and friends.

Attitudes toward work:

Deadly • Either chronically unemployed or chronically absent from whatever work they happen to have at the moment.

Shipwrecked • Job is a means of acquiring money and goods, not a source of personal fulfillment. However, in a *Materialistic Marriage*, money is the source of fulfillment. Work ethic related to the importance placed on money and financial security. "My work is what I do to make money and pass the time. I'd be just as happy doing something that paid well enough."

Conventional • High value on personally fulfilling work. Identity is highly tied to career or role: "It's not just what I do. It's who I am." Couples struggle with balancing their own needs versus the needs of the relationship and those of their spouses. Very concerned with not "losing themselves" to the relationship.

Exceptional • High value on fulfilling work but major part of identity not tied to work role. Work is less important than having satisfying relationships and intimacy. The *Partner* or *Peer* may sacrifice career opportunities for the sake of the marriage and family.

Attitudes toward raising children:

Deadly • Children in this group must usually learn to fend for themselves. Often the adults themselves are too needy to adequately care for the needs of their children.

Shipwrecked • Parenting usually resembles a power struggle more than a relationship — even from the earliest ages. Power struggle may be parents versus child, or parents versus each other. Parents constantly on guard against being "manipulated" by their children. Stay-at-home moms in this category usually don't have any other options for employment and tend to feel trapped by their role. Sometimes this resentment is played out in heavy-handed "disciplinary" measures. Caricature of the absentee father and "eternally devoted martyr" as mother.

Conventional • *Star* couples are very concerned with not letting parenting rob them of their identity. *Star* couples tend to make use of day-care facilities from the earliest possible age so as not to "lose themselves" in the parenting role. In *Storybook Marriages*, the mother is usually the primary caregiver and tends to identify with this role (sometimes excluding her mate). The stay-at-home mom's frustration is not directed at the children so much as at the husband for his domestic ignorance and inattentiveness. Women in both *Star* and *Storybook Marriages* — if they work outside the home — tend to work a "second shift" on the domestic front.

Exceptional • Couples in this group are confident in their ability to meet their own needs, so they tend not to fear the innate neediness of their children. Husband and wife are co-parents. Both are willing to make career sacrifices for the sake of their marriage and family.

Attitudes toward values groups (includes church and/or secular values groups such as men's and women's support groups, recovery groups, etc., and devotion to certain general philosophical leaders or trends):

Deadly • Usually not applicable, though they may tend to gravitate toward radical "fringe groups" or cults (left- or right-leaning) as an alternative to chemical addiction.

Shipwrecked • One or the other partner in this category usually has a tentative or suspicious mind-set toward organized values groups as characterized by any of the following: (1) Dismisses values groups as full of hypocrites or fanatics. Says, "I don't need anyone to tell me how to think or act." Considers self open-minded but is in reality wishy-washy. (2) Belongs to values group, but membership is merely inherited or habitual. No real effort to conform life to group's beliefs. "I go, but I'm no fanatic. It gives me something to do." Or, "I do it to please Mom and/or Dad." (3) Belongs to values group but mostly focused on radical outward signs of piety or devotion to group rather than a meaningful commitment to value system. May alienate spouse and children if seen as distracting him or her from "the cause."

Conventional • Actively seeking a value system to which they can be accountable. Most likely this will include an ongoing membership in a group of like-minded believers at one point or another. Couples in this category are mostly concerned with values group as its teachings relate to gender roles, sex, work, equality, politics. Tend to be fairly committed to living out the social roles as defined by the group, although they may lack a full understanding of the values or meanings behind those roles and behaviors. Can tend toward rigidity or "know-it-all-ness" when relating their beliefs to others. *Star* and *Storybook* couples tend to hate each other, but they are really opposite sides of the same coin (i.e., they both interpret "values" to mean mores and social roles).

Exceptional • Life more or less reflects a mastery of the social teachings of their values group as well as a firm grasp on the meanings behind those teachings. Tend to be less concerned with proselytizing than with conforming more and more to own beliefs. Most of identity revolves not around work or social but rather around this pursuit of actualized value system. May or may not be active members in a values group, depending upon how high a priority the group places upon the ongoing community and fellowship.

Attitudes toward spousal role. "Whether or not my mate is happy with me at the moment, I know I'm a good spouse if . . .":
Deadly • Doesn't care. "If you're happy, stay. If you're not, go. Just don't complain too much."

Shipwrecked • If . . . "I'm doing at least as much as my acquaintances say they do for their own spouses."

Conventional • If . . . "I'm conforming to the social teachings espoused by the values group I belong to *[or whose values I'm co-opting]*." Or, "As long as I am loving as much as my career or other valuable social involvements allow."

Exceptional • If . . . "I'm being faithful to my values of intimacy, love, etc. Plus I am helping my mate grow in faithfulness to her own values."

Attitudes toward social relationships and community involvements:
Deadly • Socially isolated. Acquaintances limited to drinking buddies, drug users, and the like (perhaps even partners in crime), or, if *Co-dependent*, other victims, who require help in structured environments (for example, support groups for abused women, Al-Anon meetings, and so on).

Shipwrecked • Two extremes here. Either the glad-handing, life-of-the-party person who knows everyone but (when you think of it) doesn't have any close friends, or the socially isolated, super-quiet type who tends to be painfully uncomfortable in social settings and goes to extremes to avoid them when possible. Latter type will also actively discourage mate from developing friendships. "What's the matter? I'm not enough for you?"

Conventional • Big-time joiners. Sometimes can't tell if they are coming or going because of all the committees on which they serve, projects they are planning, and/or social engagements they are attending. Busy, active, on the go. This applies to *Apprentice* couple's children as well, who probably have five thousand activities to attend — on Wednesday.

Exceptional • Couples value quality of friendships over quantity.

Concentrate primarily on own marriage and family life, plus a handful of truly intimate friends.

Attitudes toward making changes for the sake of personal growth and/or increased marital intimacy:

Deadly • "Who are you kidding?"

Shipwrecked • Women in this category tend to want change but either don't say what they want or fail to follow through on requests made. Men in this group would rather die than change — unless their mate threatens to leave them. Then it's, "I'm sorry, baby. I'll do anything — anything!" Of course, as soon as the partner returns, the status quo is restored.

Conventional • Spouses are willing to make changes to improve upon their role (motherhood or career). Less eager to make changes to enhance intimacy of marriage as this might negatively impact the role they get most of their identity from. Tend to be psychologically interested. Very interested in "rules of success" in business and/or personal life.

Exceptional • Couples in this group embrace change that will enhance both personal growth and satisfaction with marriage or family life.

Even after all this information — or, perhaps, in some cases, because of it — some couples have difficulty finding their place on *The Relationship Pathway.* Alternatively, some couples discover certain issues they have and begin asking questions about themselves and their marriages that they are not sure how to answer. In both cases, I am available for "technical support." If you would like to discuss your situation more thoroughly with me, or you would like to get information on competent counseling in your area, please call the Pastoral Solutions Institute at 740-266-6461 for a telephone consultation.

Loose Ends

1. Don't Panic ∼ As we get ready to close this chapter, I feel a strong need to emphasize that most of the marriages on *The Relationship Pathway* are basically good, loving, functioning marriages. You will recall that even many of the *Shipwrecked Marriages* (especially the *Rescue Marriages*) are, to some degree, satisfying to the couples in them. The point of identifying your marriage on *The Pathway* was not to throw you into some crisis over not having "the best" marriage in the world. You have the marriage you do because it is the best marriage God could give you at this point in your life. But, wherever you start out on *The Pathway*, it is your job to move yourself and your mate toward greater perfection in Christ. God chose your mate because more than anyone else, he or she can relate to what you've been through and have the best potential for helping you move ahead — and vice versa. Whether or not you actualize this potential is entirely up to you. My only purpose in having you identify your place on *The Pathway* is to show you what you need to do next to take even greater advantage of the sanctifying grace God wants to give you through your marriage. Don't play a relationship version of "keeping up with the Joneses." Simply work at your own pace, enjoy each step on the journey, and don't panic when the crises come, because they usually mean that you and your spouse are about to enter a new — and better — phase of your life together.

2. Balancing God's Call with Your Marital Promises ∿ By now I suspect I have beaten into your head the concept of identifying and being faithful to the identity you have in Christ. Some people have questions about what to do when pursuing this identity brings conflict in a marriage. This is a very difficult question, but the answer is fairly straightforward. St. Paul tells us that "whether we live or whether we die, we are the Lord's" (Rom 14:8). Likewise, Jesus said, "If anyone comes to me and does not hate his own father and mother and wife . . . yes, and even his own life, he cannot be my disciple" (Lk 14:26). Of course, as Christians, we must at all times attempt to grow in a way that is respectful to our marriages. But first and foremost, our duty must be to God and the mission he has given us in our lives. Everything and everyone else must play a secondary and supportive role to this mission, even our marriages. That is why it is absolutely essential to a *sacramental* marriage that you and your mate build your relationship around fulfilling your destinies in Christ. This way, your growth as a Christian and the foundations of your marriage will never be at cross-purposes.

Sometimes doing what God asks makes us uncomfortable. Following the call God has placed in our hearts occasionally causes even our mates to grow in ways they are not entirely happy about. Husbands and wives are constantly being tempted to use their special, God-given influence in a wrong way, a way that discourages and inspires guilt in their partners simply for doing what God has called them to do. Our desire to discourage our mates, to ask them to sacrifice God's call in their lives for the sake of our comfort is completely understandable — but completely inexcusable. We cannot allow our mates to stop *us* from serving our First Master. Neither should we expect our discouraging attitudes to stop our spouses from pursuing God's call. As St. Paul said: "Be subject to one another out of reverence for Christ" (Eph 5:21).

Of course, if your growth is going to cause pain in your marriage, you must make absolutely certain that it really is the way God wants you to go. (For help, I'd recommend the steps in Father Michael Scanlan and James Manney's *What Does God Want?* — an excellent book on spiritual discernment published by Our Sunday Visitor.) Having done this, you are obliged to follow the path God leads you down, hoping and praying that your spouse will follow and support you, once he or she realizes how serious you are.

C. S. Lewis addresses this point in *The Four Loves:* "So, *in the last resort,* we must turn down or disqualify our nearest and dearest when they come between us and our obedience to God. Heaven knows, it will seem to them sufficiently like hatred. We must not act on the pity we feel; we must be blind to tears and deaf to pleadings" (italics mine).

This is very difficult. As I mentioned earlier, a husband or wife must be very cautious when the path they believe God wants them to take may inflict some serious growing pains on their marriage. They should pray, discern, agonize, and seek guidance from their pastors and counselors, and listen to the good advice they are given. But if all this work points in a particular direction — specifically the direction that *leads one to closer communion with God and a greater capacity for contributing more to the marriage* — one must take that route. This is why it is absolutely essential that your marriage be built around the fulfillment of your identities in Christ, so that your primary obligation to God is never sacrificed to the idol that marriage can become.

Assuming that your marriage is primarily concerned with your fulfilling each other's identities in Christ, you will find that as you and your marriage travel up *The Relationship Pathway,* you will grow in grace, competence, egalitarianism, unity, generosity, meaningfulness, and adherence to a particular value system. I need to make one last point about this concept of adherence to a value system.

3. Of Politics and Values ∼ Some people have accused me of holding a position I do not, in fact, hold. Specifically, I have been criticized as valuing "conservative" theology over more "liberal" theology (especially because of "all that NFP stuff" in Chapter 2). The point of *The Relationship Pathway* is not to support one political position over another, even as far as religion is concerned. The point *is* that in order to travel up *The Relationship Pathway,* one's life must come more closely in line with the teachings of whatever group one belongs to. Otherwise, it is not a matter of surrendering *to* a value system — it is a matter of pursuing your version of that value system. While I do believe that some value systems, having more internal consistency and greater range of application, are better than others, I think that from a purely psychological point of view, any consistent, organized, *objective* value system is better than none. You can move up *The Pathway* by being a true feminist, just as you can by being a good Jew, or a devout Presbyterian, or even — amazingly enough — a faithful Roman Catholic. Understanding that there is complete freedom of choice as to which value system you subscribe, it only goes to follow that whatever you say you are, you must become a more faithful example of, *if* you wish to move up *The Relationship Pathway*. It is no good saying you are one thing and then acting like something else. As Scripture points out: "Would that you were hot or cold! So, because you are lukewarm, and neither cold nor hot, I will spew you out of my mouth" (Rev 3:15-16). If you prefer to act like something else, then *be* it too. But until you pick something to stand for, and then stand for it, you will not be able to move beyond the *Apprenticeship* stage in your life or marriage. Since both your identity strength and your movement along *The Relationship Pathway* are directly dependent upon how well-defined your value system is and how consistently you live that value system out, I hope you can see the truth expressed in these comments.

4. *What Now?* ∽ Finally, having identified both the ideal for your marriage and where your marriage actually is on *The Pathway*, the rest of this book is about giving you the help you need to complete the work you need to do. The advice that follows reflects the attitudes, beliefs, and practices of the *Exceptional Seven Percent*, couples on the highest end of *The Pathway* who exhibit the greatest degree of longevity and fulfillment in their marriages. We'll begin with the most basic of marital questions: "How do you know if you're really in love, and how do you stay there forever?"

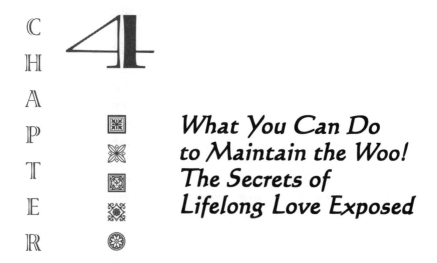

CHAPTER 4

What You Can Do to Maintain the Woo! The Secrets of Lifelong Love Exposed

> Love is a selfless surrender of everything one has and is for the sake of another. There is the expectation in this selfless gift that the other . . . will make a similar gift in return. Human beings love because they are made in God's own image. Without love, human existence is meaningless.
>
> — *R. HOGAN AND J. LEVOIR*
> *Covenant of Love*

One of the saddest things I ever hear in a marriage counseling session is, "I don't know if I love him anymore. In fact, I don't really know if I ever did."

How can you make certain that you never become the person making such a tragic statement? Or, if you already identify with this sentiment, how can you find your way back?

I believe that the secret to lifelong love starts with having a solid understanding of what love really is. Some people say that we love a person because he or she makes us feel good about ourselves. Others say that love is a mystery; it comes and goes with the wind and the best we can do is enjoy it while it lasts. Still others don't make distinctions between romance, sex, and love, believing that as long as passion lives, love exists.

The problem with all of these definitions is that they are limited at best. Of course love should uplift our spirits. But if love is simply one person's ability to make another person feel good, then what happens to love when stress, illness, depression, or other serious but common problems cause a person to resist even our best efforts to help that person feel better? As for the second definition, love is most certainly a mystery; but if it is completely incomprehensible and transient as the tide, how can we ever hope to find the safety and security that we crave from a so-called "stable relationship"? Lastly, sex and romance are an important part of married love; but I suspect that most of us are too familiar with examples of sex without love — and romance without substance — to still believe that sex, romance, and love are the same thing.

Recipe for True Love

So, what is love, and how do you really know if you are in it?

The happiest couples know a simple recipe for creating "true love": According to taste, mix seven to eight cups of companionate love with two to three cups of romantic love. Bake slowly over a lifetime.

Do you have enough of both ingredients in your cupboard? Let's find out.

The First Ingredient: Companionate Love

Dr. Harry Stack Sullivan, a psychiatrist and author, believed that "when the satisfaction or security of another person becomes as significant to one as is one's own satisfaction and security, then the state of love exists."

According to Bishop Donald W. Wuerl, Father Ronald Lawler, and Thomas Comerford Lawler, the editors of *The Teaching of Christ*, Our Sunday Visitor's popular catechism for adults: "Love is . . . the free and firm commitment of each to pursue the good of the other, for the other's sake."

Both of the above are excellent definitions of the first and most important ingredient in married love: companionate love. Companionate love is the active commitment you make to fulfilling each other's dreams, goals, and values — your identities in Christ. At its most essential and important level, to love is to will and work for the good of another. *You know someone loves you if he or she desires your well-being* and *is willing to work for it daily.* Both conditions are absolutely necessary for companionate love to exist. I'm sure you've known plenty of people who have wished you well as they slammed the door in your face. Is this love? Of course not. Even though they said the right words, they didn't *do* anything to help you achieve your well-being. This seems obvious enough, and yet, I am constantly surprised by the number of people who come to me and say, "My husband *[wife]* cheats on me *[beats me, doesn't tell me his work schedule, lies, calls me names, doesn't* come home, calls me 'silly' or 'stupid']; but he says he loves me, so it must be true."

True love requires more than saying, "I love you," or "I support you." It even requires more than a deep sense of longing or attraction for your mate. The words and feelings must be backed up with *action*. If your partner truly loves you, then every day he will make decisions with your needs in mind, make plans with your interests in mind, and prepare his schedule with you as the most important thing on his mind. To paraphrase that preeminent social philosopher *Forest Gump*, "Love is as love does."

By the same token, you love your mate if your *daily actions and choices reflect an obvious concern for his happiness and fulfillment.* One way of understanding the importance of companionate love would be to say that couples should be each other's best friends, except that many people who have an immature understanding of love also tend to trivialize what "best friendship" really entails. Many people think of friendship as "being with someone I feel good around," "having fun with somebody," or "having someone to drink *[or hunt, go to church, go to the club, etc.]* with." One person I knew in college defined a friend as "someone who fosters your illusions about yourself." Obviously, I'm talking about something significantly deeper. The following excerpts capture the essence of marital friendship:

> Friendship is — in a sense not at all derogatory to it — the least natural of all loves; the least instinctive. . . . [Friendship] alone, of all the loves, seemed to raise you to the level of gods or angels.
>
> — *C. S. Lewis*
> *The Four Loves*

> "Friendship" may seem to some a weak word for so close a union [as marriage]: but "friendship" is in fact a rich concept. Friendship is the most perfect form of love: Christ calls those bound most intensely to Him by divine love His friends. . . . For friendship, in its most authentic form, is an unselfish and mutual love persons have for each other, as each knows he or she is loved by the other.
>
> — *D. Wuerl, R. Lawler, and T. Lawler*
> *The Teaching of Christ*

Companionate love has the power to separate me from my illusions while leading me to a reality that is more wonderful and fulfilling than anything I could have imagined. Its importance cannot be overempha- sized. The essence of a good marriage is the couple's commitment to pursue the good of each other. Unfortunately, couples frequently come to marriage counseling saying to me, "I know I care about my husband *[wife]*. I mean, I love him *[her]* — it's just that I don't know if I'm *in* love with him *[her].*" What these couples are saying to me is actually very encouraging — although they don't know it yet. They are telling me that there is at least a basic friendship in their marriage, though they are lacking a certain "specialness," or passion. To use a medical analogy, what this couple is describing is the difference between being heart-dead and brain-dead. You wouldn't *want* to be either, but you can — in many cases — get a heart pumping again. Likewise, it is possible to get the romantic "heart" of a marriage pumping again, but only if there is some "brain activity," that is, a basic *friendship* that manifests a desire and willing- ness to work for the good of the other. As long as there is love (i.e., com- panionate love) the potential for being *in* love (i.e., romantic love) exists.

Which brings us to an excellent point. As vital and indispensable as companionate love is, it really can't make up the whole of married love because it is missing one important quality: passion. Any emotion that accompanies companionate love is best described as "regard" or "caring." Passion, excitement, and "warm fuzzies" are the domains of romantic love, the second ingredient in true love. In fact, without a healthy dose of ro- mance, companionate love can feel downright familial. Even so, compan- ionate love must be the more plentiful ingredient in the recipe for a happy marriage because, as any mature married person knows, romantic feelings tend to come and go — and come again — thousands of times over the life of a marriage. As essential as romantic love is, it is not stable enough to be the foundation of a marriage. We'll explore romantic love further in a minute; but first, answer the following questions to find out if you have a healthy amount of companionate love in your relationship.

~~~

The Marital Friendship Quiz

Directions: You and your spouse should each take the following quiz separately. Give yourself one point for each statement you mark True (T). Do not add your scores together. The purpose of this quiz is to discover how strong *each of you* thinks your marital friendship is.

T   F — You have a hard time identifying what is important to your partner.

T   F — You think that some of the things that are important to your partner are silly, unreasonable, or beneath you.

T F — You are not sure how you can be a part of helping your mate fulfill his dreams, goals, or values.

T F — You are uncomfortable with how much your partner expects of you.

T F — You feel love for your mate, but you are constantly being pulled away from him by other pressing matters.

T F — Having your partner along is OK, but you really prefer doing the things you enjoy on your own or with your other friends.

T F — Your partner discourages or belittles your input.

T F — Your partner disregards you when you tell him he hurts your feelings.

T F — Your partner gives you the distinct impression that you are really not welcome to participate in his interests or activities (he may not say it — but he doesn't have to).

T F — Your partner says he loves you, but he seems to disregard your needs when he makes decisions, schedules activities, or makes plans.

Scoring

0-2 — Most likely, you have a healthy amount of companionate love in your relationship.

3-5 — Your companionate love is probably closer to fifty or sixty percent (instead of seventy to eighty percent).

Talk about ways you and your mate will actively improve this. Be specific. Make a commitment to your plan.

6+ — You need to do some *serious* work on your capacity to be friends to each other. Revisit Chapter 2. If you find that discussing these issues with your mate is unproductive, you may wish to seek the help of a trusted pastor or counselor.

Discussion

Directions: Remember, companionate love is defined as your desire and commitment to work for the good of your partner. It doesn't just apply to what you think you ought to do (i.e., pay the bills or raise the kids); it really applies to the daily efforts you make to help your partner achieve the happiness and fulfillment that comes from pursuing the path he has discerned God leading him down.

Ideally, companionate love should contribute about seventy to eighty percent to the marital mix. To find out if your relationship has enough companionate love, answer and discuss the following questions with your partner.

Part One: How Well Do You Love Her?

(Answer and discuss the following.)

1a. List up to five things that you believe are most important to your mate.

1b. Describe the specific efforts you make on a daily basis to help your mate receive more fulfillment and/or enjoyment from the items you listed in 1a.

1c. Do you enjoy involving your partner in the activities and ideas that excite you, or are you a person who prefers people to stay out of your way?

1d. Do you work to develop an interest in the things that give your partner joy, or are there some activities that you wish she would drop out of, or at least stop talking to you about?

Part Two: How Well Does She Love You?

(Answer and discuss the following.)

2a. Does your partner actively solicit your opinions, encourage your growth, and work to further your interest and values? List specific examples.

2b. Does your partner look for ways to include you in her activities and interests, or does she seem to view your involvement as a burden?

2c. In your opinion alone, does your mate make decisions with your needs in mind, plans with your interests in mind, and prepare her schedule with you as the most important thing on her mind? Share specific examples of each with your partner.

Companionate love is the first part of the recipe for a healthy love life.

Now that we've discussed the cake, let's get to the frosting.

The Second Ingredient: Romantic Love

Romantic love is the snugly, cuddly, warm-fuzzy-makin', toe-curlin', make-me-feel-special, *woo! woo!* kind of love. It includes both sexuality and sentiment (i.e., romantic gestures), from love notes to pillow talk and everything in between. In Chapter 9 we'll take a closer look at the sexual aspects of romantic love. For now, it is important to remember that whatever form romantic love happens to be taking (sex or sentiment), the function of romantic love is to add a quality of "specialness" to a relationship. This is romantic love in the broadest sense.

There is some debate in certain Christian circles about the value of romantic love. Among many serious Christians, there is a tendency to write romantic love off as something those in "the worldly media" have invented for the purposes of titillating and leading us to hell. I can see their point, I guess; but these folks are missing the bigger picture. The fact is, romantic love is a very important part of a Christian marriage. Why? Because God himself uses the metaphor of romantic love as one way to explain how he loves us. The Old Testament's Song of Songs (or the Song of Solomon, also known as the Canticle of Canticles) — a completely scandalous book to many early Scripture scholars — made the cut in the canon of Scripture specifically because it was considered to be a beautiful example of love, not only between a husband and wife, but between God and his chosen people. Part of loving our mates as God loves us means manifesting the potent, stirring, intoxicating romantic love found in the Song of Songs. As I said in Chapter 2, if your mate isn't worth a couple of flowers, a love letter, a well-deserved compliment, and some generous physical affection from you, how do you ever expect her to enjoy the immense bounty of love God has prepared for her in his heavenly kingdom? I can only imagine that appearing before God after spending a lifetime in a romantically empty marriage would be like a diver who surfaced too fast and contracted the bends. Come to think of it, that is not a bad analogy for purgatory.

As I explained earlier, companionate love is a very noble and divine love. It is *the* essential ingredient in true marital love. However, emotionally speaking, it is fairly tame. But there is nothing tame about God's love for us. He is a passionate lover, a "jealous God," a God who longs for us to turn ourselves completely over to him — body, mind, and spirit. He wants us to experience the *petit mort* that comes from dying to ourselves and surrendering all to him. It was not for nothing that the great mystics referred to standing in the presence of God as being in "ecstasy." When God comes to us and we are profoundly touched by his love, we shiver, quake, cry, melt, feel special, feel humbled, feel awestruck, and fall truly, madly, deeply in love with him who constantly works for our good. If God is not ashamed to love us this way, we must not be ashamed of, or be inept at, loving our mates this way.

Having convinced you (hopefully) of the importance of romantic love, let me say that in a healthy relationship it usually doesn't make up more than twenty to thirty percent of the recipe for true love. For romantic love to be healthy, it has to flow *from* the friendship, not stand in place of it. This is the difference between wanting to be with your spouse because you become better people when you are together, and wanting to be with your spouse because of the feeling you manufacture when together. The latter reduces the relationship to a drug every bit as powerful as cocaine or heroin. In fact, it is because of such relationships that romance and/or sex addiction groups have little trouble keeping up their census. In their book *The Good Marriage*, Dr. Judith Wallerstein and Sandra Blakeslee state that when a relationship is too dependent on romantic love, it "has the tragic potential for freezing the husband and wife into a self-absorbed, childlike preoccupation with each other, turning its back on the rest of the world, including the children."

Wallerstein and Blakeslee's findings seem to mirror John Paul II's definition of a healthy unity between husbands and wives when he says that "rather than closing them up in themselves, [true unity] opens them up towards a new person [or persons, i.e., children]." Even so, in good measure, romantic love is a wonderful thing and it is a logical outcome of companionate love. In this sense, romantic love is simply one more way you are working for the good of your mate. It prevents a marriage from devolving into a brother/sister relationship or a strictly utilitarian arrangement centered on raising kids and paying bills. It adds zest to life, can be an important contributor to self-esteem (remember Rudolph the Red-Nosed Reindeer flying through the air exclaiming, "She thinks I'm cu-u-u-u-ute"?), and even — as I explained before — enhances spiritual growth. Considering the importance of romantic love, every couple needs to know a few things about why it comes and goes, and how to make sure it always comes back again.

Everybody Do the Wave

As I suggested at the beginning of this chapter, many people believe that romantic love is a magical thing with a will of its own. People think, "I have no control over it. When I feel romantic, I do romantic things." Besides being a recipe for romantic disaster, this statement isn't entirely true. The following illustration will help you understand what I mean.

The figure on the facing page shows the romantic cycle in all its glory. Let's imagine that you and your spouse are experiencing a very close time in your relationship (point *A*). For the time being, you are able to put work and other pressures on the back burner and simply concentrate on each other, doing the things you do when you feel in love. After a bit, though, the world starts knocking at your door. Work is piling up at the office, and other commitments that you have been neglecting must be attended to. As you begin to focus on these other areas of your life, your attention turns away from doing the things that made you feel so close to your mate. The dinner meeting with a client takes the place of your Wednesday night walk with your partner. Finishing that important

Everybody Do the Wave.
How Romantic Love Comes and Goes.

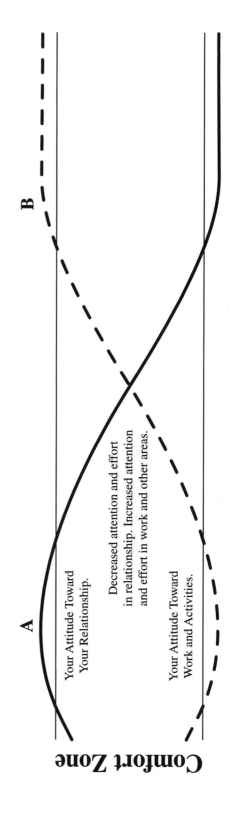

proposal — or in my case that book ("Sorry I can't spend time with you tonight, honey; I'm writing that chapter on being attentive to your spouse") — makes it impossible to take your spouse to a movie tonight. It isn't that you wouldn't rather be with your mate, it's just that you only have so much time and energy to divide between so many areas of your life.

Soon, you are on top of everything at work; but you begin to feel the effects of your lack of attentiveness to your relationship (point *B*). All of a sudden, you and your partner begin sniping at each other, forgetting to perform even the simplest gestures of affection and consideration, just because you are too busy to think about doing them.

At this point, there are two courses of action from which you may choose. Which of the following scenarios comes closest to what you would do under similar circumstances in your relationship?

A. You tell yourself that if your mate really cared he or she would make time for you. You yourself don't take any action to improve the circumstances because you don't feel like it. After all, in return for your hard work, don't you deserve a little caring now and then? You wait and hope that either your partner will stop being so insensitive, or these "blah" feelings will change and your motivation will return.

B. You think about the things you and your partner need to do to get things clicking again. You start doing some of them on your own. On top of this, one evening you tell your partner how much you've missed her lately. You ask her to get her schedule and the two of you make specific plans to take some time together.

If you chose *A,* then your romantic love will probably bottom out until such time as you and your mate have a big argument, during which each of you will accuse the other of being neglectful and unappreciative. This will result in the begrudging offer of a "date night" or "pity sex" that pacifies you for the moment but doesn't lead to any significant change over the long term. The relationship may continue having these little quasi-romantic hiccups for years, until one or both of you decide that the crust of bread you get isn't worth all the trouble. At this point, romantic love goes on life support and you and your mate console yourselves with the old chestnut "It's only natural for the fire to die out when you've been married as long as we have."

If you chose *B,* then *(survey says . . .)* you are absolutely right! *("Bob, tell our happy couple what they've won!" "Well, Greg . . .")*

You and your mate understand that romance is not some mystical thing that lies beyond your control. You understand — quite correctly — that behavior, not the Fates, drives romance. When you *do* romantic things

106

for each other, you begin to *feel* romantic toward each other. Choosing answer *B* says that you understand what the *Exceptional Seven Percent* know about romantic love. Specifically, it isn't something you sit around waiting for your partner to do for you, becoming resentful or whiny when she doesn't do it. Romantic love is a gift you give your partner — in a way that is meaningful to her. It is a gift she will return as a loving response to your loving efforts. Perfecting your ability to give this gift to your spouse allows you and your mate to fall into a gentle rhythm of love in which the highs are celebrated and the lows — because you never allow them to get too low — are accepted as a natural, even welcome, respite. The happiest spouses take great joy in knowing that they don't have to be "on" for each other at all times. This ebb and flow of romantic love actually contributes to the peace and security of the relationship, giving you a feeling not unlike the one you might have while gently floating on a raft just off the beach of some tropical island. Warm, safe, luxurious, and sensual.

Hopefully, you see that *B* is the more desirable choice. Sitting around waiting for romance to happen gives you nothing but a one-way ticket to the doldrums or, worse yet, Divorceville. Couples who make up the *Exceptional Seven Percent* understand that when they don't feel particularly romantic, it is probably because they haven't *done* anything particularly romantic for a while. Recognizing this, they don't whine to their partner, "When are you going to make time for me?" They take action into their own hands. Couples in *Exceptional Marriages* become more romantic toward their mates in the hopes of *inspiring* a loving response (as opposed to whining for one). For example, instead of sitting around feeling justifiably neglected, one spouse may go to her mate's office with a surprise picnic lunch. Or she may kidnap him for a weekend getaway. Or even do simpler things like leave loving self-stick notes pasted all over the windshield of the spouse's car, or chocolate candy hidden in places where the spouse will keep finding the candy all day, or a million other possibilities any fertile, loving mind might concoct. If such interventions aren't enough to get the romance curve swinging upward, then the neglected spouse sits down with her mate and — without accusing him of anything — calmly asserts, "I really miss doing *X, Y,* and *Z.* Get your schedule and let's make some time for each other."

In sum, the best way to resolve the number one threat to romantic love is to remember Newton's (not Isaac, uh, the other one . . .) First Law of Romantic Dynamics: "When you want to *feel* romantic again, *do* something romantic again."

This "law" leads us to examine the second misconception people have about romance. Namely, that it has to be a *big thing.* Yes, romance is weekends in the country at your favorite bed-and-breakfast, or buying that terribly expensive whatsit when your spouse least expected it; but at its core, romance is mostly about making your partner feel special by attending to her in the course of everyday life. Romance is looking into your partner's eyes when she speaks to you (instead of continuing to read the paper), kissing her when you enter and leave a room, sitting on the same piece of furniture together, going to bed at the same time (even, "just for sleeping"), remembering to say "I love you" a thousand times a day, taking time to pick up her favorite ice cream on your way home, and countless other "little things." Couples who save all their romance for that "One Big Night" are inevitably disappointed. Who could communicate all the love a person has for his or her partner in one night? Who needs that kind of pressure? No, the happiest couples actively work to develop their repertoire of both simple and grand romantic gestures. I would invite you to do the same in the following exercise.

Exercise: Twenty-five Ways to Make Love Stay — Every Day

Successful marriages are nurtured every day in the little exchanges between two people. Major efforts (weekends away, extra-special surprises, etc.) are important but tend to become less frequent as time goes by. Real romance is played out in the simple consideration, playfulness, and attentiveness that a couple exhibits every day to each other. When you complete the list below, think small. What are the simple, daily things that your mate does — or that you would like him to do more of — that demonstrates his regard for you? If you get stuck, try recalling the things people do that help you feel listened to, cared for, or appreciated. In short, what simple things make you feel special when someone does them?

1.	14.
2.	15.
3.	16.
4.	17.
5.	18.
6.	19.
7.	20.
8.	21.
9.	22.
10.	23.
11.	24.
12.	25.
13.	

Now trade lists with your beloved. Make yourself responsible for doing as many things on your mate's list as often as possible. See how many you can do every week.

✃～✃

Making Romantic Love Stay and Finding Your Balance

Remember, when you feel less warmth toward your mate it probably means that you and/or your partner have stopped doing some of the things you listed in the exercise — or are doing them less than you ought to. Referring to this list often will help you level out the highs and lows in your romantic life, and help love stay — every day. Tape it to the steering wheel of your car, the mirror in your bathroom, the fridge, or any other place where you will be constantly reminded to work for your lover's good. I like to use my list as a gauge of how successful I am in my role as a husband. I think of it as a kind of "marital examination of conscience" and I refer to it at least weekly. It helps me remember to attend to my wife's emotional welfare. Plus, it's just a lot of fun. The payoff is more good times, fewer and less-threatening lows, warmer feelings for each other in general, and a relationship that feels secure no matter what life throws at it.

Count Gabriel Riquetti is quoted in the book *Love Letters* as saying to his beloved, Sophia: "You alone have succeeded in combining . . . the most luscious fruits of friendship with the most fragrant flowers of love."

In the first part of this chapter I said that the recipe for true love is to "mix seven to eight cups of companionate love with two to three cups of romantic love." Now that we've looked at both types of love, The following example might help explain the healthy interplay between the two.

Imagine you are building a house. Unless you are building this house in Aruba (in which case, can my family and I come to live with you?), you are going to want to heat your home. You have to decide whether you are going to do this with a fireplace, a gas furnace, or perhaps electric heat. Obviously, fireplaces are very romantic. They provide a great deal of atmosphere, are nice to cuddle by, and can throw a lot of heat. On the down side, they tend to burn a lot of fuel very quickly and take a great deal of effort to maintain — all that hauling and chopping, not to mention cleaning out the ashes and the chimney (unless, of course, you use gas logs). To be perfectly honest, sometimes you just don't have the energy or the time to do all the work involved in maintaining a good fire. On those days, it would be nice to know that at least you won't freeze to death because your trusty gas furnace is chugging away in the basement. No, it's not romantic, but in a pinch, it gets the job done. Nine days out of ten, it will be your main source of warmth.

The same holds true for the relationship between romantic and companionate love. Good feelings, sentimental gestures, and a passionate sex life are indispensable for a good marriage. But if you aren't building your lives around the fulfillment of each other's dreams, goals, and values, your love doesn't exist in the real world. A marriage without the greatest measure of companionate love gets very cold very fast when the couple's normal sexual-romantic tide is at low ebb. Just as the most welcoming home would have both a fireplace and a furnace, the best marriage will include both companionate and romantic loves.

As I indicated earlier, with a little practice romantic love flows very easily from companionate love. If you are already working for the good of your mate on a daily basis, then it is a small matter to do the "little things" you listed in *Twenty-five Ways to Make Love Stay — Every Day* exercise. Let me give you a little tip, though. If you ever find your romantic love waning, don't accuse your partner of neglecting you (even if you think he or she is). You will only sound pathetic and cause him to resent you. I am constantly amazed at the people who consider themselves to be loving who, upon experiencing a little benign neglect from their spouses, begin whining, "When are you going to make time for me? Do you know *how long* it's been since you made love to me *[or took me out, bought me flowers, rubbed my back, etc.]?*"

To paraphrase John F. Kennedy, "Ask not what your mate can do for you. Ask what you can do for your mate." This is the essence of romance. Instead of whining to your mate for attention, or even worse, dragging out your romantic repertoire when you want some attention from her, get in the habit of consulting your *Twenty-five Ways to Make Love Stay — Every Day* list, and every day ask yourself, "What can I do to make her life easier today?"

Many of you will find at first that your mate will respond suspiciously, saying things like: "Why are you being so nice to me? What do you want?" This will be your biggest clue that you are not the lover you thought yourself to be. When your mate says this to you, tell her you're sorry for having taught her that you would only be loving on special occasions or when you wanted something from her. Tell her that you were hit on the head by a rock, as you deserved to be, and from now on you are going to work every day to let her know how special she is to you, because it is your job to help her learn how special she is to God. Your spouse will probably look at you as if you sprouted a third eye in the middle of your forehead. That's OK. You'll make a believer out of her.

Don't romance her because she deserves it. Don't romance her because you want something. Romance her because she is special to you and to God, and you want her to know it.

This goes as much for wives as it does for husbands. For all the popular wisdom that says women are the fountains from which all relationship knowledge flows, it has been my professional experience that too many wives think that romance is something husbands are supposed to do for them. If you are a woman who happens to believe this, I have only this to say: "Wrongo-bongo, Miss Thing. Time to get off your gilded tuffet." Remember, *true* romance is not something that is done *to* you; rather, it is an atmosphere that you and your mate work to create together. It is a by-product of a husband's and wife's mutual service to one another. It is the logical outcome of your both working daily for one another's physical, emotional, spiritual, and relational well-being. Husbands and wives, you know your mission. What are you waiting for?

In Love for a Lifetime

Earlier, I suggested that couples could guarantee that their love — both kinds — would last a lifetime. This is a shocking thing to think in a world of people who claim that their love "just died."

You might hear someone say, "I don't know what went wrong. It just happened. We grew apart." Or, "What can you do? If the love just isn't there anymore . . ."

Love doesn't ever "just die." You have to kill it. Sometimes people poison it slowly with years of mutual neglect and playing *Marital Chicken.* Sometimes people take it out and shoot it. But it never "just dies."

Life is complicated — actually, chaotic is more like it. There isn't much in this world you can control. Fortunately, everything you need to guarantee the success of your love and marriage is completely within your grasp. It all comes down to your freedom to make choices. Every time you speak, *you* choose whether to support your partner or tear him or her down. Every time you encounter a problem, *you* choose whether to let the stress ruin your marriage or to view your marriage as a refuge from the stress. Every time your partner says he needs more of your love, your time, your support, *you* choose whether to offer yourself generously or to ignore him and watch as he slowly starves. *Your* marriage, *your* choices, *your* control over *your* success. This concept can be a little overwhelming for most people. After all, it's one thing to say you have the power; but it's quite another thing to say that you know what to do with it. In moments such as these it can be helpful to sit at the feet of the masters, the married couples who have already discovered how to make choices that lead to uncommonly satisfying relationships. Over the years, I have learned a great deal from such couples. The following represents some of those lessons.

Twelve Things Happy Couples Know About Love

1. Love assumes a positive intention.

It is inevitable that your spouse will slight, offend, neglect, or otherwise step on your toes at some point. When this happens, you will be tempted to go into "fight mode" — as if your partner sat up in bed last night thinking of *Twenty-five Ways to Make My Mate's Life a Living Hell.* You may respond with comments like:

- "You're such a jerk! I can't believe you did *[said]* that!"
- "If you loved me, I shouldn't *have* to remind you!"
- "You don't give a damn about me, do you?"

In each of the examples above, you assumed it was your mate's intention to be offensive. *Exceptional* couples have a very different way of dealing with this. When an *Exceptional* spouse encounters a slight, she gives her mate the benefit of the doubt. She assumes that her partner didn't mean to hurt her. After all, they didn't get married to hurt each other. Something *must* be amiss. Perhaps the spouse wasn't thinking, or wasn't feeling well, or was having an especially bad day. The *Exceptional* spouse's response to an offensive comment or behavior sounds more like one of the following examples.

- *(Concerned)* "You're usually so considerate. What's going on?"
- *(Helpful)* "You seem really upset. What can I do to help you through this?"
- *(Firm but loving)* "Look, I love you too much to let you make an ass of yourself at my expense. What are you *really* trying to tell me?"

Couples in *Exceptional Marriages* aren't always syrupy-sweet, but they do assume that each spouse is trying his or her best *and,* with a little help from the other, can perhaps achieve such a goal. Love gives the benefit of the doubt (more on this in Chapter 9).

2. Love is always present.

Couples in the best marriages know that love is always present, even when it feels dormant at times. Healthy couples know that getting those special feelings back is simply a matter of a little time and effort. They do not respond to emotional down times with accusations of neglect. Nor do they become "St. Woe-Is-Me the First, spouse and martyr." If love was only implied yesterday, both husband and wife accept their responsibility to make love explicit today.

3. Love catches its lover being good.

Outstanding couples know that they have a daily obligation to express their love for each other. They make a point to not just criticize and complain, but to *catch each other being good.* They say, "Thank you for X" and "I really appreciate your taking care of Y," even when thanks aren't expected, necessary, or seem redundant. *Exceptional* couples are liberal with compliments and generous with affection. One major study showed that couples in good marriages have *five times* more positive interactions than negative ones. In the same study, a significant number of those couples who did not keep this five-to-one ratio were divorced within five years. Don't let your love become a statistic. Be generous with your praise, affection, and gratitude.

4. Love is a full-time job.

Some people mistakenly believe that marriage is a part-time job. Such spouses may be more committed to making their moms and dads happy or playing savior to friends and employers than they are to having a successful home life. You're not a bad person if you do this — you're just lousy marriage material.

Couples in the happiest marriages understand that promising to "forsake all others" means just that — *all* others. And that includes not only romantic interests, but also parents, friends, club memberships, and certain job placements — *if* these threaten the primacy of the marriage. This is not to say that if you love someone you may never leave the house. But it does mean that if you want an *Exceptional Marriage,* you have to require your family of origin — as well as your friends, work, and various activities — to play a supportive (and secondary) role to your relationship. Not the other way around.

5. Love is willing to make itself uncomfortable.

Love stretches you. It requires you to do things you never imagined yourself doing, to grow in ways that can be scary at times. When you married, you promised to allow yourself to be pulled, stretched, opened up, and "loved into Real," according to the Skin Horse in *The Velveteen Rabbit.* Don't hide out behind such selfish comments as "I would never do *X*, go to *Y*, or try *Z*. That just isn't me!" Challenge yourself a little. God will reward your efforts with a richer life and a more satisfying marriage.

6. Love takes care of itself.

Love knows how to meet its own needs. It does not *expect* you to clean up its emotional or literal messes (though help is always appreciated). It does not expect you to be its parent or mind reader. It would sooner die one thousand deaths than ever say, "If you really loved me, you would know."

113

7. Love is tactfully honest.

Love doesn't stuff feelings. It says what it needs to say. And yet, if love doesn't *hide* the truth, it doesn't beat you about the head with it either. People who say cruel things under the guise of "just being honest" are fooling themselves. There is no virtue in verbal evisceration. Love says what it needs to say, lovingly.

8. Love is safe.

Love behaves itself. It does not demean, humiliate, or intentionally embarrass. Love criticizes gently and responds well to gently offered criticism. Love encourages the beloved to do more, to say more, to be more.

9. Love is willing to fake it till it makes it.

You won't always feel loving or feel inspired to do loving things. But the best couples know that it is important to do loving things, especially when they don't feel like it. In the first place, their Christian dignity demands it. In the second place, sometimes you've got to prime the pump to get the water flowing again. Less mature couples say, "I can't be loving if I don't feel it. That's dishonest." That's rubbish. Love is not a feeling. It is a commitment to work for the good of your mate whether you feel like it or not. I always tell my clients that the feelings are always the last thing to change. First comes behavioral change, then comes thinking change, then comes emotional change. Sometimes, to get a desired state of feeling back, you've got to start by acting as if you already are feeling that state. That's not being dishonest. That's being hopeful.

10. Love is generous.

Loving people do not say, "I'm a loving person," and then go on to complain about how empty their marriages are. You cannot simply give as much as you are comfortable giving and then call yourself a "loving person." This is self-serving at best. If you are in a healthy relationship and want to be loved more, you've got to love your mate more, and *you've got to love in a way that is meaningful to your beloved* (see Chapter 7).

11. Love laughs.

Love is playful. Love enjoys itself. Love isn't afraid of being silly. It never intentionally makes fun of the beloved, but it can help the beloved find the fun. Love has a funny bone.

12. Love is not a feeling.

Love is action. Love is a choice. Love is hard work. Love is daily making personal choices with the good of your partner in mind. There are many other good things that are feelings. Affection is a feeling. Romance is a feeling. Attraction is a feeling. Passion is a feeling. But "love for love's sake," as Elizabeth Barrett Browning put it, is *not* a feeling.

Love Lasts Forever, But Mercifully, This Chapter Doesn't

It is my hope that after reading this chapter you will find love to be a little less mysterious, but no less wondrous. In this very busy world there are many things that compete for our attention. Many of these things are, in fact, hostile to marriage and family life. Despite these many distractions, it is my most deeply held conviction that there is no work more important than the work of loving. If I stopped counseling, my clients would quickly find another therapist (not as good as me, mind you, but still . . .). If I stopped writing, someone else would publish in my place. If I stopped acquiring material goods, someone else would spend his or her money. If I dropped dead this minute, all traces of me would be wiped out tomorrow — unless I have loved. I could never be replaced as a husband or a father. Some other body could fill my shoes, sleep in my bed, eat my food, but he could never remove the influence I have had on the people I have loved, if indeed I have loved well. You will never doubt the meaning and purpose of your life — if you love first.

When you finish this chapter, put down this book for a minute (just for a minute, now). Find a way to let your partner know that she is on your mind — right now. Call her. Write a note. Go to the store on your way home and pick up her favorite whatever, or walk into the next room and kiss her — just because. Celebrate the purpose of your life by bringing some love into hers. Do it now. When you return, *For Better . . . Forever!* will give you an exciting glimpse into the next fifty years of your life.

Love is patient and kind;
love is not jealous or boastful;
it is not arrogant or rude.
Love does not insist on its own way;
it is not irritable or resentful;
it does not rejoice at wrong,
but rejoices in the right.
Love bears all things,
believes all things,
hopes all things,
endures all things.
— St. Paul (1 Cor 13:4-7)

C
H
A
P
T
E
R

On the Road to "Happily Ever After": The Stages of Married Life

My wife once observed that being married is like climbing a mountain. There are times when the climb is exhilarating and the views are breathtaking. Other times you're scared out of your wits and it's all you can do to hang on and keep from falling to your death. In order to make it to the top, you can't look down. You've got to keep your eyes on the next peak and keep climbing. Sometimes you'll wonder why you ever decided to do this crazy thing, but once you've made it, you're never sorry.

When the marital climb gets difficult, it has been my experience that too many people panic and jump. They don't think beyond the immediate crisis; they just know they're scared and uncomfortable and they don't want to be scared and uncomfortable anymore and so it would be easier to fling themselves into the great unknown than to keep going. Of course, when you're ten thousand feet up, the first step is a doozy.

Any couple who is going to do such a foolish thing as get married ought to at least have a map, some resource to let the partners know what common obstacles they will encounter while they are going up the mountain. Otherwise, it is too easy to take a normal part of the climbing experience and make a crisis out of it, with one or the other spouse complaining, "This rock face is too sheer. This path is too narrow. We must be going the wrong way. And it's all your fault!"

While the specific challenges, crises, and celebrations you face throughout your married life will be unique to you, every marriage evolves through the same general stages and encounters similar landmarks on the ascent up Marriage Mountain. Having a knowledge of those stages is immensely helpful. It can be a great comfort to know that a particular problem you and your mate are struggling with is, in fact, a normal part of your marriage's evolution. Too often, a common challenge of married life is mistaken for a sign that love is dying or that one partner or the other is flawed. This simple ignorance can cause an otherwise vital and viable marriage to be tossed on the scrap heap, a completely avoidable tragedy, assuming that you know what you are doing.

Your Journey: An Itinerary

The chart on pages 120-121 shows the different stages that every marriage encounters. You *will* go through these stages, no matter what type of marriage you have. But your chances of surviving each stage and making it to "happily ever after" are directly related to whether your marriage is in the category of *Shipwrecked, Apprenticeship, Partnership,* or *Romantic Peer.* As we examine each stage, you will see how they affect the different types of marriages. You will also learn how to gracefully negotiate the challenges you will face and increase the likelihood of arriving successfully at the top of the mountain.

Stage One: Beginning the Climb

HONEYMOON STAGE

Major Task for Self-esteem: Pursuing intimacy.

Time into Marriage: Newlywed to six months (approximately).

Major Relationship Challenges at This Stage: (1) Establishing the strength, priority, and independence of your marriage. (2) Reconciling romantic notions with marital realities.

When you first begin your climb you are excited, to say the least. It's a clear, sunny day and you have all the energy in the world. It's a good thing too, because the work begins with the first foot you set on Marriage Mountain.

The *Honeymoon Stage* of marriage encompasses two challenges. The first is to establish the strength, priority, and independence of your marriage. The second is reconciling the reality of marriage with your romantic ideal of it. Most of you reading this will already be through the *Honeymoon Stage,* so I will not belabor it except to say that a couple's commitment to marital fidelity receives its first challenges here. I don't mean fidelity in the simple sense of not sleeping with other people; I mean fidelity in the sense of a willingness to forsake *all* others, including families of origin, friends, extracurricular activities, and even certain job placements — *if* they interfere with the primacy of the marriage. (Keep this "if" phrase in mind when questions concerning relationships, values, priorities, and the like are discussed.) Devaluing the attachments held dear for much of one's life can be a terrifying experience; but for the sake of the marriage's future, it must be done. At this stage it is especially important for a couple to remember that they got married because they believe they are each other's best hope for becoming the people God wants them to be by the end of their lives. This is the only reason strong enough to motivate a couple to establish the necessary boundaries between them and their friends, employers, and families of origin.

As I suggested, cutting loose from old attachments is hard work, and the pain involved often brings the first challenge to people's romantic ideals of marriage. But doing this work builds a solid foundation of security in the marriage. A couple can't embrace the vulnerability involved in pursuing mutual growth and intimacy unless they know that they are really each other's number one priority, after their love of God. Fortunately, the warm-fuzzy feelings that accompany this stage often make the difficult choice of forsaking all others more bearable than it might otherwise be. Making the mutual choice to gently but firmly stand up to Mom and Dad, less-supportive friends, and other obstacles to establishing the primacy of the marriage creates the security necessary for the couple to negotiate the next stage of married life as a team, instead of as "every man for himself" individuals.

Stage Two: Climbing to the First Peak

CONFLICT AND NEGOTIATION STAGE

Major Task for Self-esteem: Pursuing intimacy.

Time into Marriage: Approximately six months to three to five years.

Major Relationship Challenges at This Stage: (1) Learning that disagreements and/or differences do not equal death. (2) Establishing rules that keep arguments safe and productive.

One of the keys to successful mountain climbing is packing light. Unfortunately, on this part of your ascent up Marriage Mountain, you are beginning to discover that you have brought along a little more baggage than is absolutely necessary. Before going any further, you are going to have to decide what to keep and what to leave behind.

Following quickly on the heels of "honeymoondom" is the "I never knew *that* about you" stage. Suddenly, you begin discovering things about your mate of which you were previously unaware. Some of these discoveries are pleasant, some are surprising, and some are decidedly unwelcome. As you marvel at your spouse's hitherto unknown obsessiveness, eccentricities, and harebrained ideas, you begin to wonder who this wacko is that you married and if there is any hope for your future.

The Stages of Married Life

Note: All time frames are approximate. Actual beginnings and endings of stages may vary greatly from couple to couple.

1 • Honeymoon Stage (0—6 months)

Major Goals: Establish strength and independence of your marriage. *Individual Goals:* Foster intimacy and fidelity.

2 • Conflict and Negotiation Stage (6 months—3 to 5 years)

Major Goals: Learn safe, effective problem-solving skills. Work out unique character of your relationship. *Individual Goals:* Maintain intimacy in spite of conflict.

3 • New Pattern Stage (4—8 years)

Major Goals: Take time to let patterns negotiated in last stage take hold before starting too many other new ventures.

4 • Creative Stage (7—15+ years)

Major Goals: Maintain intimacy while pursuing goals that are important to personal fulfillment. *Individual Goals:* Develop relationship with community at large. Increase potential for caring, nurturing, and creativity. (*Warning:* Extremely difficult phase for *Shipwrecked/Rescue* couples; moderately difficult for *Conventional* couples in later phases of stage.)

5 • Homecoming Stage (14—25+ years)

Major Goals: Jettison unnecessary commitments for the sake of greater intimacy and time with family. Zero in on what's "really" important. Also, begin thinking about life after children leave home.

6 • Launching Stage (20—30+ years)

Major Goals: Successfully launching children into the world. Answering question "Now what?" about life and marriage. Midlife crises common. Second major danger area for *Shipwrecked* and lower-functioning *Conventional* couples. *Individual Goals:* Maintain intimacy while figuring out what to do with second half of life.

7 • Second Honeymoon Stage (30—45+ years)

Major Goals: Maintaining intimacy, creativity, and relevance in the world as late midlife/later life is approaching. Finding new ways to deepen intimacy and beginning new projects that you didn't feel comfortable starting while children were still around.

8 • "Happily Ever After" Stage (45+ years)

Major Goals: Enjoying late years together. Confronting loss and death. Maintaining hope and meaning as end of life draws near. *Individual Goals:* Reviewing life. Developing and passing on your wisdom.

This is the stage where couples tend to lose a lot of blood fighting over such issues as the "correct" way to wind the vacuum cleaner cord, roll a tube of toothpaste, drive the car, and assorted other life-or-death catastrophes. These arguments are never as simple as they seem because there is more going on than toothpaste. Arguments in this phase are often really about vulnerability and safety. In other words, couples engaging in such petty battles are often saying to one another, "I've never trusted so much of myself to anyone else before. I want to be certain I didn't make a bad choice. So, I am going to make a big fuss about nonsense to see if you treat me with respect even when I am acting like a complete idiot." We all play this game at one point in our marriages. Fortunately, most of us survive it. Better still, we become more mature and more confident in our marriages as a result.

The second factor that complicates arguments in the *Conflict and Negotiation Stage* is that we are often unclear about the differences between our identities and mere preferences. This stage involves so many challenges to how we used to organize our single lives that some people begin feeling as if they are "losing themselves." Learning to identify what is an essential part of our identities versus what are merely our preferences is a major goal of this stage. "How much can I let go of without losing myself?" is an important question to ponder. Obviously how you define yourself will determine how successful you are at negotiating this stage. If, like *Shipwrecked* couples, your life is built around maintaining your comfort, then this stage will be a living hell for your marriage. Every stylistic difference, from how you wash dishes to the "correct" way to conduct your morning routine, will be experienced as a real threat to your sense of self. If, like *Apprentices*, you build your life around meaningful work and roles, things will go relatively well, until you begin arguing over your inherited ideas of what husbands and wives are "supposed" to do for each other or how work schedules should be arranged. If, like *Partners* and *Peers*, you build your lives around fulfilling a particular value system, then you will limit yourself to arguments that infringe on your ability to live up to your values, ideals, and goals. You will be able to see that everything else is either unimportant or simply a matter of taste and there is no sense arguing about that.

No matter what category of marriage you fall into, to keep a proper perspective about the many changes you undergo in *Conflict and Negotiation*, you have to ask yourself the following question: "Does negotiating this issue in any way decrease the possibility of fulfilling my dreams, goals, or values?" If the answer is "yes," then by all means argue about it. If the answer is "no," you would probably do better to get over yourself and exercise a bit of flexibility. Save your energy for the battles that really count.

As I've already suggested, the *Conflict and Negotiation Stage* is only moderately uncomfortable for most *Apprenticeship, Partner,* and *Romantic Peer Marriages.* But it can be devastating to *Deadly Marriages,* and it often initiates the long slide into estrangement for *Shipwrecked* couples who view challenges to their personal comfort and style as life-or-death issues. This attitude often causes them to choose either quiet resentment or violent, recurring arguments over practical, equitable solutions.

This brings me to the second task of the *Conflict and Negotiation Stage:* establishing rules for effective problem solving. As you and your mate discuss your different preferences, styles, and attitudes toward household tasks and life, you will have to work out what "fair fighting" means to you. The implicit or explicit "rules of engagement" you develop in the *Conflict and Negotiation Stage* set the precedent for solving large and small problems in the future. The wise couple will take this opportunity to learn the difference between problem solving and arguing. Chapter 8 talks more about this subject, specifically how those in the *Exceptional Seven Percent* learn to feel closer *because* of conflict rather than in spite of it.

Stage Three: The First Plateau
NEW PATTERN STAGE

Major Task for Self-esteem: Pursuing intimacy.

Time into Marriage: Approximately four to eight years.

Major Relationship Challenges at This Stage: (1) Solidifying the unique identity of your relationship. (2) Seeking "second-nature" status.

The climb to this first plateau of Marriage Mountain was a little harder than you would have liked it to be. Still, you are grateful to have made it this far. Time for a little rest. As you finish pitching the tent and begin to warm yourself by the fire, you and your partner talk about the things you have learned so far and how these lessons will enable you to work together more efficiently when you start climbing again.

In the *New Pattern Stage,* your marriage begins to take on an organized identity that is unique to the two of you. Because — in the last stage — you were so conscientious about negotiating mutually satisfying "standard operating procedures" (i.e., acceptable ways of solving problems, resolving conflict, and conducting your everyday life as a couple), you now generally know what is expected *of* each other and what you can expect *from* the other. The main task of the *New Pattern Stage* is taking time to let these "standard operating procedures" take hold of you — become second nature.

As satisfying as this stage can be, it takes a great deal of work to get here. Couples don't usually find their feet until between three and five years into the marriage, after a whole lot more *Conflict and Negotiation* than they would have liked. This is the major reason that so many first-time marriages don't make it to the five-year mark. Couples become frightened that the conflict stage will never end. But, of course, with patience, diligence, and sincere effort, it does, and the spouses find that through all their *Conflict and Negotiation Stage* they have created a truly unique relationship that is not based on old, inherited expectations, but on what works well for them.

The most important thing that spouses can do in the *New Pattern Stage* is to relax and take some time to become accustomed to their new ways of doing things. The next stage of marital development causes partners to begin distancing themselves from each other a bit. To prepare for this, it can be helpful to avoid taking on any new, major stressors for a while so that a couple's routine can solidify. This is not always possible, but when it is, it is most certainly desirable.

Stage Four: Climbing to the Second Peak
CREATIVE STAGE

Major Tasks for Self-esteem: Creating, caring, and nurturing.

Time into Marriage: Approximately seven to fifteen years.

Major Relationship Challenges at This Stage: (1) Creating and caring for something larger than yourselves. (2) Holding on to the intimacy you have achieved.

Now that you are well rested, it's time to start climbing again. But be warned! On this part of Marriage Mountain, the path narrows and becomes considerably steeper. You are going to have to proceed one at a time, and tie a line to your partner so you don't lose each other.

This is truly one of the most interesting and exciting stages of married life, and the personal growth this stage affords will often move a marriage to the next level on *The Relationship Pathway* (e.g., from *Shipwrecked* to *Apprentice, Apprentice* to *Partner,* etc.). The seeds of your dreams and goals — which were planted in the *Honeymoon Stage,* germinated in *Conflict and Negotiation,* and rooted in *New Patterns* — now burst out of the ground and into the sunlight. This is the *Creative Stage,* the time in your marriage when you begin to create something larger than yourselves. This is the time in your lives when you start that family, build that home, further your education, launch the business you've been dreaming about, and follow through on at least one million other wonderful things.

Assuming you have taken the time to learn the lessons and resolve the challenges of each previous stage, the *Creative Stage* is like a public proclamation that the love you and your mate have for each other requires a larger package. You want to become more — to create *a world* together that reflects both your oneness *and* your uniqueness. Children will be an important part of that world, as might building a home that meets the needs of the people living in your world, and doing work that serves the dreams and dignity of all of those living in your world. This is most certainly the experience of *Partners* and *Peers*. These couples are especially adept — not by birth as much as by practice and maturity — at building one another's dreams while increasing the depth of the intimacy in their marriages. New levels of joy, hope, fear, and frustration are explored — and love is the beneficiary.

Apprenticeship couples fare pretty well at this stage too, though the ride is a bit bumpier. Usually, for a time, the *Apprenticeship* couple loses each other in all the commotion. The husband and wife become so busy attending to their own set of branches (work, kids, etc.) that they forget to nurture the tree (marriage) that is feeding their efforts. One day they notice that the leaves on their respective branches are wilting. They know that "something is missing," but they can't figure out what. This phenomenon has been popularly called "the seven-year itch" (although it has been known to occur as late as fifteen years into a marriage, depending on how long a couple postpones childbearing and other adventures). Sadly, this "itch" has been the cause of many affairs and divorces. So, what's the best way to deal with this "embarrassing itch"? Prevent it. Every day you must remind yourselves to step out of your own little worlds and meet to work on your marriage. During this hectic time of life, it will be more important than ever to recall the list you made in Chapter 4 *(Twenty-five Ways to Make Love Stay — Every Day)* and live it out every day.

Special Considerations:
Shipwrecked Couples and the Creative Stage

For those of you in *Shipwrecked Marriages*, the *Creative Stage* may be the single most difficult crisis of your marital relationship. The difficulties presented by this stage have the potential to move you to an *Apprenticeship Marriage*, but only if you survive them. Too many couples don't. If you suspect that there is any chance that yours is a *Shipwrecked* relationship, I strongly recommend that you pay special attention to the following if you hope to survive beyond the ten-year mark.

Your problem is this: The requirements for your continued mental health are now at cross-purposes with the foundation upon which you built your marriage. On the one hand, you have a normal and deeply personal longing to be more, to take risks, to expand your role in the world, to test your limits. On the other hand, your marriage was built around maintaining security and guaranteeing the basics of life. At first glance, it would seem that you cannot have both. It is impossible to quit your job to start that business you've always dreamed of without threatening the financial security of your family. You can't demand more intimacy from your mate without increasing the conflict — and thereby jeopardizing the safety — in your marriage. You can't expand your role in the world without taking the risk that you might prefer another person to your mate or another circumstance to your marriage. These are all conflicts that the *Shipwrecked* couple has tried to avoid for the last ten years but all of a sudden can't. These risks must be taken if the *Shipwrecked Marriage* is to evolve into something more; but *Shipwrecked* relationships, which are built to defend the status quo at all costs, don't *do* risk.

Until now, that is. There are only three possible "solutions" to the problem of a conflict between the needs of a marriage and the needs of the individuals in that marriage. Only one of those options is healthy. (Hint: It's number 3.)

Option 1. Sacrifice your personal needs for the sake of the marriage. (The least healthy choice.)

This is what you, if you are a *Shipwrecked* spouse, will want your partner to do when he or she starts telling you of the "bizarre and sudden" desire to join things, choose a new career path, go back to school, involve you more as a parent, or increase the intimacy in your marriage. As a *Shipwrecked* spouse (great defender of the status quo that you are), your first reaction to all of these suggestions will be to say, "What in heaven's name is wrong with you? We're not broken; why are you trying to fix it?"

Taking this tack is both unhealthy and impossible. In fact, if you cling to this approach, you will invariably push your spouse away from you and destroy your marriage. People must grow. It's what we do. If you try to stop your partner's growth, one of two things will happen: You will either be run over (divorced), or you will cause disease. You may actually be able to bully your mate into giving up her dreams, goals, and values "for the sake of the marriage." But you will only have succeeded in putting her into a high-risk category for affairs, substance abuse (she has to do something to numb that longing to be more), anxiety disorders, depression, and even suicide. Clearly, this "solution" is not desirable.

Option 2. Chuck the marriage for the sake of your personal growth. (Getting warmer . . . but still not one of the healthy choices.)

This is the option that until recently was favored by too many counselors who apparently fell asleep during their *Intro to Psych* classes. Superficially, the argument makes sense, but only superficially. The logic goes like this: Nothing should stand in the way of your personal growth and/or mental health. If anything does get in your way, you are obliged by simple, basic principles of survival to push it out of your path. So far so good, right? Now, here's the problem. As the famous psychosocial researcher Erik Erikson asserted, it is extremely difficult to move on to your second and third stages of adulthood ("generativity" and wisdom) if you feel like you failed at the first one (achieving intimacy). In other words, when you're standing there watching your house burn to the ground, it is hard to remember that you have a great job, a fascinating education, or even wonderful children. Mostly, you just feel awful that your house is a carbon briquette. Ask any divorced person if he didn't live through a big chunk of time during which he felt like a failure, not just in his married life, but in other areas as well. Just about every divorced person I have ever met has flogged himself with "What's wrong with me?" questions that spill over into everything.

Research indicates that it can take between five and seven years to overcome the various feelings of guilt, shame, depression, and anger that accompany even most "amicable" divorces. As far as personal growth is concerned, this is clearly an "out of the frying pan into the fire" situation. Before, you couldn't grow because your marriage was unsupportive. But now, having acquired that Holy Grail of personal growth — a divorce — you will probably be too depressed for the next five to seven years either to pursue your growth or enjoy your achievements. Some solution this turned out to be!

I am not saying that there are some marriages that would not be better off dissolved; I'm simply suggesting that yours is probably not one of those. Besides, there is a better way.

Option 3. The Both . . . And . . . Solution.

Since you *must* grow, and since your optimal growth *requires* you to maintain intimacy, why not learn to do both at the same time? (To borrow from an old TV series: *We have the technology . . .*) Why not make your marriage into something that allows for both intimacy and personal growth? *(We can rebuild it . . .)* This will take persistence, strength, and courage — all qualities you want more of anyway — but your efforts will be rewarded. *(Presenting . . . the Six-Million-Dollar Marriage!)* To successfully accomplish this, you and your partner must revisit the exercise at the end of Chapter 2 and give some deeper thought to the following.

1. Developing Your Personal "Mission Statement" ∾ What would it take to organize your life around the things you believe in? In order for you to feel excited when you wake up each day, what kind of work would you have to be doing, how (specifically) would your marriage need to be different, and what behaviors would you need to demonstrate in the face of irrational people and adverse circumstances?

2. Assessing the Resources and/or Support You Need ∾ What role would you need your "ideal spouse" to play in helping you fulfill your answers to question 1? Don't hold back.

3. Assessing the Support That Is Available ∾ Exchange your answers (after you've taken the time to develop them fully). Would you be willing to actively support your mate in the pursuit of her goals — even if you don't understand why she would want to make some of those choices? Would you be willing to do what your partner's version of the "ideal spouse" would do for her?

These questions are difficult ones. You may have to enlist the support of a marriage-friendly counselor to help you get through them, but one never grows by taking the easy way out. Choosing this more difficult path will increase your personal strength and self-respect, and will build true intimacy into your marriage.

Whether your marriage is *Romantic Peer, Partnership, Apprenticeship,* or *Shipwrecked,* the tasks of the *Creative Stage* remain the same: creating something larger than yourselves and holding on to the intimacy you have already achieved. To accomplish both of these goals is to allow your marriage to evolve into something more intimate, more enduring, and more vital, giving you much joy and satisfaction in the years to come.

Stage Five: The Second Plateau

HOMECOMING STAGE

Major Tasks for Self-esteem: Clarifying priorities; finding a balance.

Time into Marriage: Approximately fourteen to twenty-five years.

Major Relationship Challenges at This Stage: (1) Simplifying. (2) Reasserting the priority of marriage and family. (3) Preparing the marriage to withstand the empty-nest syndrome.

"I thought it would be good, but I never new it would be like this,"

you say as you gaze up at the stars from your camp on the second plateau of Marriage Mountain. Every muscle in your body hurts. You and your partner even slipped a couple of times on the last part of the climb. And when you encountered that stampede of mountain goats, you thought you were goners for sure. But you can chuckle about it now from the relative safety of your camp. Before settling in tonight, you and your partner are going to check your lines to make sure they're secure. You are also going to go through your backpacks and get rid of some of the things you picked up along the way. Those herbs and berries can stay, but the rock that reminded you of your great-aunt Hildegard is a little less fascinating now that you see the cliff you are going to have to scale tomorrow.

In the *Homecoming Stage,* you will continue to maintain the projects you began in the previous chapter of your marriage; but you have less to prove. You have demonstrated your ability to be successful in the world at large and you have shown yourself to be a capable parent, all while holding your marriage together. "Mazel Tov!" as the old saying goes. Even so, doing all of those things takes a lot of energy, and you are starting to wonder if you need to stay as busy as you have been the last few years. The kids are getting older and you begin to feel that "time is going by so fast." Your heart is calling you to simplify.

It is perfectly natural to go through a period of anxiety as you start to pull away from some of the less necessary commitments of your life. You are nervous that such and such will not be able to function without you, or perhaps you are concerned that not working those extra hours will hurt you financially. Soon, however, your anxiety gives way to the peace that comes from having your life in order. Accomplishments are nice; but love is better, and you find yourself becoming more relaxed and able to enjoy what time the kids still have left at home.

Which brings me to your second task: preparing your marriage for the fact that one day in the not-too-distant future the kids will be leaving the nest. Even though this is a few years off, I am bringing it up now because too many couples blow through this stage without even taking a minute to consider life without kids. When it happens, they find themselves having to cope with two major crises: saying good-bye to the little ragamuffins (who aren't so little anymore) and getting to know each other again. It will be important for you and your mate to take this time to celebrate your marriage and all you are accomplishing together. Start talking about what you would like to do with yourself and the marriage when the children are gone. Make new plans, dream new dreams; but, most of all, reconnect with your mate because the next stage can be a shock even to the best of marriages.

Stages Six and Seven: The Third Peak and the Third Plateau

Major Tasks for Self-esteem: Developing new goals; maintaining intimacy.

Time into Marriage: Approximately twenty to forty-five years.

Major Relationship Challenges at This Stage: (1) Getting the kids out into the world. (2) Answering the question "Now what?"

You are climbing up what appears to be a perpendicular wall of rock. The footholds and handholds are about as wide as your bootlace. Between gasps for air, your partner calls down to you: "This is the part of the climb that separates the big dogs from the porch puppies." You just grit your teeth and smile. Your mind can't decide whether this is the biggest thrill of your life or the dumbest thing you have ever done. You hope it's the former. Better keep climbing and find out.

You've come a long way, baby. Little Gunther, the last of your fourteen children (you had two sets of quints, plus four others) is off to study computer-assisted animal husbandry at the University of Wherever ("One of the top ten schools for computer-assisted animal husbandry" — you proudly tell your coworkers). You and your mate unpack Gunther's belongings in his dorm room and bid a tearful good-bye as you say, "See you over Christmas break."

The ride home is quiet. But one question is going through both of your minds: "Now what?"

You are smack-dab in the middle of midlife and it is a time for a mini-reckoning. Is your life going the way you thought it would? Has your marriage been what you hoped? What — if anything — stands between you and the sense that your life has had meaning? What must yet be done for you to feel as if you have fulfilled the purpose of your life?

If you have been conscientiously attending to your marriage throughout the last twenty years or so, this could be the beginning of a wonderful time in your lives. You and your mate will begin making plans for that second honeymoon and upon your return, the two of you will get down to those projects that you just didn't feel right about pursuing while you still had the little ones around. The *Launching Stage* will smoothly evolve into the *Second Honeymoon Stage* in which you and your beloved rediscover the joys of working side by side on fulfilling what remains of your most personal dreams.

If, on the other hand, you have been a little careless about your marriage — and depending on how careless you have been — this stage of your journey could include anything from mild crises to major catastrophes. What can compound the difficulties of this stage is that you begin to realize that *(Wait! Are you sitting down?)* you are not going to live forever. The major disease of this phase is the "midlife crisis." If you feel that your life and marriage have basically been on track, then this will not be cause for too much concern; after all, you did and are doing what you were put here to do. But if you have been neglecting your marriage, or have been cavalier about figuring out who you wanted to be when you grew up, you are in for a wild ride that could include affairs, divorce, cosmetic surgery, psychotherapy, remarriage, and starting all over again with the *Honeymoon Stage* — probably in that order.

The best way to prevent the collapse of your identity and marriage at midlife is to keep both in the forefront of your mind today. Socrates said, "The unexamined life is not worth living." But too many people would rather just go where life leads them. It sounds so-o-o-o romantic, but what happens at midlife is that these same people break into a cold sweat upon realizing they are nowhere near where they hoped their romantic road would lead. They then wreck a lot of lives in their crazed frenzy to get where they think they should be.

But you have nothing to fear as long as you have built your marriage around fulfilling your identities in Christ and daily working for each other's good. All this enables your marriage to survive and thrive through the *Launching Stage* and into your *Second Honeymoon* years. You will remain passionate friends and lovers long into your dotage — eating your oatmeal out of heart-shaped bowls.

Stage Eight: The Summit

"HAPPILY EVER AFTER"

Major Task for Self-esteem: "Ego integrity."

Time into Marriage: Approximately forty-five or more years.

Major Relationship Challenges at This Stage: (1) Supporting each other through retirement and beyond. (2) Financial issues related to retirement. (3) Fostering "oneness." (4) Confronting mortality.

The sun is just beginning to set as you reach the summit of Marriage Mountain. You are tired and you are a bit low on supplies, but any worries are secondary to the scene that greets you. As you look around you, you understand what all the work was about, and you think about how the two of you worked together to get here. You take your partner in your arms, saying, "We made it." You both still have concerns about the future and are aware of the challenges that face you as you make your way down the mountain again, but you are looking forward to being able to share your wisdom with those who will climb after you. For now, it is enough to be here. Together. You thank God for your partner because you see that you never would have made it without him or her.

You have survived the most serious threats to your marriage. You have protected both your intimacy and your autonomy throughout the course of your life. God willing, you have quite a few years to go (as many as twenty to thirty years, depending upon when you got married). There will be some hurdles along the way, but most of the challenges to be faced are of a more personal nature. You will encounter such issues as how to spend your retirement years, asserting your continued relevance even though you are no longer working, confronting physical problems, mourning the death of friends, and eventually facing your own and/or your mate's passing. But throughout all of this, assuming you have faithfully attended to all the tasks along the way, you are at peace with yourself and your marriage. You begin to exhibit what is called "ego integrity" — that is, when you review the years of your life you are filled with a deep sense of rightness. No regrets. You are satisfied with the choices you have made and, somehow, all the insanity of life makes sense to you. You may know things now that you wish you knew when you were younger; but life has been good, and you expect it to continue that way for the foreseeable future. You and your partner will spend this phase of your lives exploring new depths of the phrase "soul mates." You will take on new challenges, continue to enjoy each other's company, and seek opportunities to pass on your wisdom. As a bonus, your teenage grandkids *want* to be like you when they grow up.

There are some who will criticize me as being overly optimistic about this stage of life. I wish to assure those people that I am not a fool. I am painfully aware that there are many older couples who do not achieve ego integrity — too many couples who consistently make poor choices, lead tragic lives, and meet tragic ends. But this book is not about them. I am writing about the couples *you want to be like* when you "grow up," the genuinely happy couples — they really do exist — who are both satisfied with their lives and their relationships well into the twilight years. Such couples may be in the minority, but to my mind it is not necessary for that trend to continue. It is easy to get lost without a map. But armed with what I hope are the good directions contained in these pages, some persistence, and a prayer or two, there is no reason you should not achieve "happily ever after" status. Prince and Princess Charming are alive and well and living in a neighborhood near you. Maybe they *are* you.

The biggest challenge couples in this stage encounter is facing death. Some married people arrive at this point in life, only to despair at the futility of it all, lamenting, "We've been through so much together. Only to have it end like this." Very few sorrows can compare to the loss of a spouse; but rather than undermining the meaning of marriage, preparing for death *is* the meaning of a Christian marriage. "In life and death we belong to God" (cf. Rom 14:8). Our marriages are supposed to be a testament to the belief that we have a better chance of becoming all God created us to be with our mates than without them. This last stage of married life demonstrates the fruit of such a partnership more than any other stage. It can be a powerful witness.

When my grandmother died, I knelt over her coffin to offer a prayer for her soul. As I looked at the body of this woman, I noticed the wedding ring on her hand. What struck me most about it was how thin and worn it had become over the years. My first reaction was to see this as just another metaphor of our mortality. But then, right in mid-prayer, a beautiful and hopeful thought pierced my sadness. The ring, I realized, hadn't worn thin because it was corrupted by time and labor; it had worn thin because through the years the gold rubbed against her hand and, slowly, it was absorbed by her body. At some point in her life, my grandmother no longer simply *wore* my grandfather's wedding ring — she *became* my grandfather's wedding ring. What an amazing and beautiful symbol of how, through a lifetime of partnership, two people really do become one. In that moment, I could almost hear the Lord saying to her, "Well done, [my] good and faithful servant" (Mt 25:21).

For the Christian married couple, death is "graduation day." It is the beginning of everything we have been working for. The entire point of a Christian marriage is spending one's life preparing one's mate for the heavenly banquet. The couple who understands this will certainly suffer the pain of loss but will not be crushed by it.

In his book *Spiritual Passages,* Father Benedict Groeschel recounts the story of a deeply spiritual couple who had a long, loving life together. For years the two lived and worked together, rarely leaving each other's side. When the man's wife passed away, Father Groeschel went to the widower's home. He expected the man to be agonizing over the loss of his dearest friend and lover. The husband responded to Father Groeschel's condolences with a comment reflecting that peace which goes beyond all understanding: "On the contrary, I feel closer to her more than ever."

When I grow up, I want to be that man.

As you consider the eight stages of your love life, allow me to take a moment to remind you of something. The difference between a happy couple and a miserable couple is not the difficulties each couple faces along the way. Most people's lot in life is basically the same. What really makes the difference between happy and unhappy couples is that the former never stop expecting the best from themselves and their mates. They never give up, never stop striving for the good of one another. No matter what life throws at them, whether they *feel* like it or not, daily they choose to love. "Better and worse, richer and poorer, sickness and health" aren't just poetic words whispered in front of the altar. These words are reality. Good and bad times, wealth and poverty, sickness and health have absolutely nothing to do with our responsibility *to* love or our capacity *for* love. In fact, it is because we humans are so often sick, poor, and sad that we *need* marriage. A happy marriage is not an escape from reality; rather, it is a celebration of that reality and a promise to love each other "into Real" — even if that means enduring some popped stitches, worn velveteen, and sagging stuffing along the way.

Some Closing Thoughts

Throughout this chapter, I have attempted to give you a crystal ball with which to see the future of your marriage. As you are now aware, each stage of your journey involves new challenges that you must face if you are ever to arrive at "happily ever after." When people talk about marriage being hard work, it is mostly the challenges described in this chapter they are talking about. While I have done my best to spell out the tasks each marriage must accomplish, I thought you might like both a summary and a second opinion. The following is from the book *The Good Marriage*, by Dr. Judith Wallerstein and Sandra Blakeslee. It lists the nine tasks their research has identified as necessary for a marriage's healthy growth. They are not listed in any order and each is as important as the last.

✔ To separate emotionally from the family of one's childhood so as to invest fully in the marriage and, at the same time, to redefine the lines of connection with both families of origin.

✔ To build togetherness by creating the intimacy that supports it while carving out each partner's autonomy.

✔ To embrace the daunting roles of parents and to absorb the impact of Her Majesty the Baby's dramatic entrance. At the same time the spouses must work to protect their privacy.

✔ To maintain the bond in the face of adversity.

✔ To create a safe haven for the expression of differences, anger, and conflict.

✔ To establish a rich and pleasurable sexual relationship and protect it from the incursions of the workplace and family obligations.

✔ To use laughter and humor to keep things in perspective and to avoid boredom by sharing fun, interests, and friends.

✔ To provide nurturance and comfort to each other, satisfying each partner's needs for dependency and offering continuing encouragement and support.

✔ To keep alive early, idealized images of falling in love while facing the sober realities of the changes wrought by time.

Well, there you have it, the end of Part 1. By now you should have a pretty good idea of what building a happy marriage requires. In the next series of chapters, you will uncover what the most satisfied couples know about sex, how to make sure you always understand each other (in and out of bed), and the *shocking truth* behind the story of the Princess and the Frog Prince in Chapter 7 (inquiring minds want to know).

Part 2

The Road to Intimacy

C
H
A
P
T
E
R

The Road Trip (or "Der Intimacy Ist Goot, Ja?")

I propose another adventure! (As if mountain climbing weren't enough!) Pack your bags — we're taking a road trip to "Intimacy."

Imagine that Intimacy is an actual place. For the sake of argument, let's say it's located somewhere in Pennsylvania Dutch country, just northwest of Intercourse, a little town in Pennsylvania.

To get to Intimacy, you are going to need a car (good communication skills), fuel (a willingness to be vulnerable), a map (romance), and plenty of road signs (a playful, healthy, physical relationship). Successfully arriving at your destination requires all of the above to be present, plentiful, and in good working order. For example, without a map or road signs (romance and sexuality), a couple will frequently feel lost ("Just where do I stand with you anyway?"). With everything but the car (good communication), spouses can do little over time except take their fuel and set themselves on fire.

The chapters that follow are concerned with seeing that your relationship will not only be loving but also intimate.

Now Just a Cotton-Pickin' Minute!

No doubt some of you will be confused at this point. You might think that we already covered intimacy in Chapter 4 (on love), but you'd be wrong. There is a saying in Latin, *"Cognescere est distinguere"* ("To know is to make distinctions"), and there is an important distinction to be made between love and intimacy. Simply put, intimacy is the *measure* of love. If love were a tree, then intimacy would tell us how much fruit the tree could yield. If love were a body of water, intimacy would tell us how deep it was. (It is this distinction that allowed me — in Chapter 3 — to say that while *Apprenticeship Marriages* were built on love, they can be a bit shallow with regard to intimacy.)

In Chapter 4 we drilled a well — metaphorically speaking — to find out if there was any water (i.e., love) on your land. We also tested that water to make certain it wasn't too "hard" or "soft" (i.e., had the right mix of companionate and romantic loves). Now, by examining your capacity for vulnerability, communication, physical affection, and romance we are going to find out how much water your well is producing. Better still, if it turns out to be a puddle, then Part 2 of *For Better . . . Forever!* will show you how to go deeper and find an ocean. To begin, let us take a look at the first and most frightening of the four pillars of intimacy.

The "V-Word"

Vulnerability is seriously misunderstood and undervalued, but without vulnerability, people can too easily become self-righteous, self-absorbed bullies whose marriages are not so much relationships as they are extensions of their own infantile egos. The major problem with vulnerability is that people equate it with weakness. In fact, the word does mean "capable of being wounded." And I will agree that this does not sound at all desirable. Shouldn't people get married to protect each other from harm? Well, maybe. If by "protected from harm" you mean protected from indignity, humiliation, physical injury, and emotional wounding, you are absolutely right. A marriage that involves any of those is not vulnerable — it is *Co-dependent*. Every healthy marriage must above all be a safe haven from such offenses to human dignity. But there is one kind of pain from which no person should be exempt: the pain that is a necessary part of our growth as human beings. Even if we have a good sense of what our Christian identities are, we don't always live up to them. Worse still, sometimes we think we are living up to our values when in fact we are not. At such times, our vulnerability — our willingness to listen to some painful words from a trusted friend — will determine whether or not we are put right again. And that's where you come in as a spouse. If your marriage is to be a true partnership in fulfilling your Christian destiny, there will be times when you will need to gently wound, and be gently wounded by, your spouse in order to remain faithful to God's plan for your life.

Imagine that you fall down the stairs and break your leg, except you don't know it is broken because it is only a hairline fracture and you are like me — too stubborn to go to the doctor. Time goes by and there is little improvement. Weeks later you are still limping and your leg hurts

140

almost as much as the day you fell. One morning you wake up and say, "Enough is enough," and you make appointments with two different doctors. (If you are going to do this, you might as well do it right.)

Doctor A says that while he sympathizes with you, you are really doing just fine. He proposes to give you some painkillers and sends you on your way. On the other hand, Doctor B says that even though painkillers might give you some comfort in the short run, they won't really solve your problem — you will still limp, after all. This doctor would prefer to fix your leg. There is, of course, a small hitch. Since you waited so long to receive treatment, the bone has knitted itself back together incorrectly — and to fix it, he is going to have to break it again. The leg is going to hurt for a while; but, after you heal, you will be better than new. "Well, what do you think?" asks Doctor B.

Now, I admit I might be tempted to go with Doctor A. But I think when it came right down to it, I would choose Doctor B. I *want* to be better than new even if I might have to undergo some pain to get there. I do not relish pain, but I can endure it if necessary. In a sense, we are all like that patient with the broken leg. We are all limping along in pursuit of our God-given dreams, goals, and values; but we will never get there at the rate we are going. Some spouses, like Doctor A, just give each other painkillers: "Will I ever become the person God wants me to be?" "Oh, yes, dear. I'm sure you will" *(plod, plod, plod)*. Other — and I think healthier — spouses are like Doctor B: "Will I ever become the person God wants me to be?" "Honey, you know I believe in you; but I think I see how you might be getting in your own way a bit. Do you mind talking about it?"

There have been plenty of times in my marriage when I thought I was living up to my values. Times when I thought my actions were loving and my intentions sincere; but, in reality, I was being an insensitive prig. In these times, I rely on my vulnerability (my willingness to be wounded if necessary) and my wife's keen ability to *gently* break that malformed, misinformed part and get me on course again. Sometimes I perform a similar service for her (though she doesn't need it nearly as often as I do). No matter how lovingly the words are said, they always sting — sometimes a lot. But to my mind, it is more compassionate for my wife to do this than to simply leave me to my delusions and become more resentful at my ignorance over time. In short, my vulnerability allows me to be lovingly challenged to become the man I want to be when I grow up.

I Love You Just the Way You Are?

A healthy sense of vulnerability allows marriages to do the work they were ordained to do. It enables couples to move up *The Relationship*

Pathway toward greater competence, fulfillment, security, and participation in marital grace. But in my experience, there are two erroneous beliefs that stand between individuals and their ability to appreciate the need for vulnerability in a marriage. The first is represented by the following statement:

"Isn't marriage supposed to be the place where you can be yourself? You know, where you can stop pretending to be some goody-goody and just let the real you out?"

In a word, no. There are so many things wrong with this statement that it is difficult to know where to begin. In the first place, this belief usually assumes that the "real you" is the most vile, disgusting, and disagreeable version of oneself. This is clearly not the Christian view. For the Christian, the "real you" is the person God created you to be. The "real you" is the person you may hope *to become* by spending a lifetime cooperating with God's grace. Becoming who we are — whom God created us to be — takes real work, and for the most part, there is no better place to do this work than in our homes with our spouses and children.

While I will grant you that love calls husbands and wives to be more tolerant of occasional breaches of good taste and behavior, there are entirely too many people who make the mistake of thinking that being ignorant toward, or neglectful of, their mates is somehow a *proof* of love. As C. S. Lewis writes in *The Four Loves*, "[A person] knows that Affection takes liberties. He is taking liberties. Therefore (he concludes) he is being affectionate." I hope you can see the absurdity of this notion.

In Christian marriage, we are given the grace to work with our mates to *become* ourselves. Most of us are not there yet. Once we *become* who God created us to be, then, by all means, we should sit around the house being *that* all day. Until then, we have way too much work to do on ourselves to take advantage of too many "liberties." This leads me to the second misconception about relationships, namely:

"I've always thought you shouldn't try to change your mate. Shouldn't a husband and wife accept each other for who they are?"

The best answer to this question is, "Yes and no." Your partner should never try to change you simply to meet *his or her own* expectations — and vice versa. However, when you marry someone, you *are* swearing that person to help you stay true to *your own expectations for yourself* (this is why it is important to have some). Remember, the best marriages — the *Exceptional Seven Percent* — are built around both the husband and wife being able to say, "I married you because between now and the day I die, I have a better chance, with you than without you, of becoming the person God created me to be."

Think of the thousands of times you have disappointed yourself — much less anyone else. You do not really want to be accepted for *that,* do you? The healthy person may want to be loved through such things, or handled delicately in these areas, or even accepted as a "work in progress," but no one has the right to be let off the hook for disappointing himself or God. Pacifying — or expecting to be pacified — in the name of compassion is cowardice at best and enabling at worst. For the Christian, everything is an opportunity to grow in love; everything can be a spiritual exercise, from formal prayer, to kissing our spouses when we leave and enter a room, to getting off the couch when we are too tired to play with our children or wash the dishes. Every time we stretch ourselves to love, honor, and serve more than we happen to want to at the moment, we become a little more like Christ.

The renowned family therapist Cloe Madanes has said that the institution of marriage is the best kind of group therapy going. This goes double for marriage's potential for spiritual therapy. When husbands and wives celebrate their vulnerability to one another, they embrace the spiritual and therapeutic nature of all good, loving Christian marriages. They allow their marriages to help them become the people God created them to be.

A Word to Those Who Wound Others

Having heard all this, keep in mind that the obligation to help your partner remain true to him- or herself is not a license to kill. Remember St. Paul's admonition to the Corinthians, "Love keeps no score of wrongs, it does not gloat over another's sins" (cf. 1 Cor 13:6). Under no circumstances do you have permission to lord your partner's faults over her, be constantly critical, or even mildly cruel in the delivery of any feedback. In fact, nine times out of ten, it will be better for you to keep your mouth shut and simply listen as your partner tells you of her struggles. Does this seem contradictory? I do not mean it to be. While you and your partner must be willing to say the hard words when necessary, it must not be the main activity of your marriage — far from it. Dr. John Gottman's five-to-one rule applies here (see *Twelve Things Happy Couples Know About Love*, in Chapter 4). For *each* criticism you deliver you must give *five times* as many sincere compliments and perform *five times* as many loving acts if you are to be seen by your mate as anything more than a nag, a control freak, or worse. In Dr. Gottman's study, an amazing number of couples who did not maintain this ratio divorced within five years. Spouses must challenge each other to be more loving and more faithful to their own values, but they must challenge each other gently and with love. The four tips below will help you approach your partner's soft spots respectfully.

1. Don't volunteer "constructive criticisms." Wait for your spouse to ask.

Nobody likes a "buttinsky." Ideally, you should wait for your partner to ask for your input before you give it. If your mate tends to be slower than you would like in asking your opinion on how she should conduct her affairs, the solution is not to begin volunteering criticism. The *solution* is to practice your patience and build your credibility (see number 3 below). Wait to be invited to the party before offering to bring the potato salad.

2. What to do when your usually mature spouse doesn't ask for help and you can't bear to suffer — er, I mean — see her suffer any longer.

We all have blind spots. Sometimes we do not ask for assistance even when we really need it. If your spouse looks as if she is spinning her wheels and you genuinely want to help (not merely criticize for the fun of it), say something like, "I notice that you seem to be frustrated with such and such. Would you like to talk about it?" If she denies any problem, you can press a bit further with, "Well, it's just that I've noticed you pulling out clumps of hair *[eyeing the gun cabinet, sticking bobby pins in Barbie dolls, or other stress-behaviors]*. What's that about?"

This line of questioning allows you to secure an invitation to offer assistance. It has the added bonus of earning you "Brownie points" for having been so sensitive as to notice your mate's stressed-out behavior. All of this will increase the chances that any feedback you offer will be perceived as charitable and loving. At any rate, it sure beats yelling, "What the hell's the matter with you?"

3. Build credibility with the "Lord, change me" strategy.

What if number 1 and number 2 don't work? Try the following.

Let's say your mate isn't being as loving, attentive, successful, thoughtful, holy, whatever, as you think she could and should be. Moreover (stubborn person that your mate is), she is not asking for your help in solving this particular problem. Let us also say that you are like me, insofar as patience is not exactly your strong suit, and on several occasions you have broken down and, both gently and not so gently, explained the (you think) obvious solution to your mate's "problem." Again, if you are like me, you probably expected undying gratitude and an immediate change in your mate's behavior as a result of your wise intervention. But do you get so much as a "thank you" for all your efforts? Heck, no! (The ingrate!) What to do?

Both personally and professionally, I have found that when our mates

144

ignore our — *ahem* — wise counsel, and other — *ahem* — well-intentioned attempts to call them on (i.e., lead them in the path of Jesus), it is usually because, despite what we may like to think, we are not such hot stuff ourselves. In other words, we lack credibility. For example, we may ask our mates to love us the way we want to be loved, but very often we remain blind to the billion or so ways we are disappointing them. As our Lord pointed out, we see the speck in our neighbor's eye and not the beam in our own (cf. Mt 7:4-5 and Lk 6:42). In such a case, it is hard to imagine why our mates should *not* ignore us — expert lovers that we ourselves are.

No matter how high an opinion we may have of our own talents for holiness, love, romance, wisdom, success, etc., nine out of ten times our mates' ignoring our divinely inspired wisdom on how they can improve their lives is a clear sign that we need to work on our own credibility.

To truly call our mates on, rather than whine at them or nag them to change, we must become more loving *to them* and more faithful to *our own* values. Otherwise we end up playing *Marital Chicken*, as is evident in comments like "I would be more *X* if you would just be *Y*." If we want to lead our mates to the Lord, then we need to become someone worthy of following. We must ask the Lord to help *us* become more loving, faithful, *credible* spouses. When — and only when — our mates experience our loving them without a chip on our shoulders and without expecting some kind of payment in return; when they see us living up to our God-given values, dreams, and goals on a consistent basis, only then can we expect them to look at us and say, "You have it so together and you are so loving and generous to me. How can I be more like that?"

Congratulations! You have now been invited to the party. Pick up your potato salad and proceed in all haste to number 4, immediately following.

4. When asked, be gentle.

This should be so obvious as to be undeserving of mention, but my experience tells me otherwise. Be gentle when offering help, even after being invited. I find that the best way to do this is to merely talk about your observations and be prepared to be told that your observations are incorrect: "*I could be wrong,* but I seem to have noticed such and such. What do you think?"

Repeat the formula as necessary. This approach allows you to assert what you believe to be true without overstepping your bounds. Compare the above to "Y'know what your problem is?" or the ever-popular "Why do you have to be such a jerk?" and you will understand what I am getting at.

Sacrificial Love? Or Co-dependence?

Vulnerability, as exhibited by our willingness to be "broken" for the sake of our identities in Christ, and our willingness to be loving to our mates even when they don't deserve it, falls under the heading of "sacrificial love" — and good marriages have plenty of this. Unfortunately, for many, the phrase "sacrificial love" has an even worse ring to it than vulnerability. I suppose it is easy to see why. Some people confuse sacrificial love with being spineless or co-dependent. But true sacrificial love, like true vulnerability, requires that one does not surrender unless one's values and/or personal dignity require them to do so. Compare this to the *Co-dependent* person who throws down his or her arms for any reason at the first sign of conflict. If co-dependency is sensitivity in the *absence* of personal strength, then true vulnerability and sacrificial love demonstrate the *balance* between sensitivity and personal strength. The following quiz can help you see if you have what it takes to be healthily vulnerable.

Are You Vulnerable — In a Healthy Way?
Part A: Personal Strength

Directions: Write T for "True" next to each statement that applies. Answer according to how each statement applies to the way you act *in your marriage.*

1. ___ My life reflects a clear set of values, i.e., "I don't have to say, 'I believe such and such.' You can tell by looking at my life."

2. ___ I am capable of providing for my own needs, whether emotional and/or financial.

3. ___ I enjoy being by myself.

4. ___ I have strong opinions.

5. ___ I am comfortable in conflict (though I don't look for fights).

6. ___ I am not easily intimidated.

7. ___ I do not take criticism personally.

8. ___ My own satisfaction or fulfillment is important to me.

9. ___ Certain things are worth fighting for.

10. ___ I speak my mind.

Score Part A: Personal Strength _____

Part B: Sensitivity

1. ___ I am careful not to offend others with my speech or actions.

2. ___ I am quick to notice another person's pain.

3. ___ I go out of my way to help others in need.

4. ___ I am a good listener.

5. ___ People tell me I'm easy to talk to. (Or, "Everybody seems eager to talk to me.")

6. ___ Being considerate is very important to me.

7. ___ I am concerned about the happiness of others.

8. ___ I believe that the people I know are basically good-hearted.

9. ___ It would be very painful for me to lose a friend.

10. ___ I am comfortable talking about my feelings.

Score Part B: Sensitivity _____

Scoring

Compare your scores for both parts of the quiz.

• A score of *six or more in both* personal strength *and* sensitivity suggests that you probably have the skills to be vulnerable in the healthiest sense of the word.

• Scoring *less than six in both* personal strength *and* sensitivity suggests that you are neither remarkably sensitive nor do you have much strength of character. You probably don't care enough about anything — including your own personal growth — to make vulnerability seem worthwhile to you. You need to develop some passions and a greater concern for others if you want more than a perpetually stagnant life and marriage.

• A *high score* (six or more) in personal strength combined with a *low score* (five or less) in sensitivity suggests that vulnerability does not come easy to you. Depending upon the disparity between the two scores, you may tend to come across as a bully. Work on your awareness of other's feelings and perceptions of you. Being right all of the time is no fun if it eventually causes you to be alone all of the time.

• A *low score* (five or less) in personal strength combined with a *high score* (six or more) in sensitivity suggests that you may have a tendency toward being a doormat instead of vulnerable in a healthy way. Depending on the disparity between these two scores, you may also have some *Co-dependent* tendencies. Find something to believe in — starting with yourself — and stand up for it.

— Excerpted from Gregory K. Popcak Seminars, © 1997

ᡈᢍᡈ

Vulnerability: You've Got the Power

As I explained earlier, vulnerability enables your marriage to become a spiritual endeavor. It allows you to stand in awe of the transformative power of God's love working through you and your mate. When your mate has earned your trust by demonstrating his credibility and you grant him the right to rummage through the closets and cobwebbed basements of your soul, inevitably he will come across some gunk-encrusted thing, a behavior of which you are ashamed or a belief that is unhealthy or destructive. In a good marriage, the finder will not recoil with disgust; instead, he will help you uncover and reclaim that part of yourself.

The Great Divorce (an allegorical novel about heaven and hell) describes the process I am writing about. In one scene, a man is being tormented by a terrible lizard (representing his sinfulness). With the man's permission, an angel strikes the lizard with a flaming sword (the love of God), and the lizard is transformed into a stallion, which the man then rides into the mountains of heaven. To practice vulnerability is to allow your marriage to participate in the divine work of redemption and transformation. The marriage that can do this is to be both envied and imitated.

Because secrets melt in the heat of true vulnerability, you will constantly be discovering new facets of your mate and yourself. You will never have to fear becoming bored with each other because every day another defense will melt away, another "lizard" will be transformed in the spiritual fire of your love for each other. As you grow in trust, love, and vulnerability, you and your mate will fling open the doors to each other's secret chambers. Light and air will pour into the once dank and dreary corners of your soul. Each day a new piece of your heart will be captured until there is no part of you that is left untouched; until your partner has dwelt in every part of your body, soul, and consciousness — and you in his. Practicing this kind of vulnerability is the only way you will ever know what it means for two to become one. No thrill will ever come close to the fear, anticipation, and sweet release that is experienced in the presence of true vulnerability. It is a thrill that will last a lifetime.

As you might well imagine, vulnerability lends itself to an uncommonly rewarding sex life. Most of the books on sex are dead wrong. You don't have to dress up like Batman and Catwoman to add spice to your marriage. If you want a thrill befitting a "Real Man" or a "Real Woman," try exposing every aspect of your being to your mate over a lifetime. It is no great mystery that spiritual people have more intense orgasms. The *Janus Report on Sexual Behavior* (1993) states that while others are mere technicians, spiritual people "pay more attention to the mystic and symbolic aspects of . . . sexuality." No prop, costume, or role-play could ever compare to the soulfully orgasmic, transcendent ecstasy that accompanies offering one's whole self as a free, unrestrained gift to one's beloved.

148

The following will help you increase the healthy vulnerability in your own life and inspire the same in your mate.

❦

Surrendering to Love: A Discussion

1. Make a point of living out the *Twelve Things Happy Couples Know About Love* (Chapter 4). Pay special attention to numbers 1, 3, 5, 7, and 8.

2. Maintain the five-to-one ratio of positivity to negativity by checking your *Twenty-five Ways to Make Love Stay — Every Day* list at least once a week. Are you living up to your value of being a loving person?

3. Discuss the following.

(a) What are the ways you sabotage your own progress toward your fulfillment?

For example, where do you experience fear, shame, or self-doubt? When your partner sees you stumbling on the road, how could he or she be helpful — without stepping on your toes?

(b) What shortcomings do you have about which you are especially sensitive? While acknowledging your primary responsibility for correcting these faults, what can your partner do to assist you in this transformation?

(c) When your partner disappoints or frustrates you, how would your partner like to be approached with this information? That is, what does your partner think would be a considerate and respectful way to let him know of your hurt?

❦

Conclusion

Having covered vulnerability *(There now, that wasn't so bad, was it?),* we can move on to the second pillar of intimacy: the secrets of exceptional communication. As a bonus, you'll also find out the *shocking true story* behind the courtship of the Princess and the Frog Prince. Go to the next chapter — if you dare!

CHAPTER 7

The Princess, the Frog Prince, and Freud

Once upon a time . . .

There was a beautiful but lonely princess. She sought her Prince Charming among the royalty of the neighboring kingdoms — with no success. She sought her one, true love in the cities and villages of the world; but again, she met no success. One day, weary and exhausted from her travels, the Princess found a sun-dappled knoll in the middle of a forest. She lay down and fell fast asleep.

She awoke to the sound of tiny voices and laughter. A short distance from her, she saw a small gathering of children sitting around a weathered, stooped old man. "A bard!" thought the princess to herself. She crept closer so that she could hear the old man's tale.

She couldn't make out everything he said, standing as far back as she was, but she heard enough to know that his story was about a princess, like herself, who, having found a frog wearing a crown, convinced him of her love, whereupon the frog was transformed into a handsome prince with whom she lived "happily ever after."

The Princess could scarcely contain her excitement. After the story was completed and the children dismissed, she approached the storyteller. "O wise bard, I am a lonely princess, but I am encouraged by your remarkable story. I am sure that your tale was intended for my ears and that you, at long last, can help me find my prince. Will you help me?"

The old man considered her request; then, waving her to

follow him, the bard took her to some wetlands. Sure enough, looking decidedly uncomfortable among the other amphibians was a singularly distinctive frog, wearing a singularly distinctive — crown.

The Princess' heart leapt. Her search was over! The bard looked at her and smiled. "I have done what I can for you. Now you must convince him of your love. If you can do this, you and your prince will live happily ever after." With that, he left her.

The Princess immediately began thinking of ways she could convey her love to him. "This should be easy," she thought. "I'll simply do the things I would want my beloved to do for me." So she sat down and composed a beautiful love song with a profound lyric and gentle, stirring melody. With the sweetest voice in all heaven and earth, the Princess sang of her love with such feeling that the birds swooned and remained silent, as they could not compete with her song. When she was finished, she looked to the Frog Prince with great anticipation.

He began to stir, then twitch. All of a sudden, much to her astonishment — his tongue flew out of his mouth and zapped a fly that had invaded his airspace. *"BZZRRT!"*

She was crushed. How could the frog not be convinced of her love? She regained her composure and said to the frog, "Wait right here." With that, she walked to the field on the other side of the road. She picked a bouquet of flowers whose fragrance was so rich and intoxicating that the royal perfumers still seek to copy the scent of that loving gift. She carried the flowers to the frog and, laying them before him, said, "My love for you is twice as sweet as the most fragrant buds in this bouquet."

That got him. The frog's heart quickened. The Princess stood, arms outstretched, eagerly awaiting the man of her dreams. What would he say to her?

"RRRBBBBBTTT!"

That did it. She picked up the frog and his crown and ran to the village. There, she found the bard in the local pub. She grabbed the old man in a most unladylike way, and screamed, "*You gave me a defective frog!* I sing him songs, I give him gifts, but *nothing*! He still isn't convinced of my love. You old fool!"

The bard was stunned. "My child," he said, "did you not hear the story? You must kiss the frog with the passion of a thousand lovers on a midsummer's night."

The Princess froze. "Kiss him?" she thought. She fully

intended to do that — and a whole lot more — after he became a prince, but kiss the frog? Ugh. That was weird. Gross even. She looked at the bard as if to ask, "Isn't there some other way? He's slimy and that tongue . . . *Ugh!*" A shiver travelled from her feet to the tips of her strawberry-blond locks, but the bard only smiled and shook his head, "No."

"Oh well." She sighed. She closed her eyes, puckered her lips and after taking a good, deep breath, she let the frog have it right on the kisser. "Hmmm. This isn't so bad," she thought. Imagine her surprise when she opened her eyes in mid-kiss to see before her the most handsome and charming prince in the world. Knowing when she had a good thing, the Princess immediately carried the Prince to the village church and before he could say, "Excuse me, Miss, I'd like some ketchup with my flies," they were married — and they lived happily ever after.

The moral of the story is . . .

It is not enough to love. You must love in a way that is meaningful to the beloved.

The end.

— Excerpted from

The Princess, The Frog Prince and Freud

(© 1997 by Gregory K. Popcak Seminars)

A Love of Another Kind

This chapter describes those advanced communication techniques I mentioned in Chapter 3 (under the subhead *Recommendations for Star and Storybook Marriages*). We all like to give and receive love differently. There are those authors who would have you believe these differences are basically gender-related.

The popular line is that men prefer physical — and especially sexual — displays of affection, while women prefer emotional and more romantic displays. But this is an oversimplification. Research shows us that gender does not account for such differences in *at least* twenty percent of both men and women. This is an important statistic because many of us, coming home from the bookstore with one of the more popular relationship tomes, think that we have it all figured out: Wives will do X for their men, husbands will do Y for their women, and everyone will live happily ever after. But a large number of husbands and wives simply don't fit the pithy "Mars and Venus" formula. So, if gender isn't the primary determining factor in affection styles, what is? Believe it or not, it's neurology.

"Love-speak"

Originally identified by linguist John Grinder and mathematician Richard Bandler, there are three major "love languages," that is, three different ways people prefer to give and receive affection. These "languages" are based on our senses (sight, hearing, touch, and so forth) — specifically, which sense is most highly developed in any given person. To best explain how this works, I need to take you back to grade school for a minute.

Kids all learn differently, and teachers spend a great deal of time trying to figure out their students' "learning styles." For example, children who learn better by reading and taking notes are said to have a "visual learning style." Students who learn best through lectures, songs, and being "talked through" tasks have an "auditory learning style." Finally, kids who learn best by doing hands-on projects and activities have a "kinesthetic learning style." These styles can change over time, but they never go away completely because they are *neurologically based*. That is, they are dependent upon the senses that are most highly developed in a particular student. When we grow up, our "learning styles" become our "communication styles," or, for our purposes, the three major "love languages."

Flash forward to adulthood. You are married. Imagine that your mate "speaks" a visual love language while you have a more auditory love language. You will *tell* him, "I love you," about a million times a day. This will be very meaningful to you (auditory people love to hear themselves — and everyone else — talk); but *your mate* (visual person that he is) will probably think, "Ho-hum. That's nice, dear."

You see, if you *really* want a visually attuned person to understand the depth of your love, you must *show* him you love him — literally. Get that person a silly card and write a poem that he can *read* over and over. Leave love notes for him. Get him a present and wrap it in beautiful paper. Cook a fancy dinner and (this is the important part) light candles, set the table, use your best china, and the good silver, and dress up. For visual people, atmosphere counts — a lot.

Likewise, if you are "in the mood" and want to make sure your visual mate is similarly inclined, wear something sexy. Better still, make love to him with the lights on. He wants to *see* how much you love him. If you do any or all of these things for your visual spouse, then he will really understand your love in a meaningful way. Why? Because you are speaking your partner's visual love language. Cognitively, he *understood* what you meant when you (in your auditory way) *said*, "I love you"; but he *experienced* it when you *showed* him.

You, however, as a person with an auditory love language, would consider many of the things that mean so much to your visual spouse irrelevant and distracting at best or completely stupid at worst. Let's take this same example and flip it around. Because your mate has a visual love language, he is going to bring you flowers, cards, or other tokens to *show* you how much he loves you. But, after the novelty of this wears off, because you have a primarily auditory love language, you will probably think, "Ho-hum. That's nice and all, but why don't you *tell* me you love me more often? I love *hearing* you *say* it."

More than getting flowers, cards, or notes, you would probably rather stay up all night with your mate talking about your feelings, or your plans for the future, or, for that matter, about nothing at all. You will want him to sing you songs, call you pet names in a silly tone of voice, leave you cute messages on the answering machine, or read you love poems. When you are in the mood to make love you will want him to *tell* you what he is thinking and how wonderfully you are making him feel. In and out of bed, you want to *hear* how much he loves you. If he's not talking to you, he's not being loving to you.

As time goes by, if neither of you learns to understand the reasons behind the way you communicate love to each other, one of you is going to accuse the other of neglect. For the sake of argument, let's say it's you.

"You don't ever tell me you love me unless I say it first. What's wrong with you?"

Your partner will probably be insulted and become defensive at your accusation. He will probably say that since *your* gums never stop flapping they don't have half a chance to "say it first." Next, he will point out all the things he does to *show* you that he loves you, bringing up such things as the cards, flowers, candy, and love notes he's given you over a period of time. Depending upon how bad a day he is having, he may even "diagnose" you as being "insecure" because he has to *tell* you how much he loves you so often: "You should know I love you by now. Why do I have to tell you all the time?"

You will eventually become disgusted with your spouse and decide he just doesn't get it. More than likely you will have a big argument, or a series of big arguments, in which you will accuse each other of being *"insensitive."* (Little will either of you know how literally true this is. Keep in mind that love languages are neurologically based on the five senses.) As a result of these arguments, you will probably come to one of two conclusions.

1. You were never meant for each other and should proceed, post-haste, to divorce court.

2. You decide that each of you loves the other "in his or her own way" and even though it is basically meaningless to you, you'll try to choke down your disappointment and get on with it. "Nothing's perfect. Right?"

Well, very little is perfect, but love can be. For the Christian, it must be, since Jesus said: "Be perfect, as your heavenly Father is perfect" (Mt 5:48). That is, perfect in love. In order to perfect our ability to love our mates, we must learn how to love them in a way that, literally, makes *sense* to them (i.e., appeals to the *physical sense* to which they are most attuned).

The problem is, in the above example, it would never have dawned on you that some of the loving expressions your mate values would be valued by anybody. You just think he's a big, dumb idiot. In our example, you were *literally* not wired (neurologically) to think the way he does. Furthermore, when a person with a different "love language" than your own expresses his preferences, you will be apt to forget what he said, not because you are inconsiderate, or don't love him enough, but because your brain simply isn't wired to understand what he is telling you.

It is like the first day in an immersion Japanese-language class. You nod politely, act as if you understand the instructor, but you really won't get it until she has repeated herself a hundred (or maybe a bazillion) times and your brain has *literally* acquired the neurological connections it needs to make *sense* of her message. You may think I am overstating this. You may prefer to believe that your mate is insensitive. He is. Just not the way you mean. If you identify with anything you are reading so far, your partner may literally be "out of sense" with you. It takes real work to make the neurological connections necessary for translating across a couple's conflicting sensory styles (i.e., love languages); but it can be done. A great deal of research on both remedial education and the physiological effects of psychotherapy show that it can be done. Several well-respected studies have indicated that when a person changes his or her behavior, communicative ability, and life experiences, he or she actually causes structural changes in the brain and nervous system. When spouses talk about "struggling to make a connection" with each other, they don't realize they are describing a physiological reality. Understanding and loving your mate in a meaningful way *is* hard work. Fortunately, God gives Christian married couples the grace they need to be up to the task.

So far, I have described visual and auditory "love-speak." Let me take a minute to explain the third major love language: kinesthetic (i.e., pertaining to touch). Stereotypically, this is the style most often attributed to "guys." However, *at least* twenty percent of women exhibit this style as well.

Kinesthetic spouses tend to be very physical. They can never get enough touching, holding, hugging, kissing, cuddling, and/or lovemaking. They need to "be in touch" with their partners to "feel connected." People who have a primarily kinesthetic love language tend to love quiet times together, just sitting and being, and when they feel *really* ambitious, sitting, being, *and* holding. That's not to say that kinesthetics are lazy (quite the contrary, they are often very hard workers); they just aren't super-showy about their love. They tend not to say much or be very talented at the things many people would consider to be romance. For the kinesthetic, romance is best demonstrated by faithfully carrying out the common duties of daily life. The best kinesthetics are usually very good at quiet, humble service. (Contrast this with auditory people who tend to ask for feedback about everything they do, or visual people who want to make sure you saw their gesture.) Most often, to demonstrate their affection for you, kinesthetics will *do* things to make your life easier. They will get you coffee, wash your car, clean the house, pay the bills. Visual and auditory spouses often hate this. They are usually very critical of their kinesthetic partners for trying to get relationship points for "doing stuff they would just have to do anyway." Visual and auditory people tend to believe love is something you have to make a fuss about. Kinesthetic spouses, on the other hand, tend to view love as something they live, feel, and are, commenting, "Why do we have to try so hard all the time to analyze everything? Can't we just *be* together?"

When stressed, the purest kinesthetics tend to withdraw into themselves, immerse themselves in work, or exercise vigorously. Kinesthetics tend to come across as stoic and aloof until you get to know them. They are the people who like to hang on the edge of a crowd and remain quiet until they *feel* comfortable with their surroundings. Kinesthetics are often criticized as being unemotional, but nothing could be further from the truth. In fact, because their sense of touch is so acute, they tend to *feel* emotions in their body more strongly and deeply than either visual people (who tend to live in their heads) or auditory people (whose feelings change with the subject they are discussing). The problem is, the purest kinesthetics don't *show* their emotions or *talk* about them. They just *feel* them. In arguments that exceed their comfort level, they are easily overwhelmed and may either agree with their partners just to shut them up, or react explosively when they can't keep it in anymore. Kinesthetics tend to be impulsive, making decisions based on how they *feel* at the moment. They tend to have an intense dislike of conflict (it just feels too stressful); they also tend to abhor schedules insofar as they hate committing themselves to anything they might not *feel* like doing later. Again, contrast this with auditory people who love to debate everything, and visual people who would post their morning shower routine on a schedule (in triplicate) if they could — because if they can *see* it, they know it will be done correctly.

Do you see the potential for problems here? Obviously mismatched love languages can become a serious problem. But, believe it or not, of all the marriage problems I see in counseling, differences in love languages are the easiest to fix. There are three steps: (1) Determining your language. (2) Separating who you *are* from how you're *wired*. (3) Rewiring.

Becoming Multilingual: Step One
DETERMINING YOUR LOVE LANGUAGE

When a husband and wife speak different love languages, they may know they are loved by their partner — in their own way — but a wife won't really experience the fullness of that love unless her husband takes the trouble to learn her love language and vice versa. So far, we have taken a cursory look at the three major love languages (visual, auditory, and kinesthetic). Some of you may wonder why — if they are truly based on the five senses — there are only three love languages. Elementary, my dear reader. The other two senses (taste and smell) are not usually dominant enough for either one to be a person's primary love language. (I suppose you *could* smell how much you love your mate — but, frankly, I don't want to know about it.) At best, our senses of taste and smell add spice and freshness to our experience of the three primary love languages: visual, auditory, and kinesthetic.

The first step to overcoming the communication barriers between you and your mate is to identify the specific ways in which you are different. The following exercise describes the behaviors, speech patterns, and preferences of each love language. See if you can identify the languages you and your partner speak most fluently.

***

Love-Speak Exercise

Directions: Chances are you use all of your five senses, but you will *favor* one or two of them when it comes to giving and receiving love. The following are some of the most prominent characteristics, speech patterns, and preferences associated with each love language. Write *M* for "me" next to each quality that describes you. Write *P* for "partner" next to each quality that describes your mate. You will probably check some in each category. You are looking for the category you check the *most* items in. This will be your primary love language.

The Visual (Seeing) Love Language

Check the statements that describe how you are *most* of the time.

___ "*Show* me that you love me."

___ Flowers, love notes, cards, etc., *most* meaningful (not just liked).

___ "Presentation" important (i.e., presents wrapped nicely, meals arranged decoratively on a well-set table, etc.). Think "Martha Stewart."

___ Lighting important to mood.

___ "Turned on" by candlelight, lingerie that looks sexy even though it may be horribly uncomfortable, other visual stimuli.

___ Clothes important. *Looking good* more important than comfort or practicality.

___ Desktops and visible surfaces neat as a pin. Desk drawers and closets, however, may be a disaster. Out of *sight*, out of mind.

___ Always making plans. Very productive. Tracks a hundred projects at once.

___ Good at decorating or other visual arts (photography, painting, etc.).

___ Good at matching unusual colors and patterns in attractive ways (clothes, house decorations, etc.).

___ A house that "looks clean" more important than a house that *is* clean.

___ Unconsciously makes neat piles out of anything that happens to be in front of you.

___ Mess *causes* stress.

___ Thinks more clearly when house is neat.

___ Cleans or tidies up *when* stressed.

___ Daydreams a lot.

___ Speaks quickly. Uses a lot of words.

___ Tends to be "anal retentive" (i.e., uptight, proper, or detail oriented).

___ Enjoys books with vivid descriptions and/or pictures.

___ Loves to keep journals, makes plans, and write lists.

___ Charts, graphs, or other visual aids helpful. "Learns by watching."

___ Uses visual metaphors in speech like, "I've got to focus," "Imagine that," "It seems vague," "It seems clear," "I can see right through you," "I'm seeing things in a new light," "I'm drawing a blank," "See my point?"

Visual love language scores: "Me" _____ "Partner" _____

Auditory (Hearing) Love Language

Check the statements that describe how you are *most* of the time.

___ "*Tell* me that you love me."

___ Talks constantly about everything.

___ Has an opinion on every subject. Sometimes told, "You analyze and/or think too much."

___ Likes hearing and saying "I love you" a million times a day.

___ Loves to have extended conversations about anything.

___ Important to "talk things out."

___ "If you talk to me, that means you love me."

___ No such thing as a "rhetorical question"; he or she answers everything.

___ Likes music, poetry, etc.

___ Speaks with a certain rhythm or variations in tone.

___ Very sensitive to other's tone of voice.

___ Hums, whistles, talks to self, perhaps constantly.

___ Radio or TV on at all times, "Just for the noise."

___ Sounds (music, tone of voice) affect mood.

___ "Turned on" by romantic, emotional, and/or sexual *conversations.*

___ When arguing, doesn't know when to stop. May follow other person from room to room talking, whether or not the other is listening.

___ When moderately stressed, tries to talk about it. When maximally stressed, needs quiet to restore calm.

___ Phone permanently connected to head.

___ Always gets the last word.

___ Always late because he or she "just stopped to talk for a minute."

___ Would rather die than be quiet.

___ Uses auditory comments, "Hear me out," "I could tell by your tone," "I need some feedback," "We need to talk," "Just *listen* to me," "It made me want to scream," and other auditory metaphors in speech.

Auditory love language scores: "Me" _____ "Partner" _____

Kinesthetic (Touch) Love Language

Check the statements that describe how you are *most* of the time.

___ "You love me if you're touching me."

___ "I love when we're both quiet and we can just *be* together."

___ "Why do we have to talk all the time and/or work so hard on our relationship?"

___ Likes touching and hugging more than any other expression of affection.

_____ Dresses for comfort. Appearance secondary if considered at all.

_____ Tends to withdraw or shut down in arguments fairly quickly.

_____ Easily overwhelmed in verbal conflict. Often feels picked on. "I never know what to say . . ."

_____ Has a hard time making decisions. Tends not to reason things out. Gives "gut reactions" to things.

_____ Poor organizer. Lots of unorganized piles. "Don't touch my mess. I'll never find anything."

_____ Gestures, grunts, and shrugs more than talks.

_____ Works off stress physically. Either by exercising and/or "working it off," or by taking "spa time" (i.e., hot bath, pampering one's body, naps).

_____ Talks slowly. Has trouble finding the right words.

_____ "Turned on" by touching, hugging, kissing, massage, other physical contact. May have a hard time not "going all the way" when physical affection started.

_____ Tends to have a hard time delaying gratification. Sexually, may rush through "preliminaries" to get to "the good stuff."

_____ After arguments, looks for physical reassurance (hugs or sex) to make sure "we're still OK."

_____ Loves sports or other physical activity.

_____ Hates making plans. "I don't know what I'll _feel_ like doing that day."

_____ Tends to be impulsive or spontaneous.

_____ Sometimes hard to get motivated. Can't get past how he or she _feels right now,_ in that particular moment.

_____ Learns by doing. Often a slower learner in school.

_____ Doesn't like to read, or prefers books and movies with "action."

_____ Tends to be a slob. Doesn't see mess unless he or she trips over it.

_____ Says things like, "Get a grip," "I'll handle it," "Take it easy," "We're really connected," "I just feel that way, that's why," and similar physically attuned metaphors in speech.

Kinesthetic love language scores: "Me" _____ "Partner" _____

Scoring

✔ In which category did you mark the _most_ checks?

"Me" _____ "Partner" _____

These are your primary love languages.

✔ Which category had the second most checks?

"Me" _____ "Partner" _____

These are your secondary love languages.

✔ Which category had the least number of checks?

"Me" _____ "Partner" _____

These are your tertiary love languages.

❦〜❦

Love-Speak Continued

As you can see, there are significant differences between each style. But don't be too surprised if you checked some items in each category. Most of us have five senses and use them all to one degree or another; it's just that our life experiences have made some of those senses more acute than the others. In the exercise, you identified your primary, secondary, and tertiary love languages. Even if you and your mate's primary love languages are different, you will probably share a highly developed secondary "language" together. If you didn't, it would have been hard to understand each other well enough to get together in the first place. For most couples, wanting to increase proficiency in a secondary or tertiary love language springs from the desire to develop even greater intimacy than already exists. As such, differences in love languages tend to be a greater concern for *Apprentices* and *Partners.* Still, differences between spouses in their primary love languages can be fairly problematic.

Early in our marriage, my wife and I struggled with this very issue. As I mentioned before, I tend to be highly visual (my primary love language). But I am also very auditory (my secondary love language). My wife, on the other hand is highly kinesthetic (primary love language) *and* highly auditory (secondary love language). We really connected when it came to our love of long conversations, saying, "I love you" a million times per day, and all that auditory stuff. But when it came to other areas, we kept missing the boat. I would bring home cards and flowers and she would say, "Thank you, honey," and leave them sitting on the table for a week. "How insensitive," I thought. "Such things should be displayed prominently on the mantle so that all the world could *see* how much I loved her. How dare she just let them sit there!"

Meanwhile, my wife would sit on the couch and say to me, "Come and hold me. Why do we have to always be running somewhere? Let's just sit together."

Please understand that I am much different than I used to be, but back then my definition of hell was "sitting still." It wasn't that I didn't *want* to sit with her; it was just that everywhere I looked, I *saw* something else that had to be done.

Until my wife and I started learning about love languages we just felt that the other person was being an intractable idiot.

Me: "I wish you would get *me* some flowers or a card sometime, just as I do for you."

Wife: "Anybody can do that. Come here; let me hold you."

Me: " 'Hold you?' Gee, a whole lot of thought goes into that!"

Me: "Let's make plans for Saturday." (Visual people can't *stand* to look out into the future and see a blank space on their mental calendar.)

Wife: "Can't we just see how we *feel* when we get up?" (Kinesthetic people can't *stand* to be committed to something they might not feel like doing later.)

Me: "I don't understand. Why can't we plan something for a change?"

Wife: "Why do you have to be so compulsive?"

No matter how many times we tried to explain our positions to each other, they never made *sense*. It was getting to the point where we began thinking that the other was thoughtless, inconsiderate, "just didn't love me enough to remember what was important to me," or worse. Once we learned what our love languages were, we began to understand that the reason we weren't being loving in as meaningful a way as possible (i.e., working hard, not smart) wasn't that we didn't love each other enough — we were simply wired differently. And once we learned how to do it, we could "rewire" ourselves to increase our understanding of the true depth of love that existed between us.

This brings me to step two.

Becoming Multilingual: Step Two

SEPARATING WHO YOU ARE FROM HOW YOU'RE WIRED

It is at this point that most couples I am counseling say, "So, that's it? We're wired differently? You mean, we're doomed?" *Au contraire, mes amis.*

Remember what you read earlier? You and your mate must understand each other on some level or you never would have gotten together at all. If you and yours don't speak the same primary love language, chances are you at least share a highly developed secondary or tertiary one. What we are really addressing here is the fact that at some point most couples hit a wall where there will be no more growth in their intimacy unless they develop their proficiency in a second or third love language. This wall will take the form of a minor crisis. That is one of the many times spouses look at each other over the course of a marriage and say, "Uh, now what?"

The second step to successfully bridging the differences between you and your spouse is realizing that your love language is not who you *are*. It is not who God created you to *be*. It is simply how you are *wired*. While you may only be *proficient* with one or two of your senses, God *gave* you five senses and he expects you to learn to use them to the fullest extent possible. As we are told in the New Testament: "To whom much is given, much is required" (cf. Lk 12:48). Why would God want you to do this? Because God reveals himself to us through the created world almost as much as he does through Scripture. (This revelation is what theologians call "Natural Law.") To put it in the words of the late, great Catholic physician-philosopher Dr. Herbert Ratner, God is one, so "the revelation of the Father [in Creation] does not conflict with the revelation of the Son [in Scripture]."

God wants to share his "natural" revelation with all of us, but we will be completely unable to receive it unless we open up all the channels he has given us (our five senses). Limiting yourself to your preferred sense (or senses) while attempting to understand how God is appearing to you, speaking to you, and reaching out to you through his world is as absurd as trying to appreciate a painting by one of the great masters while wearing sunglasses, listening to one of Beethoven's symphonies while wearing earmuffs, or running your fingers over *The Pietà* while wearing gloves. No less an authority than Pope John Paul II, in his *Theology of the Body. . .*, has encouraged us to prayerfully contemplate our bodies as a way of understanding God's plan for us and the world. What I am describing in these pages is simply one more way psychology can help us do what the Holy Father asks. If marriage was instituted by God to give us the grace we need to become who we were created to be, then becoming fluent in all the sensory love languages is just one more way marriage makes this possible.

Before I met my wife, I was perfectly content to live in my own visual/auditory world. I appreciated the arts, especially good music. I dressed as well as my budget would allow. I was creative and productive. I lived life to what I thought was the fullest. But then along came my wife, who introduced me to a world that God created and I knew little, perhaps nothing, about. This was a kinesthetic world where people could just sit and not do anything (good grief!) except maybe, if they were really ambitious, hold hands. This was a world in which people were quiet (heaven forbid!), and closed their eyes (scandalous!), and just *felt* the breeze on their skin. This was a cozy, comfortable world where sometimes it was enough to just "be." In the same way, I like to think that I introduced my wife to a more visual world. A world where little things matter, where structure and feelings work together to make poetry out of

164

life instead of mere prose. It is my hope that she has benefited by these small gifts I could give her, just as I have benefited by her gifts to me; but neither of us could have gotten to such places on our own. Because of our unsanctified, *insensitive* neurology, we didn't even know God created such places. God is using my marriage to open my eyes, ears, nose, mouth, and hands to all the wonderful worlds he has created, and I am better able to praise him because of it.

Husbands and wives, we need to stop hiding out behind phrases like "That's just not who I am" or "That isn't the way people are *supposed* to relax *[or communicate, make love, wash dishes, express affection, clean the house, etc.]*." We need to humble ourselves and learn to benefit from our partners' unique experiences, preferences, and styles — especially the ones that don't readily "make sense" to us. By doing this, we become more well-rounded individuals and have happier relationships.

Let's do some rewiring.

Becoming Multilingual: Step Three

REWIRING

Now that you know *how* you and your mate are different, *why* you and your mate are different, and *what* your motivation is for challenging those differences, it's time to get to work.

You were "wired" by your experiences. You "rewire" yourself by participating in experiences that, to this point, you have decided are just "not you." As you read earlier, the last thing I, as a visual/auditory, busy, productive, noisy, hyperactive person, wanted to do was sit still and hold my wife for more than 2.5 seconds. But because I understood this *would demonstrate my love* to her in a more meaningful way than all the notes I could write and flowers I could bring home, I forced myself to do it.

No doubt there are those of you who think that love should just "come naturally." Well, it does to a degree, but sometimes even the most natural of loves requires a bit of heroic effort to help it along. It was important to me that my wife know how much I loved her; so I *sat there* and I controlled my urge to get up and adjust the crooked picture frame. I resisted the impulse to start gabbing about nothing, or making plans for what we were going to do after we were done sitting there. I sat, and I held, and you know something? I learned to really like it! Pretty soon I wanted to do more of this "sitting and being quiet thing." Next, I started noticing some kinesthetics creeping into other areas of my life. I became less compulsive, more able to tolerate petty concerns and offenses. I could relax more easily. I used to be the kind of guy who wore a jacket and tie to bed and now I found myself *(quelle horreur!)* wearing sweaters and open-collared shirts — to work! I know all this probably sounds pretty silly to you, but I am trying to make a point. In order to grow both as a person and in intimacy with my wife, I had to stop saying, "I am not the kind of person who . . ." I had to humble myself, tell myself that maybe my wife really did have something to offer that I didn't understand, and then I had to try it. Not just once, but over and over until I developed an appreciation for it as well. Maybe not as great an appreciation as my wife had, but an appreciation nonetheless. I had to try these new experiences until they literally wore a new groove in my brain through which my kinesthetic senses could — to use a computer metaphor — interface with my vast auditory/visual network.

My old rule was, "I don't do anything that makes me uncomfortable." Now my rule is, "As long as it doesn't violate the qualities I stand for or my moral principles, I'm game." I find that this newer rule encourages me to be a more well-rounded person, a more exciting, vital person, a better lover to my wife (in and out of bed), and a more flexible, effective servant of God.

To derive similar benefits in your life, complete the following exercise with your mate.

꿍〜꿍

Rewiring: An Exercise and Discussion
Part One

1. What real differences in preference *come between* you and you mate? What activities and/or interests does your mate enjoy that you simply can't relate to, or couldn't care less about (in fact, you'd be happy if she never did — or asked you to do — *X, Y,* or *Z* again)?

2. Excluding anything that violates your personal dignity or morality, what expressions of affection has your mate asked you to give or show her, but you have resisted because it's "just not you" or "I just don't want to, that's why"?

Part Two

1. Over the next week, what steps will you take to begin challenging your shallowness, trying to develop at least a moderate understanding (or respect, interest, etc.) of the things that are important to your mate but, until now, have not been important to you?

(Refer to your answers to question 1 of Part One for the starting point.)

2. Of all the expressions of affection that may be important to your mate but seem unimportant or "stupid" to you, which of them could you

bring yourself to do or show if you were genuinely conscientious about it? Be honest. Remember, you are not going to do these things because your spouse necessarily deserves it; you are going to do these things because your Christian dignity demands that you be loving in a meaningful way — especially to your mate.

Write your answers to questions 1 and 2, and then carefully review the *Twenty-five Ways to Make Love Stay — Every Day* list in Chapter 4. Check this list weekly — at least — to see how you are measuring up to your own goal of becoming a more loving servant to both God and your spouse.

Part Three

The following are some suggestions for activities that demonstrate love in either a visual, auditory, or kinesthetic way. Review and discuss them with your mate. Which would your spouse like you to do more of? Which would you like her to do more of for you? What are some of your own ideas for novel visual, auditory, or kinesthetic expressions of love?

HOW TO INCREASE YOUR VISUAL LOVE LANGUAGE

If your mate has a primarily visual love language and you want to *show* your mate you love him or her, see if he or she would like any of the following.

___ Write love notes.

___ Buy or make an "I love you" card. Just because.

___ Have a glamorous, professional photo taken and give it to your mate.

___ Learn to tie bows and wrap gifts decoratively and/or neatly.

___ Keep all clutter out of sight. Concentrate on making your home "look clean" even if it really isn't.

___ Leave love messages on Post-It notes and stick them all over your home and your mate's car.

___ Read books together.

___ Have a candlelit meal. Use the good china and silver. Even if the meal is just hot dogs.

___ Get a blanket. Lie out under the stars at night and count constellations or make up your own.

___ Wear lingerie or attractive pajamas to bed.

___ Make love with the lights on.

___ When making love, spend lots of time on foreplay.

___ Keep the bedroom free of laundry and clutter.

___ Look into each other's eyes and don't say anything for a whole minute.

___ Have lots of candles in your bedroom, bathroom, or on your mantel.

___ Go to a movie together.

___ Make a silly video of you and your beloved making snow angels, building sand castles, baking a cake, or whatever. Make popcorn and watch it later.

___ Make a sign that says "I Love You, *(name)*!" and hang it from the door.

___ Dress up in your best clothes for a date with your mate. Even if you are just going to the mall. Don't worry about overdressing; just look good for *your partner.*

___ Buy your spouse flowers regularly. They don't have to be expensive. Anything pretty and thoughtful will do.

___ Write your own card at one of those "create-a-card" places.

___ When you look at your mate, smile.

___ (Other)_____

___ (Other)_____

___ (Other)_____

INCREASING YOUR AUDITORY LOVE STYLE

If your mate has a primarily auditory love language and you want to express your love more effectively, ask your spouse if he or she would like any of the following . . .

___ Say, "I love you" a million times a day. Say it in a genuinely loving tone.

___ Call your partner from work as often as you can just to say, "Hi."

___ Regularly compliment the things your spouse does and the way he or she looks.

___ Read aloud to each other.

___ When making love, talk about how your spouse is making you feel. Tell your beloved what you like. Make noise.

___ Make an audiotaped "love note." Put it in your mate's car stereo so that it automatically clicks on when he or she is driving to work.

___ Leave cute messages on the answering machine.

___ Buy your spouse some CD's of his or her favorite music and favorite groups.

___ Compliment your spouse publicly. *Don't ever* criticize him or her in public.

___ *Tell* your mate often how glad you are that you married him or her. Be prepared to answer why you think this way.

___ Ask your partner's opinions. Listen respectfully. Contribute to the conversation.

___ Make a habit of remembering jokes and stories from your day. Share them with your beloved.

___ Talk about current events.

___ Whisper "sweet nothings" in your spouse's ear.

___ Give him or her a "pet name." Use a silly voice when you say it.

___ Be very careful of your tone of voice.

___ On stressful days, be available to talk but keep noise to a minimum.

___ Buy your mate an "ocean waves" tape to listen to while he or she takes a bath.

___ Write a song and sing it to your spouse. Write a love letter or poem and read it to your beloved.

___ Hum your mate's favorite love songs when you are around him or her.

___ Auditory people remember every single word that comes out of your mouth. Learn to choose yours carefully.

(Other)_____

_____

(Other)_____

_____

(Other)_____

_____

INCREASING YOUR KINESTHETIC LOVE LANGUAGE

If your partner has a primarily kinesthetic love language and you want to demonstrate your love for him or her more effectively. Do the following.

___ Hold your mate's hand.

___ Sit on the same piece of furniture with your beloved (instead of across the room).

___ Kiss and hug your spouse a million times a day.

___ Spend a quiet evening just sitting with him or her watching the tube. Don't talk. Give your spouse the remote control, and don't complain about what he or she picks!

___ Snuggle.

___ Give your mate massages.

___ Scratch his or her back. Rub your beloved's neck.

___ Keep your hands on him or her at all times. (Please be discreet in public!)

___ When at home, or if you're *sure* no one is looking, pinch your mate's butt.

___ Nibble his or her ears.

_____ Work with your mate side by side on household projects or other fun activities.

_____ Don't talk while making love. Don't tell your beloved what you want him or her to do; just take your spouse's hands and passionately demonstrate what you like.

_____ Be sexually assertive.

_____ Skip foreplay once in a while and "go right to the good stuff."

_____ Wear nothing to bed. Turn off the lights. Make your partner feel his or her way around.

_____ Cuddle under the blankets with your spouse.

_____ Give him or her a "spa day" to be alone (soak in the tub, exercise, whatever your beloved needs to recharge his or her body).

_____ If your mate likes to watch or play sports, learn to love watching or playing them too.

_____ Go to a bath and body store. Stock up on massage lotion, bubble bath, and other comfy stuff.

_____ Don't pick on your mate when he or she wears that ratty and old but very comfortable whatever-it-is.

(Other)_____

_____

(Other)_____

_____

(Other)_____

_____

Some General Tips

1. If your partner has indicated that he or she likes something on the above lists, do it for him or her.

It doesn't matter if it makes sense to you or not. It doesn't matter whether you happen to like it or not. It doesn't even matter if you think your spouse deserves it or not. You *claim* to love her. Love means working for your mate's good. Now that you know what she thinks is good, get to work.

2. Don't *ever* criticize your mate for behaviors and preferences related to her love language. If you do, you might as well smack her in the head with a board while you are at it. Since love languages are so personal, criticizing your partner will be taken very personally. Don't criticize; instead, compliment.

3. Challenge your comfort level. If a particular request is not offensive to your dignity or your value system, then *fulfill that request*. We have to love our mates even when it makes us uncomfortable. "That's

just not me" or "I'm not comfortable with such and such" isn't good enough. Stop whining. You'll never *get* comfortable sitting on the edge of the pool; you've got to stick your toe in — at least.

4. There comes a time in every couple's life when the spouses are getting as much intimacy as they are going to get from their lives unless they really shake things up. Becoming fluent in a second and third love language is a great way to do this. It stretches you to go beyond a merely "comfortable intimacy"; it also empowers you to develop an intimacy based on actualization, becoming who God created you to be. An intimacy that has this kind of power is to be envied. It is this latter form of intimacy that separates *Partnership* and *Peer* couples from *Conventional/Apprenticeship* couples.

〜〜〜

One Final Shot in the Arm

Frequently a client comes to counseling saying, "Something's missing in my marriage, but I don't know what. I know he *[she]* loves me. Everything just feels so dry and dull."

Very often, what's missing is a particular love language, and my client is suffering from a kind of *marital sensory deprivation.* For example, if you are a primarily kinesthetic lover, your nervous system will literally crave touch. If you are primarily a visual lover, your nervous system craves visible demonstrations of love. If you are primarily an auditory lover, your nervous system aches to hear the words "I love you" and similar messages. If you don't receive enough loving input through your most acute senses, you will *physically* feel dried up and dull when with your spouse. Why wouldn't you? The neural pathways that carry loving signals to your brain are dried up and dulled. They are literally atrophying from a lack of stimulation. If this continues over a long period of time, you may become depressed, possibly seriously so. For many individuals, love languages aren't just a cute thing they read about in some book. Love languages can actually mean the difference between mental health and mental anguish. As a husband or wife, you get from God an immense amount of power to affect the health of your mate's body, mind, and spirit. Will you love your spouse the way she *needs* to be loved, the way God wants you to love her? Your marriage. Your choice.

For his part, Christ reaches out to each one of us through every channel we leave open to him. We are called to be Christ to one another, but we can't do that unless we too are actively seeking to love our mates through whatever channels they leave open to us. Sometimes this causes us to be uncomfortable, and we become reluctant to give of ourselves in our marriages. But God is not too proud to put himself out for the sake of loving us. Scripture tells us, "He emptied himself and became a slave" (cf. Phil 2:7). How much more uncomfortable can you get? We all know this, but admittedly it's a tough act to follow.

In one of his "sower's seeds" books, Father Brian Cavanaugh tells the story of a teenager who lived in the early 1900s. It seems this young man had an accident on his bicycle and sliced open a vein on a piece of glass. He lost a lot of blood and would have died if the family doctor hadn't been familiar with what was then a brand-new medical treatment called a "blood transfusion."

The doctor tested the other family members. The only person with a similar blood type to that of the teen was his four-year-old brother. The doctor asked the little boy if he would be willing to give blood to his brother. The four-year-old thought for a minute, swallowed hard, and nodded his head. Using a hypodermic needle, the doctor took blood out of the little boy's arm and injected it into his brother. Over and over. Finally, the procedure was complete and the injured brother was resting comfortably.

Though he had been so brave and not even flinched during the procedure, suddenly the four-year-old burst into tears. His father scooped up the boy and asked if he was hurting. "No," the child sniffled. "But my blood is gone, and I'll miss you when I'm dead."

With each vial of blood the doctor took, the little boy thought he was losing his life.

Becoming fluent in another love language sometimes requires us to give more of ourselves than we want to give. Too often, we experience the littlest pricks of love's needle and immediately panic.

"I'm losing myself!"

"This hurts!"

"How dare you ask me to do that!"

"You know that's just not *me*!"

We think and act as if we are going to die, but in reality, it's such a small thing. Jesus did the hardest part of loving. He emptied himself and all of his veins so that we wouldn't have to. He just asks us to give a few drops of our blood to our spouses when they need it.

Of course it hurts. But if you don't do it, who will?

CHAPTER 8

The Secrets of Red-hot Loving (How to Be Loving When Conflict Heats Things Up)

> Lord and Savior, you have told us that we too must accept
> crucifixion if we are to accept resurrection with you. Help us to
> rejoice in the sufferings that come with the fulfillment of our daily
> duties, seeing them as the royal road of the cross to the
> Resurrection.
>
> — *THE WAY OF THE CROSS*
> *(Prayer at the Eleventh Station:*
> *"Jesus is nailed to the cross")*

No section on intimacy and communication would be complete without a chapter on what I call "Red-hot Loving." That is, how can we fulfill our call to love even when conflict heats things up? Needless to say, this can be very tricky; but mastering this skill is one thing every Christian must do. After all, doesn't the Lord tell us: "Love your enemies, do good to those who hate you" (Lk 6:27)? How can we resolve problems, maintain our integrity, be loving, *and* not be a doormat, all at the same time?

"Problem Solving" Versus "Fair Fighting"

First, I need to explain the difference between what I mean by "problem solving" and what some people call "fair fighting." Just as war is the failure of diplomacy, fighting is the failure of problem solving. Don't misunderstand me. I don't mean to suggest that couples should experience the kind of bliss usually reserved for deodorant commercials every time they have an argument. Far from it. Problem solving can and does become heated at times. But while problem solving is mainly concerned with finding solutions, fighting — even so-called fair fighting — is mostly about getting one up on your sparring partner and winning at any cost. As far as marriage goes, I don't believe there is such a thing as "fair fighting." Once you and your mate are actually fighting, it's probably way beyond fair already, and whether you box with fists or gloves, someone's still going to get hurt.

I would much rather we all stop thinking about marital arguments as boxing matches and start thinking about them as business meetings where you and your mate solve problems as a team. Stop chuckling at me and think for a minute.

When a problem arises at the office, do you pout, threaten, stamp your feet, pretend it doesn't exist, put on a big crying show, call your boss evil names, or just walk out the door if you don't get your way, and then expect to have a job when you get back? Probably not. (If you do, you need more help than *this* book can give you.) Most likely, you take a breath, think before you speak, outline your position, write a couple of memos, argue back and forth a bit with coworkers, go out with your team for a coffee break, table discussions when they get too hot, and keep coming back until the problem is solved. After all, the wheels of commerce must grind smoothly, no? Effective *marital* problem solving is very much like this. Why? Because pouting, threatening, whining, grandstanding and/or running away doesn't solve problems at the office, and such "options" won't work at home either. Moreover, don't try to bring up that "Let it all hang out at home" excuse, because I already dealt with that in Chapter 6. If you want a fight, take a karate class, buy an exercise dummy, or better still, call the IRS tax help line. But, if you want to be married, you are going to have to learn problem solving.

Massaging Your Marriage

The *Exceptional Seven Percent* have a lot to teach us about conflict management. While couples in more-or-less *Conventional Marriages* often leave arguments feeling beaten up, a little distant, and worn out, *Exceptional* couples actually grow in intimacy *because* of their arguments. In the words of one *Exceptional* husband, "Our arguments are like a deep muscle massage. It hurts a little while you're going through it, but you always feel better in the end, and your relationship seems looser and more comfortable than when you started."

To master the art of marital massage, you need to know a little about what separates healthy arguing styles from unhealthy ones.

The Three Arguing Styles

There are three major arguing styles. Each of them could be healthy or unhealthy, depending upon whether or not each meets certain criteria. You'll learn about those criteria in a minute, but first I need to describe the three major arguing styles. They are: Validating, Volatile, and Avoidant (cf. *Why Marriages Succeed or Fail* by Dr. John Gottman).

The Validating style is the most civilized of the three and the one therapists — as opposed to normal people — like to promote. The Validating style is typified by such behaviors as taking turns, not getting too emotional, making sure everybody understands each other, solving one problem at a time, etc. At its best, the Validating style is a very caring and efficient way to get things done. At its worst, people can get so concerned with "validating" each other, smoothing over emotions, and playing armchair analyst, that they never solve any problems.

Alternatively, the Volatile arguing style is the style therapists tend to like the least. It is loud. It yells. Sometimes it even calls names, slams doors, and pounds fists (although it is *never* physically abusive — no remotely healthy arguing style ever is). At its best, it would be better to say that the Volatile style is a "passionate" style, demonstrated by a person who is *even more passionately demonstrative* of his or her positive emotions (affection, love, praise, etc.). If you will forgive the stereotype, the image that a healthy Volatile style calls to my mind is that of a few large Italian families I knew growing up, who at one moment were shaking the rafters with their yelling and screaming and the next moment were hugging, kissing, crying, and swearing eternal fealty to one another (this went for the women as well as the men).

Jesus himself had a fairly Volatile arguing style. The phrase "Get behind me, you Satan!" (Mt16:23 and Mk 8:33) was not exactly in the warm-fuzzy category. Nor, for that matter, was, "Woe to you, you den of vipers!" (cf. Mt 3:7 and Lk 3:7). And the idea for turning over the money changer's tables didn't come from a Dale Carnegie *How to Win Friends and Influence People* course either. In certain contexts, with certain people, the Volatile style can be a perfectly acceptable way of arguing. On the other hand, at its worst and decidedly *least* Christian, the Volatile style can be just plain mean.

Finally, there is the Avoidant style. Its name says it all. These folks really hate arguing and avoid conflict as much as possible. At its best, the Avoidant style prevents a couple from having a whole bunch of genuinely unnecessary arguments. At worst, it stops spouses from dealing with issues that really need to be addressed until they have swallowed so much anger that it nearly causes an aneurysm.

As you can see, there are pluses and minuses to each arguing type. But particular style notwithstanding, the thing that makes an argument healthy or unhealthy is its ability to meet three criteria: (1) A mutually satisfying solution results from the argument. (2) There are certain lines the couple just doesn't cross no matter how heated things get. The spouses have explicit or implicit "rules of engagement." (3) There is a five-to-one ratio of positivity to negativity. That is, the partners are five times more loving and affectionate than they are argumentative, critical, or complaining.

Why are these things necessary? The first point is self-explanatory. If an argument never reaches a solution, either that couple just like beating up on each other or they lack the skills they need to solve their problems. Either way, it's unhealthy. With regard to the second point, every person has hot buttons, topics, words, or actions that — if you love the person — you just won't bring up, say, or do in an argument. This is true even of Volatile couples. For example, a Volatile husband might not think twice about his Volatile wife calling him stupid. But she would never, ever say that he reminded her of his abusive, alcoholic father who abandoned the family when he was a child. Healthy Volatile people are very savvy. Their arguments are like fireworks. That is, the families who make them are proud of them, the explosions are loud and amazing to watch; but, somehow, no one ever really gets hurt.

Finally, the five-to-one positivity-to-negativity ratio is extremely important. First of all, it builds credibility (see Chapter 6). Second, when spouses are arguing, they need to be able to remember that things were not always so unpleasant. In order to do that, a couple must have ready access to an overwhelming bank of positive experiences to draw from. This enables the couple to give each other the benefit of the doubt, so that even in the midst of an argument, they will be able to say to themselves, "Let's see, eight times out of ten, I am absolutely sure my spouse is on my side and working for my good. Even though I feel otherwise right now, the law of averages says he [she] is probably not out to get me. Maybe I should try a little harder to understand his [her] point."

Learning how to have arguments that meet these three criteria is the basis of healthy marital problem solving.

Christian Problem Solving

Now that you understand the three criteria for healthy arguing, I want to combine this with what our Lord teaches us about handling conflict. To understand how to solve problems in a way that is consistent with our Christian dignity, we need to meditate long and hard on the following words of Scripture (Lk 6:27-38):

> [Jesus said:] "But I say to you that hear, Love your enemies, do good to those who hate you, bless those who curse you, pray for those who abuse you. To him who strikes you on the cheek, offer the other also; and from him who takes away your cloak do not withhold your coat as well. . . . And as you wish that [others] would do to you, do so to them.
>
> "If you love those who love you, what credit is that to you? For even sinners love those who love them. And if you do good to those who do good to you, what credit is that to you? For even sinners do the same. And if you lend to those from whom you hope to receive, what credit is that to you? Even sinners lend to sinners, . . . But love your enemies, and do good. . . . Be merciful, even as your Father is merciful.
>
> "Judge not, and you will not be judged; condemn not, and you will not be condemned; forgive, and you will be forgiven; give, and it will be given to you; . . . For the measure you give will be the measure you get back."

That doesn't exactly leave a lot of wiggle room, does it? Christians are called to be loving no matter what our spouse/sparring partner throws at us. When we argue, no matter how "crazy" our mate gets, we must be able to say that we are proud of the way we conducted ourselves. Not because our mate deserves such displays of temperance, but because God demands it of us, and our Christian dignity requires us to respond to our Lord's call.

The following rules are some ways you might apply Jesus' words to your marital problem-solving sessions. *Exceptional* couples use many of them, and that is why their intimacy grows *because* of their arguments instead of in spite of them. You may initially be inclined to balk at some of the rules as being "not what normal people do" or simply "too hard." I see your point, but to be frank, when you decided to live life as a Christian (especially a Catholic one) you gave up every chance you ever had of being anything close to normal. Christianity just isn't "normal," and neither is anyone who truly practices it. Had Adam and Eve not fallen, godliness (or righteousness) would be the most normal thing in the world. But they did, and it's not. And yet, with God's grace — and a lot of work on our parts — it could be once again. In fact, if you and your mate master the skills outlined below, you might just come one step closer to becoming that new Adam and new Eve you are called to be. Go figure.

The Fifteen Commandments of Red-hot Loving

As you can see from the figure on the facing page, the first six "commandments" are problem-solving habits that thou shalt practice regularly instead of fighting — fairly or otherwise.

I: Thou Shalt Know When to Hold 'em and Know When to Fold 'em

The *most* important thing to do before any argument is to decide whether or not it is really an argument worth having.

✔ *Red-hot Loving Technique: Hold 'em or Fold 'em?*

Ask yourself the following questions to decide whether to hold an argument or fold it before it starts.

(a) Is the thing you are upset about a problem that is going to stop you from fulfilling your God-given dreams, goals, or values? Or is this just a petty offense to your comfort level?

• If this issue really is a challenge to your God-given dreams, goals, or values, skip to (c).

• If "you're just being petty," go to (b).

(b) Don't give up. You might still get to argue. Even though this seems like a petty issue, ask yourself the following: Are you using this petty thing as a way to demonstrate your anger over another, more vital issue? What might that issue be?

• If you can identify what you're really angry or upset about, go to (c).

• If you really are just being petty, it's time to take a breath, swallow your pride, and spare yourself and your mate the unnecessary stress. This would be a good time to practice the patience and prudence given to you at your baptism. Besides, every time you argue you make a withdrawal from your emotional bank account. Spend wisely. "Offer up" your frustration for the intention of becoming a more accepting, loving, Christ-like person. Hey, if it worked for St. Thérèse of Lisieux, it might work for you too.

(c) Well, it looks like some problem solving is called for. Make some time to sit down with your mate (don't ambush him or her) and, after you read the rest of this chapter, you'll know exactly how to get your needs met every time. And, you'll be able to do it gracefully.

178

FIFTEEN PROBLEM-SOLVING COMMANDMENTS

The first six "commandments" will help you and your mate solve problems as a team.

I. Thou Shalt Know When to Hold'em and Know When to Fold'em.

II. Thou Shalt Begin with the End in Mind.

III. Thou Shalt Get Thy Thinking Caps on Straight.

IV. Thou Shalt Always Assume a Positive Intention or Need Behind Thy Spouse's Words, Actions, and Behaviors.

V. Thou Shalt Use Respectful Deadlines Instead of Ultimatums or Nagging.

VI. Thou Shalt Never Negotiate the "What" (But Always Negotiate the "How" and "When").

The remaining "commandments" will help keep your problem-solving sessions healthy and productive even as things begin to heat up.

VII. Thou Shalt Take Thy Emotional Temperature.

VIII. Thou Shalt Do Loving Things.

IX. Thou Shalt Take Respectful Breaks.

X. Thou Shalt Set Respectful Limits.

XI. Thou Shalt Use "I" Statements Instead of "You Stink" Statements.

XII. Thou Shalt Not Be Contemptuous.

XIII. Thou Shalt Put It in Writing.

XIV. Thou Shalt Not Go Crazy at the Same Time.

XV. Thou Shalt Pray, Pray, Pray.

II: Thou Shalt Begin
with the End in Mind

Would you ever start a business meeting without an agenda and expect to get anywhere? Of course not. In the same way, no couple begins an *effective* argument without a plan. Too many husbands and wives treat their marital problem-solving sessions like pointless, meandering bitch sessions. They have nothing more on their problem-solving agenda than "demonstrating my pain to you and proving what a pig you are." This is a recipe for disaster. Even if you were "successful" in proving your pain and demonstrating your mate's piggishness, then what? Can you really say that such a discussion would do anything except let off some steam? Would having such a "discussion" actually prevent the problem from ever happening again? Of course not. All you did was emotionally vomit all over each other.

To have an effective argument, you must begin with the end in mind. That is, you must know the goal you want to achieve by initiating the discussion. Before you open your mouth and say something stupid, calm down enough to at least have some possible answers to the following questions:

1. What do I need to know from my mate to feel better about this problem?

2. What do I think needs to happen so that we can avoid this problem in the future?

3. What changes will I have to make to solve this problem?

4. How will I be willing to support my mate in making any changes she decides she needs to make? (That is, "What am I willing to do besides tell her what to do?")

Only when you have at least some general answers to these questions are you ready to begin an effective problem-solving session.

III: Thou Shalt Get
Thy Thinking Caps on Straight

At one point or another, all of us think our spouses are out to get us — especially when we are arguing with them. Sometimes it's hard not to believe that our mates don't wake up in the morning with their *Twenty-five Ways to Make My Mate's Life a Living Hell* list fresh in mind. But this is simply not true. In the first place, our mates love us, and because of this, under most circumstances, they would not hurt us *intentionally*. Most likely, any hurt we do encounter is the result of either a misunderstanding, or their frustration at our own neglect or thickheadedness. (That is, sometimes they do hurt us "on purpose," but only because we have not given them a more reasonable way to get through to us.) We would do well to respond to such slights lovingly, as Christ himself does.

In the second place, even if we are questioning our mates' love for us, no living creature seeks to bring harm to itself. At their most selfish level, our spouses would not hurt us intentionally because they know or believe we would respond by hurting them in turn. When two people live in a house, if one of them isn't happy, "ain't no one happy!" Again, when we are emotionally wounded by our mates, chances are that the pain was inflicted unintentionally, or because they sincerely didn't know how else to get through to us. Think about it: Aren't those the only two reasons *you* ever cause another person pain? Why would it be any different for your mate?

We *must* train ourselves out of thinking and responding as if our spouses were out to get us. Whenever we experience those negative thoughts like "She is such a bitch," or "I can't believe that jerk would do that to me," or "He must not *really* love me," or anything even remotely similar, we must check ourselves because reality tells us that *we are thinking irrationally*. Study after study has shown that both mental disease and marital deterioration increase in proportion to the degree of irrational thinking present in a couple.

✔ *Red-hot Loving Technique: Clarify, Clarify, Clarify*

When your spouse offends you, in word or in deed, give her the benefit of the doubt. (No, she doesn't deserve it, but do it anyway.) Assume *you* somehow misinterpreted her. Say, "I'm sorry. I didn't understand what you meant by that." Or, "I really want to give you the benefit of the doubt. Could you please explain why you did that?"

For example:

Your mate: "Sometimes you're such a jerk. You make me so angry."

You *(taking a calming breath):* "I'm not sure I understand what I could have done to make you feel that way. Could you please explain?"

Notice, nowhere in this example did you admit to, or apologize for, anything. How could you? You don't even know what she is upset about yet. In the example I gave, you simply assumed that your usually loving spouse would not say such an obnoxious thing if she didn't have a good reason for doing so. Because you love her and respect her opinion, you are going to find out what she meant by the comment instead of immediately jumping down her throat for being so blunt. You are going to make an effort to assume that she is not out to get you, but rather have some good information for you, which, unfortunately, she has expressed rather indelicately.

Responding to slights and offenses in this manner is rational, firm, loving, and efficient. It lets your mate know that even if she *did* mean what she said, you are going to be kind enough to not let her make an ass of herself at your expense. Likewise, it gives you a chance to find out what's really going on (instead of just mind-reading what you *think* is going on). It stops you from having those arguments in which you get to the middle and realize that you don't have a leg to stand on, but you'll be damned if you're going to let *her* know you don't have a leg to stand on and so you commence fighting to the death. Finally, it builds your credibility (reasonableness is always respected) and stops potentially explosive arguments from actually exploding. This technique is shored up by the next "commandment."

IV: Thou Shalt Always Assume a Positive Intention or Need Behind Thy Spouse's Words, Actions, and Behaviors

As I mentioned above, no living creature seeks to injure itself. Behind even the most idiotic and self-destructive behaviors is a positive intention or a need. Even people who attempt suicide don't think about it so much as a self-destructive act as they do a means of relieving stress. When your mate does something you consider to be obnoxious, inconsiderate, or rude, you must operate under the assumption that he *does not actually intend to come across that way*. The ability to assume a positive intention behind another's disagreeable behavior is the essence of loving the sinner but hating the sin. There is no other way to do it. Jesus, hanging on the cross, practiced this concept. "*Father, forgive them. They do not know what they are doing*" (cf. Lk 23:34; emphasis mine).

Please don't think I am attempting to excuse obnoxious or self-destructive behavior. Finding the positive intention behind an offensive behavior is not an excuse *for* the behavior; it is a respectful way to begin changing the behavior. For example, if you learn that the reason (intention) behind your spouse's temper is that it is the only way he knows to get you to take him seriously, you can suggest some more respectful and efficient alternatives. If you discover that the reason your spouse isn't "pulling his weight" around the house is that he is sitting up nights worrying about something, you can brainstorm some solutions. Finding out the intention behind a problem behavior is the first step to changing it. It sure beats judging and alienating your spouse. Remember what Jesus has told us: "Do not judge. . . . For the measure you measure with, will be measured back to you" (cf. Lk 6:37-38). Use the following technique to help your partner through an obnoxious relationship habit and toward a more respectful solution.

✔ *Red-hot Loving Technique: Finding the Positive Intention*

Problem: Mate consistently does something that you consider to be obnoxious, thoughtless, or unloving.

What you used to say: "You are such a thoughtless pig!"

What you will do from now on:

1. Say to mate, "When you do *[or say that obnoxious thing]*, what reaction are you hoping to get from me?"

2. After some initial confusion (he wasn't expecting the question) your mate explains how he wishes you would respond to him when he does or says *X*.

3. Say to mate, "Well, I could understand why you'd want that; but if that's what you really need, could you please do *A*, *B*, or *C* instead of what you're doing? I would like to give you what you're asking for, but I'll never be able to bring myself to doing that if you keep going about it the way you've been."

For example:

You: "When you refuse to speak to me after an argument, what reaction are you hoping to get from me?"

Mate: "I felt like you didn't care about what I had to say, so what's the sense in talking to you?"

You *(taking a breath, not reacting, trying to understand):* "I'm still not sure I understand. What do you need from me?"

Mate: "I want you to stop trying to force your ideas down my throat and listen to me."

You *(again not reacting):* "I never meant to give you that impression." (Aha! See? *Your* intention was misunderstood.) "It really *is* important to me that you know I care about what you have to say. Could you do me a favor?"

Mate: "What favor?"

You: "Since I don't know when I'm doing that, the next time could you just tell me, 'You're not listening'? It would sure help me change a lot faster than your pouting *after* an argument."

Mate *(suspicious, but considering how well you've responded, he is willing to give you a chance):* "If you really think that'll work, I'm willing to try it."

You: "Great. I promise. I love you.

Mate: "I love you too."

Granted, this kind of maturity in problem solving is difficult to achieve, but it is something that must be done. You may have to repeat this several dozen times before the lesson really sinks in. Remember to be patient and respectful. Look for the positive intention behind your spouse's offensive behavior and, taking a cue from the Skin Horse, gently "love it into Real."

V: Thou Shalt Use Respectful Deadlines Instead of Ultimatums or Nagging

Your well-meaning spouse doesn't want to disappoint you, so he tends to promise more than he can deliver. This leaves you disappointed and resentful. How to solve this problem?

✔ *Red-hot Loving Technique: Don't Nag; Give Mate a Choice*

Instead of asking your spouse to do something for you and then becoming angry if he forgets or neglects your request, assume a positive intention to his oversight and have an alternative plan in mind.

What you used to do:

You: "Honey, can you do *X* for me?"

Mate: "Uh-huh." (Three weeks later, your request is still unfulfilled and you must either begin nagging, or give up on your spouse and assume that you will never get your needs met.)

What you will do from now on:

1. Set an *arbitrary* deadline.

You: "Honey, I need to get such and such done. I'd really like your help, but I'd like to have it done by Tuesday. Can I count on you? Or should I call so-and-so to do it?"

Mate: "Huh? Oh, yeah. I'll take care of it."

Tuesday comes and your spouse has forgotten. Don't remind him.

2. Call for help.

First thing Wednesday, call the plumber (or housekeeping service, auto mechanic, landscaper, etc.) and ask for the required service. Your spouse will come home and find the task done. He will either be relieved or irritated. Either response is OK. If he is irritated, simply say in your most sincere, innocent voice, "I'm sorry, honey. When you didn't do it by the day you said you would, I just assumed you didn't have time. Rather than pester you, I thought I'd do you a favor and take care of it myself."

Granted, this technique may cause some short-term tension; but, let's face it, it solves the problem. It lets your mate know that: (a) You mean what you say. (b) You're not going to wait around forever for his help. (c) It really is OK if he can't do something for you. You simply need him to be honest about it and help you figure out an alternative way to address your need.

Compare this option with the long-term tension and resentment that accompanies nagging (or whining, pestering, sulking) that not only doesn't solve the problem but also causes the heart of a marriage to rot.

The fact is, if you need to have something done, the most you can rationally do is *invite* your mate to help. If he can't do it, simply come up with an alternate plan for getting it done. This idea will be strongly repulsive to anyone who has compensatory roles in a marriage (see *The Unitive End of Marriage* in Chapter 2). But to have a *Partnership Marriage* or better, we need to overcome our desire to be taken care of, and learn how to become experts at making plans to take care of our own needs. We've got to stop making every little thing be yet another test of our mate's devotion. Of course your mate's help is a gift that should be given freely and generously. But like any gift, you can desire it, and you can be grateful when it is given to you, but — sadly, perhaps — you have no right to demand it.

VI: Thou Shalt Never Negotiate the "What" (But Always Negotiate the "How" and "When")

You are a spouse, not a parent. It is not your job to ever give or deny permission for your mate to do or have anything. It is merely your job to raise concerns about your mate's plans, taking care to do so supportively, and respectfully. Use the following rule: *Never negotiate the "What." Always negotiate the "How" and "When."*

In other words, you will never tell your grown-up spouse, who can think for herself, that something she wants (or needs) cannot be had. You will simply state the conditions (the "how" and "when") under which you would be comfortable helping her get her "what."

For example:

Your mate: "Honey, I would like to start an ostrich farm."

What you used to say: "Are you nuts? Why would you want that?"

What you will say from now on: "Well, I guess I'd be OK with that as long as we could work out *[insert your concerns here]*. What are your thoughts about the concerns I raised?"

Expressing your concerns and/or objections in this manner lets your mate know you care both about her and the big picture. Feel free to be very firm about requiring your concerns to be addressed even while supporting your mate in the pursuit of her goals. After all, for your marriage to become more intimate, you both must learn to respect each other's needs while pursuing your own dreams, goals, and values. This technique is the essence of a good partnership. In fact, mastery of this skill is one of the things that separates *Partnership* and *Peer* couples from more *Conventional* couples. *Don't* ever issue an edict that says your mate can't have or do something. *Do* raise your concerns and let *her* decide whether or not what she wants is worth the work it will take to get it. If she decides it's not worth it, then she has made up her own mind to drop the idea. On the other hand, if she does decide to figure out a way to address your concerns, she has you to thank for helping her fulfill her dreams, goals, and values in a way that is respectful of the entire family. Remember, never negotiate the "what." Always be willing to negotiate the "how" and the "when."

♣ ♣ ♣

The remaining "commandments" will help keep your problem-solving sessions healthy and productive even as things heat up.

VII: Thou Shalt Take Thy Emotional Temperature

On an emotional-temperature scale of 1 to 10 (with a 1 meaning that you are heavily sedated and a 10 meaning that you are climbing a clock tower with an AK-47 strapped to your back) no productive problem solving goes on above a 6. Let me give you some examples.

At 1-3, you are perfectly calm, content, and relaxed.

At 4-5, you and your mate are having a purposeful, respectful, and honest discussion.

At 6, you are beginning to become frustrated. You are starting to think some moderately unkind thoughts about your mate, but you are able to keep things under control and remain outwardly civil and cooperative.

At 7, you are now openly disgusted with your mate. You may not be calling him names but you are considering it. You are exhibiting behaviors that show your disgust (e.g., rolling your eyes, making dismissive hand gestures, shaking your head, and the like). Physiologically, your heart rate and blood pressure are beginning to increase.

At 8, rationality is completely suspended. You are now calling your mate the names you were thinking about at 7. The argument is becoming more hostile and personal.

At 9, you are now thinking about either hitting him or running away. Physiologically, your heart rate is approaching one hundred twenty-five beats a minute (compared to eighty at rest). Your blood pressure and respiration rate are also through the roof. Fight-or-flight response is kicking in.

At 10, you are striking your partner or storming out. You don't care what you do, or if you ever see your spouse again.

It is very important that you keep your arguments at a 6 or lower. If an argument rises to a 7 or above, there are few, if any, ways to stop it. The couple is simply too far gone to think rationally at that point. Past 7, the only choice you have is to ride the emotional roller coaster until one of you jumps off — or is pushed.

Some people tell me that they go from a 1 to a 10 in a second. This is a serious problem. It implies a lack of self-control, a long history of perceiving oneself to be a victim, a high level of perfectionism, and/or a tendency to disregard the other's feelings for the sake of being right. Counseling may be indicated.

For the rest of you, whose rage is not connected to an on/off switch, the following rules will help you maintain your problem-solving sessions within a healthy range.

VIII: Thou Shalt Do Loving Things

If you remember the scriptural quotation earlier in this section, Luke 6:27-38, you will recall that Christians have a responsibility to be loving and nurturing even in the presence of conflict. In fact, it is in conflict that such qualities are needed the most. When you suspect that either you or your partner is getting a little too close to a 6.5 on the emotional-temperature scale, *do something loving* to decrease the tension and increase the teamwork. Offer to get your mate a cup of coffee. Thank her for hanging in there with you. Tell her you love her and appreciate her patience. Tell her that you are glad that she is your partner, both when things are easy and when things are hard. Ask if you can sit next to her, give her a hug, or hold her hand.

If you view arguments as competitions in which the dirtiest fighter wins, then none of these things will make a bit of sense to you. If, however, you think of arguing as problem solving and your mate as your partner in solving the problem, such suggestions make all the sense in the world. After all, you realize that even in an argument, your partner is not the problem; rather, the *problem* is the problem, and you and your mate must work together to solve it. The key to this is learning how to separate *how much your mate means to you* from how much she is irritating you right now. This comes more naturally to people than you might think. I have met many couples in session who argue constantly — and fairly cruelly — but would never leave each other "because my spouse means the world to me." Of course he or she does. Just because you are angry with someone doesn't mean you don't love that person. So, if you are already showing your spouse how irritated you are, don't forget to also show her how much she *means* to you (even though you *feel* irritated). This is the practical reality behind Wallerstein and Blakeslee's suggestion to "confront the realities of marriage while safe-guarding early romantic feelings" (see other suggestions, or tasks, at the end of Chapter

5). The more you do loving things and demonstrate affection even in conflict, the deeper your intimacy becomes, and the more your relationship will grow *because of* your arguments instead of in spite of them.

IX: Thou Shalt Take Respectful Breaks

If you or your mate is approaching a 7 on the emotional-temperature scale, take a short break. Go to the bathroom, get a drink (offer him one while you're at it), or cause some other short, polite interruption in the arguing process. At an emotional temperature of 6, all that is needed for a break to be successful is three to five minutes to pull yourselves together and remind yourselves that you are a team.

Some people think taking a break from arguing means storming out of the room and/or not speaking to one's mate for a couple of hours or days. This is not a respectful break; this is the running away that occurs at an 8 or 9 on the emotional-temperature scale. Doing loving things and taking plenty of short respectful breaks *while you are still at 4, 5, or 6* will keep you from ever getting to an 8 or 9 where you desperately feel that you must get away — *now!*

X: Thou Shalt Set Respectful Limits

Besides being able to be loving, and to be a generous servant in conflict, effective problem solving also requires you to be able to set respectful limits when you feel that the argument is getting out of control. As I hope you gathered by reading about the three major arguing styles (Validating, Volatile, and Avoidant), there are no hard-and-fast criteria to determine when an argument is getting out of hand (besides when it turns physical). Every person must decide for himself what the line between problem solving and fighting is. It is up to you to tell your mate when she has crossed your boundary. It is up to your mate to respect your limit regardless of what she thinks of it. You may recall that being loving means working for another's good. Part of working for another's good means respecting her limits even when those limits don't make sense to you.

✔ *Red-hot Loving Technique: Setting Respectful Limits*

A respectful limit looks something like this:

Spouse says or does something that you consider out of bounds.

Say, "Honey, I love you, and I want to keep working on this, but I can't let you talk to me *[or treat me]* that way. Can you calm down and talk about this with me? Or should we take a break?"

Regardless of what your mate says, let her behavior speak her answer for her. If she makes a concentrated effort to cool down, continue the discussion. If she can't get a grip on herself, respectfully say, "Look, this is obviously getting too hot. I want to solve this, but we're not going to do it this way. I need a break. Let's pick it up at *[insert specific time here]*."

A respectful limit includes:

1. A "warning shot," and an assessment of your mate's response.

2. If the offensive behavior continues, remind your spouse that solving the problem is important to you *but . . .*

3. You have decided a break is needed. *Period.*

4. Finally, suggest a specific time to pick things up again. This is very important because it demonstrates that you really aren't trying to weasel out of anything.

Setting limits according to the rules above is not always easy; but it sure beats storming out of the room, saying things you will regret later, "getting back" at your partner for hurting you, and other escalating behaviors that adversely affect the emotional-temperature scale. Setting limits this way teaches a couple that if finding a solution is important, then the solution must be sought while making a concerted effort to protect the dignity of all involved. This is one of the major skills required for having arguments that build intimacy instead of simply wounding the participants.

XI: Thou Shalt Use "I" Statements Instead of "You Stink" Statements

This old therapy chestnut really does work if you know why and how to use it. When conflict is heating things up, the last thing you want is someone telling you how *you* screwed up and what's wrong with *you* and what *you* need to do to fix it. Most likely, under such circumstances, you are going to start thinking, "Who the hell does he think he is?" — and you will feel obliged to direct a few rather pointed *"you"* statements at that person. Obviously, this just increases the tension. The people playing this game are more interested in determining who is at fault than discussing solutions to a problem.

Instead of diagnosing, analyzing, or blaming your partner, it is sufficient to describe your own thoughts and feelings. Perhaps the following example will help you understand the subtle but significant difference between "I" statements and "You stink" statements (or even "I think you stink" statements).

Imagine someone looking fiercely at you and saying, "You are so thoughtless, you make me angry *[crazy, ready to kill, etc.]*."

In response, you probably feel defensive or dismissive. You may be thinking something like, "Well, who do you think *you* are?" Or, "For heaven's sake, what's wrong *this* time?"

Now imagine that, instead, the same person looked at you and said, "I'm trying to hold it together, but I just feel so angry."

In response, you probably feel curious, or even slightly sympathetic. You may be thinking something like, "I wonder what happened?" Or, "Is there anything I can do to help?"

A subtle word change made all the difference. Practice using "I" statements to describe your own insights and feelings about yourself, not your mate. Some other examples include:

• *Instead of,* "You need to get control of yourself," *say,* "I need a break."

• *Instead of,* "You are such an ass," *say,* "When you did that, I felt so hurt."

• *Instead of,* "You're nuts!" *say,* "I don't understand."

So many people think that "I" statements are silly, but when you start practicing them, you will begin to see that people respond to you more respectfully. Since you aren't threatening them, they have nothing to lose by listening to you. As the commercial used to say, "Try it. You'll like it."

XII: Thou Shalt Not Be Contemptuous

You need to avoid all contemptuous gestures, phrases, and actions in a problem-solving session because they just aren't helpful. Some examples include rolling your eyes at your partner, shaking your head in disbelief, agreeing with him so he'll shut up, walking out in anger, letting arguments become even moderately physical, stonewalling your spouse, calling him hurtful names, etc. One very well-respected longitudinal study demonstrated that a statistically significant number of couples who exhibited a high incidence of these behaviors divorced within five years. One of the worst examples of a contemptuous act is threatening to file for a divorce.

Threatening to divorce your mate in the heat of an argument makes you look as juvenile, petulant, spoiled, pathetic, whiny, and utterly contemptible as a person who threatens suicide every time he or she runs out of socks. While you're at it, you might as well hold your breath until you turn blue. It's that mature. Not only does threatening divorce destroy your credibility, it undermines your mate's ability to trust you, damages the security of your relationship, and offends the dignity of your marriage.

If you believe that either your marriage is so hopeless or you are so

190

helplessly pathetic, that the best problem-solving intervention you can come up with is to threaten divorce, then either you need some serious counseling or your marriage requires a detailed examination. Either way, if I ever hear of a person who has read this book using a divorce threat as a bargaining chip in marriage, I will personally come to that person's house and cut out his or her tongue. As far as I am concerned, it is better to enter the kingdom of heaven with no tongue than to be cast into the fires of hell with your mouth forming that despicable phrase, "If that's the way it's going to be, then we might as well get a divorce." (Can you tell this is a pet peeve of mine?)

Anytime you are tempted to demonstrate any of the contemptuous behaviors I listed above, especially threatening divorce, remember the acronym *D.U.M.M. (Don't Undermine My Marriage!)*.

XIII: Thou Shalt Put It in Writing

Sometimes an issue is just too hot to talk about. Try as you might, you and your mate just can't be civil when discussing such and such. Further, the problem just gets worse when you try to ignore it. What to do?

I recommend writing letters to each other. These letters should describe the problem as you see it, how that problem affects you, and your thoughts about solving the problem. If you are going to use this technique, ideally the husband and wife should both write their own letters and exchange them. Then they should write responses to the letters they received. Both Marriage Encounter and Retrouvailles have built their long histories and strong reputations on just such an intervention. Writing letters back and forth allows you to think about what you really need to say. When you get such a letter back from your mate, you are able to read it in small digestible pieces. You are able to react to it, calm down about it, and write a reasonable response back to your spouse. Writing problem-solving letters requires some discipline, but sometimes it is the only way to solve a problem when talking about it just doesn't work.

XIV: Thou Shalt Not Go Crazy at the Same Time

Perhaps the best advice I ever received before I got married was from an elderly husband who told me the secret of his good marriage, which was: "Don't ever go crazy at the same time."

If you've been working up a good lather all day, but your insensitive spouse (who has been "lathering up" all day as well) beats you to the screaming-lunatic role, do whatever it takes to bite your tongue, and wait your turn. In the meantime, use all the techniques you learn in this chapter to gently and lovingly help her through her tantrum. On the surface this might not seem fair, but there are some built-in benefits for you. Helping your mate get through her (nonviolent) tantrum increases your credibility and the likelihood that she will hear you out respectfully — and meet your needs more willingly — when you finally do get your turn to speak. Maintaining your cool under fire earns her respect (and makes her feel a little guilty to boot). All this translates into greater pride in yourself and, eventually, a more sympathetic audience from your mate.

Cooler heads will always prevail. Take turns going crazy.

Now, for the most important commandment.

XV: Thou Shalt Pray, Pray, Pray

Sometimes the only way through an argument is to pray your way through it. I cannot tell you the number of times I have been in heated discussions with my wife, or anyone else for that matter, and there was no way I could think of anything to do that would move things along. But as soon as I prayed, it was as if a switch clicked on in my head and I knew exactly what I needed to do or say. When I have listened to this prompting of the Spirit, I have never gone wrong.

To be perfectly honest, my problem-solving prayer lacks a lot; but just to show you that yours doesn't have to be elaborate, I'll share mine with you.

Dear Lord,

I am about to kill [insert name here]. *Somehow I know that's not the right thing to do. But if you don't give me your wisdom right away, I know I'm going to do something stupid. Please, I'm desperate. Help!*

That's not a particularly inspired prayer. It isn't very holy, and honestly, I can't say I'm proud of ever having to pray it. But it is definitely sincere, and God has never failed to come to my aid when I pray it. When you get stuck and your own wisdom fails you, don't ask our Lord to change your mate, ask him to show *you* what to do. Call, and he will answer. "Knock and the door will be opened for you" (cf. Mt 7:7 and Lk 11:9).

You're probably asking yourself: "I'm supposed to remember all that? In an argument? Are you crazy?" On the one hand, there is so much to learn about effective problem solving that what you have read is just scratching the surface. On the other hand, it *is* an awful lot of information to have to try to remember under stress. Relax, I don't really expect you to. The best thing for you to do is choose *one* of the skills that you think would be most helpful to you, and practice it until you have mastered it. Then, if you feel the need, choose another arguing skill to master. Don't try to use them all at once — you'll only frustrate yourself.

192

Take it one argument at a time. After all, you've got the rest of your life to practice.

A Shortcut

Besides this one-step-at-a-time approach, all you really need to remember to transform your fights into problem-solving sessions is to remember one word, an acronym really: L.O.V.E.

L — *Look* for the positive intention.

O — *Omit* contemptuous phrases and actions.

V — *Verify* that what you think your spouse said is what he or she really meant to say.

E — *Encourage* each other through the conflict and toward a solution.

The *Roman Missal* tells us: *"Ubi caritas et amor, Deus ibi est"* ("Where there is charity and love, God is there"). Let God help you and your mate solve your problems respectfully and as a team. Before you begin discussing a problem with your mate, talk it over with God. Ask him to show you how to present your concerns firmly, but with love and wisdom. Ask him to give you his words when addressing your mate, and when you open your mouth, make certain that only his words come out. We are supposed to be Christ to our mates. Would Christ say and do the things you say and do in an argument? I hope so. Besides this, every day pray that the Lord will make you better helpmates so that even in your arguments you will be grateful for a partner who is truly flesh of your flesh and bone of your bone.

The Selfish Person's Guide to Love

Many of you are probably like me. I know God wants me to be loving even when things get hot. Just look at the Lord's example, when he prays, "Father, forgive them . . ." (Lk 23:34). But, sometimes, I just don't feel like it. Knowing that I should do something often proves to be a less than effective motivator for actually getting me to do it. Sometimes when I am choked on my own self-righteousness I need a more immediate, more "selfish" reason for doing what I know is the right thing. God, in his mercy, gives me not one but two reasons to answer his call to love. I would like to share with you what he has taught me.

1. Choosing to love others helps us feel God's love more.

When I bring a difficult situation in my marriage to the Lord, an odd thing happens. Somewhere in the middle of my prayer (which goes something like, "So help me, God, you *better* do something about this *right now* because if you think for one minute that I'm going to be loving . . .") I hear a quiet voice that stops me in my tracks.

"You know, Greg. Now that you mention it, sometimes you do that to me."

"What are you talking about, Lord?" I say, irritated at having been interrupted in the middle of my ranting and raving.

"That thing you're complaining about. Sometimes you do that to me."

It doesn't matter what it is. Invariably, God uses the circumstances of my anger to teach me about the latest way I have been putting him off, selling him short, or otherwise treating him with unintentional contempt. Moreover, where I might be tempted to whine, complain, or argue with my wife to get what I want, God reminds me that he does none of these things when he wants me to change. He just loves me more persistently until I realize, "Hey, this God of mine isn't so bad after all. Maybe I *should* trust him with more of my life."

When I ask God to help me in my marriage, he begins by leading me to see my own bouts of resistance to his love. When I confess them, seek his pardon, and ask for his grace, he not only fills my soul with a peace beyond words, he shows me that the answer to my current marital struggle is simple: I must love more, love better, and love now. Opening myself up to his love, I receive from our Lord the courage to try and become the husband he would be.

2. Choosing to love increases my self-esteem.

There is a second reason I must choose to be loving even when I don't feel like it. I simply don't like the person I become when I choose not to love. If, as the Holy Father says, the call to love is innate, then to *not* love is to *not* be true to myself. When a person does things that are inconsistent with his or her nature, it has a horrible effect on that person's self-esteem. I see examples of this all day long when people tell me that they despise how they've let their marital problems turn them into "a bitch," "an abuser," "a miserable person," or worse. When I can help these people make more loving choices in their marriages (not because their spouses deserve it but because their own dignity demands it), two remarkable things happen.

First, they begin to like themselves again. There is a great deal of satisfaction that comes from being able to say that at the end of each day, no matter how "crazy" your spouse was, you behaved in a way that you can be proud of.

Second, when the husband and wife respond to their calls to love, acting in a manner that is consistent with their personal dignity, nine times out of ten the marriage problems disappear; sometimes in a matter of weeks, sometimes overnight, but always faster than the couple would have ever dared dream was possible.

194

Jesus said, "Love your neighbor as you love yourself" (cf. Mt 19:19,

Mk 12:31, and Lk 10:27). But I have found that if I want to love myself, the only logical choice I have is to be loving to others whether or not I *feel* like it; whether or not I think "my neighbor" (in this case, my wife) deserves it. To do otherwise is to become bitter, self-righteous, angry, and isolated. I deserve better than that. You do too.

God rewards our choice to love with deeper submersion in his joy, greater self-satisfaction, and more fulfilling relationships. The call to love is indeed the most invigorating and most important call we could ever answer. It is our beginning, our middle, and our end. To help you learn how to build intimacy because of your arguments instead of in spite of them, complete the following exercise.

~~~

Exercise: Becoming a Red-hot Lover
Commandment Quiz

Take the following quiz to see which of the skills in this chapter you need to work on the most. On a scale of 1 to 10 (1 is *completely false*, 10 is *completely true*) circle how much each of the following statements applies to you. The number of the statement corresponds with the same number "commandment" explained in this chapter (e.g., statement 1 applies to "commandment" 1, and so on).

1. My spouse and I often have arguments about "stupid things."

(Completely False: 1) (2) (3) (4) (5) (6) (7) (8) (9) (Completely True: 10)

2. Our arguments tend to wander all over the place and never solve anything.

(Completely False: 1) (2) (3) (4) (5) (6) (7) (8) (9) (Completely True: 10)

3. I frequently feel that my spouse is picking on me or is otherwise intentionally out to hurt my feelings.

(Completely False: 1) (2) (3) (4) (5) (6) (7) (8) (9) (Completely True: 10)

4. I have no idea why my spouse does the obnoxious things he or she does, or how to stop such behavior.

(Completely False: 1) (2) (3) (4) (5) (6) (7) (8) (9) (Completely True: 10)

5. I often have to pester or nag my mate to do things for me.

(Completely False: 1) (2) (3) (4) (5) (6) (7) (8) (9) (Completely True: 10)

6. I think my mate is controlling. *Or* my mate tells me that *I* am.

(Completely False: 1) (2) (3) (4) (5) (6) (7) (8) (9) (Completely True: 10)

7. Our arguments tend to get pretty hot, pretty quickly.

(Completely False: 1) (2) (3) (4) (5) (6) (7) (8) (9) (Completely True: 10)

8. In an argument, I often feel as if my mate is more an enemy than a partner.

(Completely False: 1) (2) (3) (4) (5) (6) (7) (8) (9) (Completely True: 10)

9. Our arguments usually end when one of us storms out of the room. *Or* when one of us stops talking to the other for a few hours or days.

(Completely False: 1) (2) (3) (4) (5) (6) (7) (8) (9) (Completely True: 10)

10. I often feel that my mate overwhelms or overpowers me in an argument.

(Completely False: 1) (2) (3) (4) (5) (6) (7) (8) (9) (Completely True: 10)

11. I pride myself on my insight into other people's lives and I freely share these insights in my discussions with them.

(Completely False: 1) (2) (3) (4) (5) (6) (7) (8) (9) (Completely True: 10)

12. Either I or my mate or both of us tend to obviously show our disgust and/or frustration with each other in arguments. (e.g., eye-rolling, threats, head-shaking, dismissive comments, etc.).

(Completely False: 1) (2) (3) (4) (5) (6) (7) (8) (9) (Completely True: 10)

13. My mate and I have at least one problem that is just too hot to ever talk all the way through without things getting out of control.

(Completely False: 1) (2) (3) (4) (5) (6) (7) (8) (9) (Completely True: 10)

14. My mate and I often try to one-up each other in arguments.

(Completely False: 1) (2) (3) (4) (5) (6) (7) (8) (9) (Completely True: 10)

15. I do not pray during arguments.

(Completely False: 1) (2) (3) (4) (5) (6) (7) (8) (9) (Completely True: 10)

Scoring

Which three statements did you indicate to be most true (i.e., circled the highest number of)? List them here. Number ____, number ____, number ____.

Reread the problem-solving "commandments" with the corresponding numbers. For example, if you listed statements 2, 4, and 8, you will want to reread "commandments" 2, 4, and 8. Concentrate on mastering these skills first. Practice them regularly in your daily discussions and arguments with your mate and others as well. Add more skills as you master these.

Emotional-Temperature Exercise

The goal of this exercise is to help you more closely identify your unique anger behaviors at the various points on the emotional-temperature scale, then to apply the things you've learned in this chapter to a particular argument in your marriage.

Pick a topic that you and your mate frequently argue about. Write it here:

_____

_____

When you are arguing about the above topic, identify the things you say or do at each point on the emotional-temperature scale. For example, "At a 6, I start 'organizing' whatever is in front of me. At a 7, I am usually rolling my eyes. At an 8, I start pacing," etc.

How do you act when you are at a:

1 _____

2 _____

3 _____

4 _____

5 _____

6 _____

7 _____

Stop! What new behavior or skill will you use from now on to prevent yourself from going to an 8, a 9, or a 10? Write it here:

_____

_____

Now complete the scale to see what you are saving yourself from by interrupting your anger at a 7.

8 _____

9 _____

10 _____

Discuss and do the following.

1. What are those special "dirty tricks" or "gotcha's" you use in arguments that serve no purpose other than to irritate your mate and increase the tension?

1a. Which of the "commandments" will help you overcome this bad arguing habit? How will you remind yourself to practice this new skill? Is there anything your mate can do to support you in this change?

1b. Write a love note to your mate apologizing for using those dirty tricks in the past. Explain how you plan to change. Be specific. Use examples from your life together.

2. How is God speaking to you through the things that irritate you about your mate? Do you do to God what you complain about your mate doing to you?

2a. How do you plan to address these shortcomings in your relationship with God? Can your mate support you in doing this? How? Or why not?

2b. Spend some time in prayer. Thank God for making use of even the difficult times in your marriage to facilitate your spiritual growth. Ask him to make you more sensitive to these insights and to your mate in the future. Meditate on the parable of the ungrateful servant (Mt 18:23-35).

Suggested Reading

To become truly great problem solvers, I highly recommend the following books. (For publishers and dates of publication, see the Bibliography.)

Why Marriages Succeed or Fail: And How You Can Make Yours Last (Dr. John Gottman) ∼ This is an excellent book. It contains the results of the groundbreaking study of which arguing behaviors destroy a marriage and which build it up. The study was able to predict with ninety-five percent accuracy which couples would still be together after five years.

Divorce Busting: A Revolutionary and Rapid Program for "Staying Together" (Michele Weiner-Davis) ∼ Not just for troubled marriages, this book (especially part II) is chock-full of practical, effective, and remarkably simple problem-solving techniques to transform almost any marriage. (I also recommend her book *Fire Your Shrink!*)

Love Is Never Enough (Dr. Aaron T. Beck) ∼ A profound book that teaches couples how irrational thinking destroys marriages and how to overcome their own irrational marital beliefs and practices.

As this chapter draws to a close, I would ask that you find your mate and pray the following together.

The Partnership Prayer

Lord God,

You have called my mate and me to be partners — flesh of each other's flesh and bone of each other's bone. Let everything we do, especially the way we solve problems, reflect the intimate partnership to which you are calling us.

When we struggle through hardship, give us your wisdom, love, and grace, that we might speak only your words to each other, and serve each other humbly and generously. Compel us to love even when it is difficult, even when we don't feel like it. For it is only through your holy love that we will conquer all.

Holy Family, pray for us.

Amen.

Gregory K. Popcak

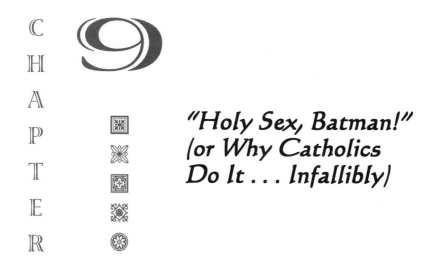

CHAPTER 9

"Holy Sex, Batman!" (or Why Catholics Do It . . . Infallibly)

> "Aslan," she said, ". . . there must be some mistake, . . . [the Witch] can't really mind the smell of those [magical golden] apples. . . . She ate one."
>
> "Child," he replied, "that is why all the rest are now a horror to her. That is what happens to those who pluck and eat fruits at the wrong time and in the wrong way. The fruit is good, but they loathe it ever after."
>
> — *C. S. Lewis*
> *The Magician's Nephew*

Walk into any bookstore. Its shelves will be positively pregnant with texts on "Spiritual Sexuality." Of, course, the "spirituality" they are hawking is usually some ancient Eastern thing that not even the "Easterners" practice any more. For example, how many people do you know actually practice *real* "Tantric Sex," in which the man is rarely, if ever, allowed to reach orgasm? Give me a break. This trend is more about spiffy packaging than spirituality. If it's true that "there is a sucker born every minute," then, gentle reader, the secular publishers think that sucker is you.

But does that mean there is no such thing as spiritual sex? Is there nowhere couples can turn to discover the secrets of a completely toe-curling, eye-popping, mind-blowing, *and profoundly spiritual* sexuality? Doesn't Christianity have *anything* to say about good sex? "Yeah," claim the cynics. "Christians say: 'Don't have any.'"

The cynics are wrong.

Sex, Lies, and the Church

Probably not unlike many of you reading this book, I used to believe that Catholicism took a rather dim and ignorant view of sex. It seemed to me that there were two prevailing schools of thought among Catholics. The first I call the "God Doesn't Care What I Do in My Bedroom School." This is the more Mediterranean must-leave-morning-Mass-early-so-I-can-have-breakfast-with-my-mistress laissez-faire relationship between faith and fornication. The thinking here is that God has more important things to do than keep score of my conquests. As long as I pray, donate to the Church, *and make sure my heart is in the right place*, everything is A-OK with the Big Guy. Needless to say, this is a very popular school, with a very impressive alumni mailing list.

The second group I call the "Aunt McGillicuddy's Antique Urn School." This is the more Anglo-Irish view, which is considered by many in America to be "the official Catholic position" on sex. This group grudgingly admits that sex is beautiful — in a somewhat grotesque Gothic sort of way — but more importantly, sex is *holy* (in the Old Testament "touch it and die" sense of holiness). Therefore sex must be approached *delicately, cautiously,* and — ideally — *infrequently,* like Aunt McGillicuddy's antique urn: "Don't ye be fussin' with *that* now, Missy! We only touch it if we have to dust it, and then only once a month er soo!"

You may be surprised to learn that neither of these schools of thought is Catholic. In fact, both reflect attitudes that have been *condemned by the Church as heresies* (Gnosticism, Jansenism, Manichaeism, etc.). Because so many people — even some in the clergy — confuse these heresies with the truth of the Church, Catholicism has gotten an unjustly bad reputation for being "sexually oppressive." To be perfectly honest, in contemporary America, the real sexual oppression comes from *feminists* like Catherine "All sex is rape" McKinnon and those present-day Fundamentalists who have raised the "Aunt McGillicuddy's Antique Urn School" to an art form. So I'll ask the question again: What does *Catholicism* have to say about good sex?

The Truth Is Out There . . .

I think the best way to introduce you to the truth about Catholic sex is tell you about how I discovered it in, of all places, a seminary.

I was a freshman in college planning an Easter Vigil Mass with a group of undergraduate seminarians and their spiritual director. We had gotten to the blessing of the baptismal waters when Father Cain, ever on the lookout for a teachable moment, smiled wryly and said, "Oh, that *erotic* rite."

Eleven pairs of eighteen-year-old eyebrows shot up.

Father Cain proceeded to explain that during the blessing, the Easter candle is plunged into the baptismal font as a symbol of Christ impregnating the womb of the Church, from which new children of God would be born in the coming year.

His words stunned me. Until that moment I had believed the popular notion that "Catholics fear sex." Yet, here it was, a sexual act as the cornerstone of the chief sacrament of initiation — baptism. Clearly, not the action of an "erotophobic" faith.

The truth is, we Catholics do not fear sex — we esteem it. Sex is one of the greatest goods God has ever given us. The non-Catholic mind cannot even begin to imagine how much real Catholics honor, esteem, and *enjoy* sex. Sex to the true Catholic is like what relativity was to Einstein, the vaccination was to Pasteur, or the electric light was to Edison. We Catholics believe that great sex *belongs* to us. As far as we're concerned, everybody else is just playing children's games where sex is involved. In fact, the only reason there are no pop-psych books called *The Mysteries of Mind-Blowing Catholic Sexuality* is that it is so powerfully spiritual, so eye-poppingly amazing, so wonderfully awe-inspiring, that most modern-day sexologists couldn't get their puny little minds around it even if they *would* put down their "sex toys" long enough to think about it, and then all they would end up with is a bad case of "crosier envy." Just as Christ crucified was folly to the Gentiles of St. Paul's day, *truly Christian* sexuality is a stumbling block to the "Gentiles" of today.

Can *you* handle the truth?

The Four Truths

There are basically four truths Christians hold regarding sex.

1. Sex is holy.

"Aha!" you say. "A contradiction!"

Not at all. Sex *is* holy; but as I suggested above, not in the Old Testament "touch it and die" sense of holiness. It is holy in the sense that is given to us by the New Testament, through the Incarnation.

Before Jesus, holiness was something "out there." Holiness was something so beyond us that if we ever came in direct contact with *"it,"* we would surely die. That's why a rope used to be tied around the high priest when he entered the "Holy of Holies" once a year. This way, if he got zapped by the awesome presence of God, his assistants could drag out whatever was left of his toasted carcass for a decent burial.

But then along came Jesus, Word of God, true God, true man, the Christ. The "out there" came down here. The transcendent, unknowable

"I Am" became "Emmanuel, or God is with us." He emptied himself and became one of us, and in so doing, he shared his holiness with each and every one of us. His holiness became encoded in the spiritual DNA of all humanity for all time. In fact, the Eastern Fathers of the Church were fond of saying that through the incredible mystery of the Incarnation, Christ "divinized our nature."

> The Word became flesh *to be our model of holiness:* . . .
> The Word became flesh to make us *"partakers of the divine nature"* [2 *Pet* 1:4]: "For this is why the Word [that is, God] became man, and the Son of God became the Son of man: so that man, by entering into communion with the Word and thus receiving divine sonship, might become a son of God" [St. Irenaeus, *Adv. haeres.* 3, 19, 1: PG 7/1, 939]. "For the Son of God became man so that we might become God" [St. Athanasius, *De inc.*, 54, 3: PG 25, 192B]. "The only-begotten Son of God, wanting to make us sharers in his divinity, assumed our nature, so that he, made man, might make men gods" [St. Thomas Aquinas, *Opusc.* 57: 1-4].
>
> — CATECHISM OF THE CATHOLIC CHURCH
> Nos. 459, 460

Talk about optimism!

Sex is holy because it is the most profound way one "divinized nature" can give itself to another. Sex is holy because *you are holy.* God came to make it so. "We are a chosen race, a royal priesthood, a holy nation, a people set apart. Once no people, now God's people!" (cf. 1 Pt 2:9-10). Sexual intercourse is holy because it is the most complete way to share the gift that you are with another person. As Pope John Paul II says, sex is a "self-gift." It is a sharing of all the holiness you are with all the holiness of another.

Holy sex is not glum sex, boring sex, or polite sex. It is godly sex. More than anything, "God is a lover" *(OSV's Encyclopedia of Catholic Doctrine).* Even *The Imitation of Christ* refers to God as "Divine Lover." And make no mistake, God is no slouch as a lover either. Saints who experienced theophanies (i.e., powerful, personal, and very real encounters with the divine presence of God) didn't refer to the experience as "being in ecstasy" for nothing.

If you will permit me to bring this concept of theophany a little closer to home, the Eucharist is overflowing with powerful imagery of God as our Divine Lover. To ransom his beloved (us, his Church), he suffered, died, and rose again by means of a love so strong not even the gates of hell could prevail against it. Having won his prize, our salvation, he gives himself to us completely, body and blood, soul and divinity, through the Most Blessed Sacrament. We draw him close. He enters us. His flesh becomes one with our flesh. His blood courses through our veins. Fearful and eager at once to be completely vulnerable to him, we fall prey to his all-consuming love. Inspired by his passion, nourished by his loving embrace, and propelled by the power of his Holy Spirit alive within us, we enter the world again, refreshed, to do the great work of bringing new children to him through the waters of baptism.

Don't you see? For the Christian, there is nothing shameful or second rate about holy sex. Page 625 of *OSV's Encyclopedia of Catholic Doctrine* tells us: "God created the whole universe so that new beings might be able to share in the unimaginable riches of his being. He created human beings to share eternal bliss with him." To experience sacred sex is to experience the cataclysmic eruption of love that was the cosmological orgasm we call the "Big Bang," *through which* the entire universe was created and *from which* the entire universe continues to reel even today. Who wouldn't give his eyeteeth for a night like *that* with his beloved? When Christian married couples celebrate holy sex, it is just one more way they celebrate "the 'trinity' that the human being images" *(OSV's Encyclopedia of Catholic Doctrine)*.

2. Sex is sacramental.

The Church teaches that when married people make love, they are celebrating the sacrament of matrimony. But sacraments are chiefly concerned with salvation. What could sex possibly have to do with the achievement of eternal life? Well, besides participating in the mysteries I have already described, when I die, I am going to stand before the Almighty and all his glory — in all my glory (so to speak). Every blemish, wrinkle, crease, and bump of my physical and spiritual being will be — for all eternity — exposed to his penetrating gaze, completely vulnerable to his pervasive touch. Under such circumstances, for me to experience anything other than the sheer terror of hell, I must be able to stand confidently in the presence of that gaze, like Adam and Eve while they still enjoyed their original innocence. What better way to prepare myself for this awesome responsibility than to challenge whatever vulnerability or shame I may feel when my wife gazes upon me in my nakedness and makes love with me? It is this unique power of sexuality to challenge shame and expand vulnerability at the deepest level of our personhood that, in addition to its unitive and procreative aspects, makes lovemaking a spiritual exercise, first and foremost.

3. Sex is unitive.

Sex has the power to take two hearts and melt them into one. "And the two shall become one" (Mt 19:5). I don't mean this in some schmaltzy, Hollywoody sort of way. When spouses build their marriage around helping each other fulfill their identities in Christ, intercourse becomes a celebration of the physical reality of that partnership. When couples make love the Christian way, it is as if they are saying, "How wonderful! We spend our days working toward the same ends, helping each other fulfill our God-given dreams, goals, and values. Look, even our bodies work for each other's good. Praise God!" (See also *The Unitive End of Marriage* in Chapter 2.)

4. Sex is procreative.

I treated this fairly thoroughly in Chapter 2 (under the subhead *The Procreative End of Marriage*). God is a lover, and because he is a great lover, he creates more creatures to love. So . . . if you want to have great, godly sex, you've got to at least be *open* to life. Though it is true that the "Church does not teach that couples must have as many children as their bodies can bear" *(OSV's Encyclopedia of Catholic Doctrine),* an ongoing, prayerful, responsible openness to life is what transforms mere eroticism into "real sex."

If you don't currently practice real grown-up sex in your marriage but would like more information on how to use your sex life to grow in love and spiritual maturity, then reread *The Procreative End of Marriage* in Chapter 2 of this book and call the Couple-to-Couple League at 513-471-2000 or your diocesan Family Life office for a natural family planning (or NFP) class in your area. Tell them I sent you. You won't be sorry. I promise. More importantly, the Church promises.

Summary of the Four Truths

Appreciating sex for all it is — holy (in the New Testament "hands on" incarnational sense), sacramental, unitive, and procreative — allows Christian married couples to both experience the fullness of their sexuality, and derive more joy from their lovemaking than couples belonging to any other group.

As I wrote in Chapter 6, the *Janus Report on Sexual Behavior* (1993) demonstrates that couples who live out their faith have more satisfying sex lives because they "pay more attention to the mystic and symbolic dimensions of . . . sexuality." This same finding has been reported in several other respected studies. God asks so little of us, and gives so much in return. By giving our sexuality to him, he enables our enjoyment of it to increase by a hundredfold.

A Rose (or a Narnian Apple) by Any Other Name . . . Stinks

"Wait a minute!" you say. "I know plenty of people who have had sex that was not holy, sacramental, unitive, or procreative, and they seemed to enjoy it well enough. Sex isn't all those things all the time. Nor does it have to be."

I see what you're getting at, but you are missing an important distinction. For the Christian, sex is *always* holy, sacramental, unitive, and procreative. If it isn't, then it isn't sex. It's eroticism (see Mark 7:21-22 in the *Philipps Modern English Bible*, which refers to the sin of "sensuality"). Eroticism comes in many forms (e.g., contraceptive sex, solo and mutual masturbation, fornication, adultery, etc.). But its hallmark is that it values your personal pleasure *over* either the dignity of the person, the dignity of the act, or both. Eroticism treats your God-given, holy body as a mere *thing* to be used as you please. It treats a person — even a married person — as a *thing* to be used to satisfy oneself (or a *thing to be resented* when the person refuses to be used). Likewise, eroticism treats sex like a common street drug you take to make yourself feel better. Again, this turns lovemaking into an act that is more about meeting your own needs than about giving yourself to your mate. This very sentiment tends to breed resentment in a marriage. Further, contraceptive practices of eroticism reduce lovemaking to sexual bulimia in which all the pleasurable sensations of sex are sought while any real spiritual or physical effect is disallowed. (Bulimia is the binge-purge eating disorder.) Like all sin, eroticism is superficially very attractive — but it's fool's gold. It eventually causes sex to become boring. After the novelty of "eroticism as sex" wears off, those practicing this form of sex are either led to believe that "sex isn't all it's cracked up to be" (thus devaluing the gift real sex is — and fulfilling the C. S. Lewis quote that began this chapter) or they find they must practice even more extreme forms of eroticism ("swinging," S&M [sadomasochism], sex toys, pornography, etc.) to derive the same emotional benefits from their sexual drug.

The problem is that everyone thinks of eroticism as "naughty sex." But that couldn't be further from the truth. They are two completely different things. There is no more such a thing as "naughty sex" as there is a "putrid-smelling rose" or a "hot snow." A putrid-smelling rose isn't a rose — it's garbage. A "hot snow" isn't snow — it's rain (Duh!). Eroticism is to real sex what dumpster diving is to dinner at your favorite four-star restaurant. Sure, you *could* do either, but why in God's name would you want to?

Think about it. If you saw a Rockefeller, or a Mellon, or a Kennedy climbing out of a dumpster, you'd be shocked! (Well, maybe not a Kennedy.) You'd say, "That poor bastard. Someone should commit him." How much more shocking for a son or daughter of the Most High God to make his marriage bed a dumpster?

If Real Sex Is So Good, Why Is It So Hard?

The reason that real sex does not come easy to us but eroticism does is something called concupiscence (pronounced con-CUE-pih-sense). That's a technical term theologians use to describe the longing for the mud we have even after baptism washes away the stain of original sin. Perhaps a metaphor will help you understand this.

Imagine that you left your garden hose curled up every which way in the driveway. Moreover, imagine it took you a while to put it away and you ran over it with the car about a half-dozen times. (Please tell me I'm not the only one who's done this!) When you get around to it, you find that the hose cleans up well enough, and you can straighten it out just fine. But as you attempt to coil it back up, it starts fighting you. Why? It's a matter of simple physics. The hose physically "remembers" the distorted shape it was forced to lie in for weeks, and it will continue to "remember" that distorted shape (and vex you) every time you try to roll or unroll it for many years to come.

In the same way, while baptism "washes us clean" and straightens us out — so to speak — our humanity retains the "memory" of the distorted thing it was before our baptism. (From the Fall to the Resurrection was a long time to lie in the driveway.) Try as we might, when we aren't paying attention, we have a tendency to want to return to this distorted shape. (Our love of eroticism and our tendency to treat our bodies and others as sex objects are two examples of this tendency.) But Jesus came to show us how the Father really created humans to live and act, and he demonstrated how to keep our humanity in line — as it were. If Jesus himself (who was perfect, and like us in all things but sin) used fasting and abstaining, prayer, and knowledge of Scripture to discipline his flesh (see chapter 4 of Matthew's Gospel on the temptation of Christ for one striking example), how can we say we are not called to do the same? We Christians must follow Jesus' example so that we can overcome the natural longing our humanness has to return to its old former distorted shape. This way, when the Master wants to "use" us to water his garden, we won't vex him too much. Practicing real sex and abstaining from eroticism are two ways to overcome concupiscence, thereby continuing and furthering the process of sanctification that was begun and made possible at baptism but whose actualization takes a lifetime.

GREGORY K. POPCAK

And this brings us back to the original point. Just like the "old us" (i.e., who we were *before* our baptism in Christ) was so inferior to the "new us" (i.e., who we are now *because* of our baptism in Christ), eroticism is a sin because it is so *inferior* to "real sex." Real sex incorporates erotic elements; but, unlike *eroticism*, there is so much more to it (i.e., the four truths). Eroticism is sinful because it is copulation that is *not* holy, *not* sacramental, *not* unitive, *nor* is it procreative. Real sex, however, because it is always *holy, and sacramental, and unitive, and procreative,* is never sinful. Married Christians are free to have as much of the latter as they want *and* they should enjoy it as much as their bodies, minds, and spirits are able.

Now that we've got that straightened out, I don't ever want to hear another person bashing Catholic sexuality. And, if *you* hear someone criticizing it, just look that person in the eye and say, "You should *be* so lucky, you poor, love-starved, ignorant neo-pagan."

Renew Your Vows

The Church teaches that every time Christian married couples make love, they are physically restating their marriage vows and recommitting themselves to all the promises they made at the altar. Every time Christian married couples make love, they promise — using a language that can only be spoken by one ensouled body to another — to love, honor, and cherish, in good times and bad, sickness and health, wealth and poverty, all the days of their life, till death do them part. So many couples look forward to their twenty-fifth anniversary when they, by popular tradition, get to stand up and renew their vows; but no married couple has to wait that long. You can renew your vows tonight — or right now — if your mate is available.

Because lovemaking is a reenactment of all the joys and promises of the wedding day, Christian married couples must *never* take their sexuality for granted. Think about it. Did you take your wedding day for granted? Did you *miss* the ceremony because you were tired or stressed out? (I was both, but it didn't stop me — nor, thank God, my wife — from coming down the aisle.) Did you say to the pastor witnessing your ceremony, "Can we move this along, Father? We've got a lot to do tomorrow and I'd like to turn in early tonight." Of course you didn't. You had been looking forward to your wedding day your whole life and planning it since the Paleozoic Era (or at least many months). Tired as you may have been, you drew strength from your wedding day. You hung on every word, sign, and gesture. All married couples who understand the truth of Christian sexuality view their ongoing sexual relationship in the same way.

In today's work-centered (as opposed to love-centered) world, one of the fastest-growing sexual disorders is "inhibited sexual desire disorder" (or ISDD). The chief cause of ISDD, according to research, is that most couples place their sex lives at the bottom of their priority list. They have so many other things to do that by the time they fall into bed at night, they barely have enough strength to acknowledge that there is someone else in the room, much less make love. But Christian married couples who understand their lovemaking as a restatement of their wedding vows rarely, if ever, fall prey to ISDD. How could they? Just as the first wedding ceremony is energizing and life-giving to spouses who should otherwise be dead on their feet from months of fighting with caterers, in-laws, musicians, and assorted other wedding nuisances, the Christian couple experiences each private "wedding celebration" as a beautiful, life-giving, energizing, desirable event. No matter how tired they are, the spouses can't wait to walk down the aisle to their bedroom (or any other room for that matter) and renew their vows on the altar that is their marriage bed (or sofa, or dining-room table, or stairway, etc.). To such couples, sex is not "just one more thing to do," it is the fountain from which they drink to grow in love and celebrate the partnership that daily helps them become who God created them to be. Christian married couples with a deeply spiritual sexuality spend as much time and energy nurturing, planning, and rejoicing in the private, physical celebrations of their wedding day as they did nurturing, planning, and rejoicing in the public celebration of their first wedding day. They do this because they realize how beautiful and essential lovemaking is to the core of their married vocation.

To pursue this ideal in your marriage, as you are called by your vows to do, follow these "five paths to sacred sex."

The Five Paths
1. Guard each other's dignity.

Spiritual sexuality cannot exist in the face of cruel humor, blunt criticism, name-calling, neglect (benign or malignant), abuse, or other affronts to one's personal dignity. It also cannot exist as long as either of you has any sense that you are being used by your mate as a mere object for the other's gratification.

According to research, the only way to avoid or overcome these obstacles is for you and your mate to be *five times* more affectionate, generous, complimentary, thoughtful, and kind, than critical, nagging, arguing, nit-picking, or contemptuous. Likewise, it has been both my professional and personal experience that this five-to-one ratio is only the *beginning* point of spiritual sexuality. If spouses exhibit a solid, sacred sexuality, then it is more likely that their positivity-to-negativity ratio is seven to one, or even ten to one.

If you want to achieve a spiritual sexuality, then the only answer is to love. Love more, love better, love every day. Love by doing the little things. Love in a way that is meaningful to your mate, not necessarily because your spouse deserves it but because your Christian dignity demands it. (Revisit Chapters 4, 7, and 8 for hints on how to make this a reality.)

2. Be a servant.

There are two sets of behaviors spouses exhibit in their attempt to build a more satisfying sex life with their mates. The first is whining: "When are you going to make time for me? Do you know how long it's been since we had sex?" Or, "You never take me out anywhere! How come you're not more like so-and-so?"

Any romance or sex resulting from such pathetic "interventions" will be born of guilt, will not be remarkably satisfying for anyone involved, and will be deeply resented by all concerned — probably for a very long time.

The only way to truly develop the love life you want is to become an expert at the second way: being a servant. Sex will never evolve into the mutual self-gift it is supposed to be until both you and your mate are equally skilled at serving each other charitably, generously, and joyfully outside of the bedroom. To better understand what I mean, take the following quiz.

✔ Do you base your spousal roles more on compensation than on complementarity? (See *The Unitive End of Marriage* in Chapter 2.)

✔ Do you criticize your mate? Do you discourage the pursuit of her dreams, goals, values, interests, or ideas?

✔ Do you pout, or act disgusted and/or uninterested when accompanying your mate to some place or function that is meaningful to her but not to you (e.g., shopping, in-laws, corporate functions, church, hobbies, etc.)?

✔ Do you use your marriage as an institution of convenience, saying, "Now that I'm married I never have to do *X* again; that's what my spouse is for"?

✔ Do you refuse or resist loving your mate in a way that is meaningful to her?

✔ Do you consistently give more time and energy to work, social roles, hobbies, or other interests than you do your marriage and family?

✔ Do you refuse or resist doing things your mate asks you to do, not because those things violate your morals, but because you "just don't feel like it"?

✔ Do you tend to do loving things for your mate and then become resentful if you are not rewarded in kind?

✔ Do you or your mate leave arguments feeling beaten up?

✔ Do your arguments end with no mutually satisfactory solution in sight?

✔ Do you tend to do loving things only when you want something from your mate?

✔ Do you tend to be *more* loving than usual when you want something from your mate?

If you answered "yes" to any of these, you now know the reason for your less-than-awe-inspiring sex life. The solution to this problem is not whining for your mate to change. It is becoming a better servant yourself. How? By supporting your mate and being actively interested and involved in the things that are important to her. By loving your mate in a way that is meaningful to her. By being a loving, respectful problem solver. By being able to identify all the million or so tasks involved in making your home, family, and social lives run smoothly, knowing how to do each one of those tasks relatively well, frequently doing any or all of them without being asked, and by doing them cheerfully and without expecting any repayment for having done them.

This is a tall order, but it can be done. The *Exceptional Seven Percent* do it most days. You can too. Cheerful, generous, mutual service is the *only* way to achieve a truly satisfying marital sex life. Why? Because a vital sexuality is the *logical, loving response* to joyfully given marital service. Nothing else works. The less joyful service there is in a marriage, the less satisfying that couple's sex life will be (or the more dependent upon eroticism the spouses will become). The more joyful service . . . the more satisfying the sex life. This is true every time. If you want better sex, don't whine. Serve.

3. Approach lovemaking joyfully.

Catholics are encouraged to celebrate the sacraments frequently and joyfully. Marriage is one sacrament I hope you will celebrate in such a way. Sex is not about "marital duty." It is not a chore, an extra, or even a "nice thing" to do when you have the energy. If you are married, and you think of your sexual relationship in *any* of these ways, then your sexual mind-set is decidedly out of order. If you are married, then lovemaking is the foundation of your vocation. It is the joyful renewal of your wedding vows. It is your loving response to God's first commandment to all of humanity. (According to the Book of Genesis, when God said, "Go forth and multiply," he wasn't giving math homework.)

A second major obstacle to a joyful sexuality (besides a lack of service) is that too many Christian husbands and wives confuse modesty with shame and awkwardness about their sexuality. While "modesty protects the intimate center of the person" (*Catechism of the Catholic Church*, No. 2521) and prevents us from being reduced to sexual objects, modesty also "authorizes sexual display where genital fulfillment is allowed, that is, in marriage" *(OSV's Encyclopedia of Catholic Doctrine)*.

Shame, on the other hand, causes us to hold back just where we are called to be generous. It prevents sex from being the "self-gift" the Holy Father says it ought to be. For the Christian, one of the greatest sexual temptations is to dress shame in spiritual garb and use it as a way to avoid confronting our fears of intimacy, while allowing ourselves to feel self-righteous at the same time. (This is the essence of the "Aunt McGillicuddy's Antique Urn School.") Be this as it may, we must never forget that our sexual and bodily shame is a "direct descendent" of the shame Adam and Eve encountered after the Fall, standing before God in their nakedness. If we are ashamed of being exposed and vulnerable before our spouses, how will we ever tolerate an eternity standing exposed and vulnerable before our Divine Lover? Challenge your fears of vulnerability, of "losing control," and you will find amazing joy in the arms of both your earthly beloved and your Heavenly One.

4. Maintain a responsible openness to life.

"True, not every upright genital act will originate a new life; neither need one intend that it will," according to Father Ronald Lawler, Joseph Boyle, Jr., and William E. May, authors of Our Sunday Visitor's *Catholic Sexual Ethics: A Summary, Explanation, and Defense (Second Edition)*. "There are other worthy goals of sexual activity also. But the life-giving aspect of sexual activity must always be guarded and respected, or sex is trivialized and made inhuman."

As I explained in Chapter 2, Christian spiritual sexuality represents the attempt to balance two equally important sets of virtues, virtues that are contained within the phrase "Responsible Parenthood." On the one hand, being open to life enables us to increase our trust in God's providence, helps us identify with the Fatherhood of God, and inspires us to greater generosity, sacrifice, and love, among other things. On the other hand, practicing this openness *responsibly* causes us to exercise such virtues as self-mastery, discernment, chastity, prudence, and temperance, to name a few. For a married couple's sexuality to be truly sacred, the partners can't opt out of practicing one set of virtues or the other; they have to learn to balance both. The best — and only — way to do this is to practice NFP, or natural family planning (as explained in detail in Chapter 2). NFP is the key to having a true, grown-up, joyful, and spiritual sex life. If you don't currently use it, I encourage you to at least learn more about it. Experience for yourself the richness it will afford your spiritual and sexual life.

5. Approach each other in prayer.

Some people turn up their noses at the notion of joining prayer and lovemaking as if prayer serves the same function as reciting baseball statistics. But prayer is absolutely essential to a spiritual sexuality. Mine goes something like this:

"Lord, let me kiss her with your lips, love her with your gentle hands, consume her with your undying passion so that I may show her how precious and beautiful she is to you."

Every day ask God to make you a better lover to your mate, both in and out of bed. Read the Song of Songs in the Old Testament. It is a beautiful allegory of God's love for his people, and also a model of ideal human love. Meditate on it. Ask God to help you become the lover (literally and figuratively) he would be to your spouse. Develop your own "lover's prayer" and see if the Lord doesn't help you become a more respectful, passionate, generous, loving, and attentive partner.

Another Reason . . . For Makin' Whoopee!

Through her wise teaching, the Church shows us that God *deeply desires* Christian husbands and wives to have a loving, rewarding, fulfilling, passionate sexual relationship. *It is extremely important to God that you have a satisfying sex life with your spouse.* To those who confuse eroticism with real sex, this statement will be absurdly silly at best, or revoltingly scandalous at worst. What can I say? I am afraid that the truth is the truth. It cannot be changed just because it makes some people uncomfortable.

God cares about your sexuality because it manifests beautifully a spiritual reality. Sacred lovemaking challenges shame and expands healthy vulnerability. It draws a couple closer together, renews the spouses' vows, celebrates and invigorates their partnership, brings new life into the world, and *helps the spouses experience, in a physical way, how passionately they are loved by God.*

Physical spirituality is *very* important to the Catholic. It is why we have sacraments (which are physical manifestations of a spiritual reality). Take confession (the sacrament of penance and reconciliation), for example. *Of course* we could confess our sins directly to God. In fact, we do! But the Church understands that people are not just souls — they are bodies too. Just as our spirits need forgiveness, our *bodies* need to go through the *experience of being forgiven* in order for the process to be complete. After all, it wasn't just Adam's and Eve's souls that experienced the Fall; their bodies' integrity was compromised as well. That's why we die.

I confess my sins to God all the time, but I never *know* his forgiveness as I know it when, *through the senses God gave my body*, I *hear* the priest say, "I absolve you in the name of the Father, and of the Son, and of the Holy Spirit."

Through the sacraments of the Catholic Church (all of which were instituted by Christ — or, in the case of marriage — the Father), God reveals his love to our souls *and* bodies. This strikes many people, especially Protestants, as odd. "Why would God want to minister to our bodies?" they ask. These people would do well to remember that Christians believe in spiritual *and* bodily resurrection (cf. 1 Cor 15:12-20 and the Apostles' Creed). If our bodies are to be raised like Christ, God has to get our souls *and* bodies ready to spend eternity with him. He couldn't very well put new wine into old wineskins (glorified souls into unglorified bodies), could he? Being able to *physically* experience the spiritual realities of God's love is extremely important to our sanctification and, ultimately, to our salvation. Seen in this light, certainly you can understand why your sex life is important to God. It is the celebration of the sacrament through which he most powerfully and *physically* (as well as spiritually) reveals his love to us. In marriage, good sex is both a fruit and mechanism of sanctifying grace.

And Another Thing . . .

Christians have let pagans both take sex from us and poison it for us. This is tragic, because God gave sex to the godly, to our first parents, who dwelt in original innocence, and enjoyed their nakedness, vulnerability, and sexuality under the loving eyes of the Lord who made them. Remember, every married couple is called to be a new Adam and a new Eve. The completeness of your sanctification hinges upon your willingness to let God prepare both your soul *and* your body to spend eternity in heaven with him. It is time for Christian married couples to reclaim what is theirs; to redeem sex and celebrate it in joy and responsibility.

Well, what are you waiting for?

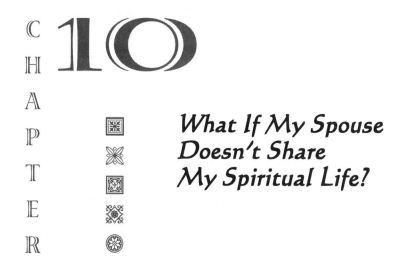

C
H
A
P
T
E
R

What If My Spouse Doesn't Share My Spiritual Life?

"Do you think that I have come to give peace on earth? No, I tell you, but rather division; for henceforth in one house there will be five divided, three against two and two against three . . ." (Lk 12:51-52).

Throughout this book, I have referred to sacramental marriage as a partnership in Christian destiny designed to help you and your mate become all God created you to be. Some of you may be despairing at this thought, especially if your spouse does not share your love for Christ or the Church.

Don't despair. God is providing you with an admittedly painful yet wonderfully powerful opportunity for spiritual and personal growth by being witness to your mate. This chapter will address some of the concerns you may have as you struggle to remain faithful to both God's call in your life and the partner he has given you.

A Painful Problem

Margeaux was referred to me by her pastor. It seems that in the last year she had experienced a "reversion" to Catholicism. The problem was that her husband did not share her enthusiasm for "all that superstition," as he called it, and it was tearing her apart. Tearfully, she told me, "I always wanted the kind of marriage where you could share everything. Now, I finally find something that really matters to me and I can't share it. It's killing me, and I don't know what to do. . . ."

In my marriage counseling practice, one of the more painful problems that arise is when one spouse has a conversion experience and the other spouse does not. It is especially difficult to watch something that should be the source of a couple's unity and strength become a club the husband and wife use on each other. While it could easily be the husband who discovers his spirituality first, most often the wife beats him to it. It has been this way since the earliest days of the Church. For example, in the year 370 the Roman Emperor Valentinian, responding to complaints from his pagan male constituents, wrote a letter to Pope Damasus I demanding that Christians stop converting pagan women. As you can see, this problem isn't something new.

Still, "post-conversion" life is rarely easy on a marriage. How do you grow in your faith in a less-than-supportive environment? And how do you share your faith with those closest to you without being obnoxious (an easy trap to fall into)? The following tips will help you find your feet.

1. It's not your job to convert your spouse.

You may be your mate's best hope for arriving properly attired at the heavenly banquet, but anything you can do is secondary to the saving work of Jesus Christ and your mate's own free will. You cannot convert your mate. Nobody ever had a *true* conversion to the faith because of someone else's begging, pleading, scolding, or cajoling. The only thing that makes conversions is a personal encounter with Jesus Christ. The temptation to be your mate's savior is a strong one, but there are three potent reasons for avoiding this trap.

The first reason is that the more your spouse suspects you are out to convert him (it is usually a "him"; but even if this is not true of your situation, the information still applies), the more he will dig in his heels. Nobody likes to be told what to do, especially when it is something as apparently "useless" and "Neanderthal" as going to church. The more you push, the more your mate will push back, and the more everyone loses.

Second, the more your mate resists you, the more you will come to hate him for his resistance. This is especially true if your marriage was not always the most joyful union on the block even before your conversion. As one person I know put it — only half-jokingly, of course —"I always thought my husband was an idiot, but now he's a *damned* idiot to boot!" Obviously, this is a poor example of the loving servanthood Jesus is commanding us to share with our mates.

Finally, and perhaps most importantly, the more you argue with your mate about the faith, the less credibility you will have. An example from Margeaux's experience may help clarify this point. Her husband once said to her, "Ever since you've been going to church, all you've been doing is bitching at me. I don't want to go because I don't want to become the kind of person you are now." Margeaux thought her husband was just being cruel; but, sad to say, there was probably a bit of truth in the comment. Often, people who are new to the faith (or have returned to it) don't just become Christians — they become Crusaders as well. And if you know anything about history, the Crusades did not go remarkably well for the Church. For the sake of your marriage, and your sanity, take a lesson from Church history. Get out of the Crusader business.

2. Make your spouse an offer he can't refuse.

But if you are not to be a Crusader, what are you to be? Simply put, you must be Christ. You must be a cheerful servant, an attentive friend, and a generous lover. Your Christianity must turn you into the spouse your mate always needed you to be but you couldn't become because you previously lacked the grace to do the job.

Earlier, I explained that only an encounter with Christ will convert your mate. You must be the chief facilitator of that encounter. If your mate won't come to Christ, then by God (and I mean that literally), you're going to have to bring Christ to him — by being Christ for him. Every day make up your mind to serve your mate as Christ would serve him, love your mate as well as Christ would love him, and upbuild your mate as Christ would upbuild him. Stop criticizing him about every little thing. Look for ways to upbuild him, emphasize his competencies, compliment his simple thoughtfulness, and in general, catch him "being good." Also, make a list of all the things your mate ever asked you to do for him, and add to that list all the things you have ever wanted your mate to do for you. Every day do as many of these things for your mate as you can, not because he deserves it, not because you necessarily feel like it, but because your Christian dignity demands it.

Being a true Christian spouse means taking all that Crusader energy and channeling it into becoming a better servant and lover to your mate. Every time you would normally criticize your mate about something, or ask him to go to church with you, or pray with you, stop yourself and instead give him a kiss, or say, "I love you," or buy him a small token of your affection, or write him a love note, or make love to him, or cheerfully do that chore he hates to do — even if it takes you twice as long and means learning an entirely new skill. If you do this with the right spirit, your mate is eventually going to ask you why you're being so nice to him. When he does, simply say, "Because every time I pray, I find out how much more God loves you, and I have to love you that much more too. I'm just sorry it took me so long to figure out how special you really are." Then give him a kiss and walk away.

This is true evangelism. Every day your spouse will see the face of

Christ shining through you and he will be knocked off his feet by love, just as Paul was. This approach of ministering to your mate may best be summarized by St. Francis, who once said to his disciples, "Go out and preach the Gospel. Use words if you must."

3. Pray.

Being Christ to your mate is hard work, and you will be unable to do it without some powerful help from the Holy Spirit. God will give you his grace, but you must ask for it every second of every day. When you pray, first ask that the Lord would change you. Ask that you would learn to be a powerful witness to your mate, inviting him to Christ without even having to say a word. Second, pray that the Lord would use others and the circumstances of your mate's life to reveal himself in an unmistakable way. Finally, and only after you have first prayed for these other graces, pray for your mate. Pray that the Lord would help him be open to all the love that is being poured out.

I believe it is absolutely essential that you pray in this order to avoid the fate of one woman I knew who — sad to say — was one of the coldest, most shrewish, and most spiteful people I have ever met. After telling me — in front of her husband — what an incompetent, unsupportive, thickheaded man she was married to, she finished her litany with, "I have prayed so many novenas and said so many Rosaries for my husband's conversion! I just don't know what else to do. I guess God is just going to have to zap him one day."

Get help when you pray. Ask St. Monica to intercede for you. She's an expert at converting pagan family members. Though it took fifteen years, her son, St. Augustine, eventually left a life of debauchery to become a great saint and Doctor of the Church.

Likewise, meditate on the following Scriptures: 1 Corinthians 7:13-14, 1 Peter 3:1-2, and Luke 6:27-49 (especially verse 41). One final caution: If you seek others for prayer support, limit yourself to partners of the same gender. I have seen too many affairs start "accidentally" by having too many clandestine meetings with a sympathetic prayer partner of the opposite sex. Trust me, these relationships are never God's will for your life and marriage.

The key to converting your mate is as simple and as hard as loving him as Christ would love him. Ask God for the courage to be the spouse you are called to be. Then, as St. Francis told his followers, go and preach the Gospel to your mate — using words only when absolutely necessary.

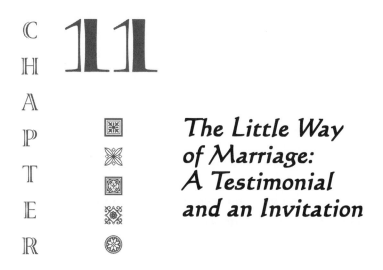

11

The Little Way of Marriage: A Testimonial and an Invitation

> It is, no doubt, impossible to prevent his praying for . . . [her],
> but we have means of rendering the prayers innocuous. Make sure
> that they are always very "spiritual," that he is always concerned
> with the state of her soul and never with her rheumatism. . . .
>
> — *C. S. Lewis*
> The demon Screwtape to his nephew,
> Wormwood, in *The Screwtape Letters*

If you've stayed with me this far, I wish to both thank you for your patience and beg your indulgence a bit longer. I need to make one final point that I believe to be the most important in the book. It is about marriage's power to transform your prayer life. But to make this point, I need to tell you a little bit about myself.

My prayer life has changed radically over the last several years, and marriage has had everything to do with that. I am a cradle Catholic who literally grew up in the Charismatic Renewal (I was born the year the Renewal started, in the shadow of Duquesne University, where it all began). I was faithfully attending prayer meetings with my parents at the age of five. By the time I was eight, shortly before my First Confession, I was "baptized in the Spirit." This experience had an indescribably positive effect on me. It empowered me to have an emotionally profound and deeply personal connection with each sacrament from the first time I encountered them, all the way to the present. I still remember my First Confession. Having been absolved of an eight-year-old's sins, I was so overwhelmed at the thought of my soul being "washed clean" (as Sister

James said it would be) that I burst into tears and couldn't stop sobbing for God only knows how long. The poor priest didn't know what to do with me. Needless to say, I was quite a sight coming out of the confessional.

Besides my connection to the sacraments, I have always loved being in the Real Presence of the Lord. From second grade through college, I spent almost every lunch break sitting in the church at my school, thinking, praying, and talking to Jesus in the Blessed Sacrament. I look back fondly on those quiet times spent in dark, empty churches. I related to Jesus as my "best friend," and the Lord and I grew very close over those years. This closeness, as well as my love for Perpetual Eucharistic Adoration, has continued into my adulthood.

But in spite of all the spiritual opportunities afforded me, I always experienced prayer as something I *did*. Prayer (especially the Rosary), Mass, the sacraments, and Perpetual Eucharistic Adoration — these were all things I was actively involved in and drew comfort from so that I could go out into "the world" refreshed and prepared to take my lumps. Over the last several years, however, my marriage has enabled prayer to become less something I *do* and more something I *am*. I realize how pretentious this might sound; but please understand, I am not making claims to any exalted spiritual state. I simply mean that I am beginning to understand how to use my *life* and marriage as a prayer; how to find God, and spiritual growth, in the "little things," the daily activities, sacrifices, and challenges that are part and parcel of my vocation of husband and father.

My work schedule and family commitments prevent me from praying and meditating like I used to. Not so long ago I felt guilty about this, but then I had a realization. At this point in my life, I reap even greater spiritual benefits by getting off the couch and playing with my children when I am tired, finding more ways to be a better servant to my wife, and working to trust God's providence in my family's finances. I have found that daily working to become a better husband and father is the best spiritual exercise I can do. I am learning to identify more closely with the fatherly love of God, the sacrificial love of Jesus Christ, and the transformative love of the Holy Spirit. Rather than always feeling as if I must travel *to* church to be with God, I am learning to appreciate the presence of God in my "domestic church": my family. The things that used to be the main dishes in my spiritual banquet (the Rosary, Perpetual Eucharistic Adoration, long periods of meditation, retreats, and the like) have now become wonderful side dishes I take advantage of as I can. The meat of my spiritual life today is learning to use the nourishment I receive

220

through the Eucharist to live out more fully the sacrament of my marriage. Every day I work to give more of myself to my wife and children in an attempt to grow in my understanding of God's selfless giving to me.

I probably could *make* more time for formal prayer; but this would be at the expense of time I spend serving my family, whom I believe God has called me to spend my days loving and serving. In this season of my life, if I do not make myself abundantly present to my children, how will they ever learn to appreciate the eternal presence of their heavenly Father? How will my wife learn how special she is to God unless I make the daily effort to show her how special she is to me? I am, after all, the husband *God* gave to her. I don't ever want the Lord to look at my relationship with my wife and say to himself, "Some gift *this* guy turned out to be."

Right now, taking time away from my family for "formal prayer and meditation" would make me a little too much like the Levite in the parable of the Good Samaritan who was in such a hurry probably to get to the synagogue that he couldn't serve the man God placed in his path. At this point in my life it would be too easy for me to use church and "formal devotions" as an escape, an opportunity to avoid the sacrificial love and service God requires me to give to my family. Someday I will return to those long prayer times and other devotions, and as they mature, I will share these jewels with my children. But until that time I will be happy to learn to appreciate God's presence in the service I give to my family. I will continue to offer up my frustrations and setbacks, and I will seek to hear his voice speaking to me in the events of everyday life.

I believe very strongly that God gave me the wife and children I have because loving and serving them is my best hope for becoming the man God wants me to be. They are my best hope for arriving, properly attired, at the heavenly banquet. I hope to be theirs as well. But I am still far from becoming the husband and father God calls me to be, the husband and father my family needs me to be, the husband and father Christ himself would be. And so, this is how I pray now. Today, and every day for the foreseeable future, I ask that God would help me give more of myself — and his love — to the family he has entrusted to my care. I ask him to help me give more of myself to them so that I might better understand the gift he is to me.

If all you got from this book was a handful of techniques you can use to make your life and marriage a little more easygoing, then I have failed you. More than presenting interesting information, practical techniques, or anything else, I have had as my real purpose all along to suggest how you might turn your everyday married life into a prayer, because whether you realize it or not, everything you do in the context of your sacramental marriage — from your work and other roles, to the little pecks on the cheek you give each other, to your getting off the couch when you're tired in order to play with or serve your family, to the arguments you have, to your lovemaking — *is prayer.* Marriage is perhaps the most beautiful prayer in the world. It is a prayer that was written by God at the beginning of time. It is the prayer our first parents spoke with their mouths, souls, minds, and bodies in order to most completely glorify God and actively participate in his creating and sustaining love. Marriage is a powerful reality. It is like the "pearl of great price" (cf. Mt 13:45-46) buried in your own back yard. It is one of the most profound ways God is reaching out to you, calling you to him, deepening your appreciation of his love for you, and preparing you to spend eternity in his holy presence. Please, don't ever take it for granted.

PARABLE OF THE GENEROUS MAN

There was once a kind and generous man. He attended church faithfully. He ran a successful business. He gave generously both to charitable causes and to the poor and homeless he met on the street. His pastor praised him because he always took the hours no one else wanted at Perpetual Eucharistic Adoration. His community praised him for being such a wonderful civic leader. He was a great witness because everywhere he went he brought his rosary. When he would have a few minutes, people would see him quietly praying in the back corner of the room. He felt full of the Spirit. He defended the faith. His wife and children admired him. Everyone said he was a good man.

One day, this generous man died. He was surrounded by a beautiful light and warmth, but also filled with a strange sadness. Standing before him was Christ — a vision more awesome, tender, and fierce than the man could have ever imagined. But when the Lord looked into the man's eyes, a tear rolled down Christ's cheek.

"Why are you crying, Lord?" asked the man.

The Lord said nothing, but pointed to something the man hadn't noticed before. There was a small group of people huddled in the darkness behind him. The man walked over to the people, and then stopped. He couldn't go any further. The sight sickened him. There, at his feet, were the emaciated forms of his wife and children. They were alive, but barely. Terrified, the man cried out, "Lord, what happened to them?"

"You are looking at the souls of your wife and children. They are starving for me. You did not show them how to find me while you were with them. Now, they don't know where to look."

"But, Lord," stammered the man, "how can you say that I didn't show them how to find you? I led scores of people to you. I donated money. I served my community. I gave my time and effort to the Church and a hundred other worthy causes."

The Lord just shook his head, saying, "Oh, child. Do you still not understand? Your family admired you, but they never knew you well enough to love you, much less see me in you. You gave to others so that you could avoid giving to the ones I gave to you."

Whatever your prayer life is like, whatever spiritual exercises you are currently practicing, I invite you to pray your marriage as well. Every time you give more love than you think your spouse deserves, you are being Christ to your mate, and you have a better chance of understanding what it is like for Christ to love you. Every time you make yourself vulnerable by giving more to your family than to your own comfort, work schedule, and other "priorities," you join your suffering to the Lord's. Every time you serve the members of your family, you show them the generous face of God. Every time you sweep your mate off her feet, you demonstrate God's own passion for your beloved; and every time you bring a smile to your partner's face, you are giving her one more reason to praise the God who gave you to her. Saints are transparent. Their love and service always lead their admirers to God, who shines through them. Be a saint to your spouse and children. Let the Lord shine through the loving, generous service you give — joyfully — every day. Pray your marriage, and let God's grace transform you and your loved ones through that living prayer.

May the Lord bless us and keep us.
May the Lord make his face to shine upon us.
May the Lord grant us pardon and peace,
All the days of our lives.
Amen.

— Traditional blessing based on Numbers 6:24-26

Marriage: An Owner's Manual

Cars, boats, homes, gardens — all have them. In fact, just about every valuable thing has them. Why don't marriages have maintenance schedules? Most people know how often they have to change their oil, till their garden, rotate their tires, replace their furnace screens, etc. But do you know how often to oil your marriage? This "owner's manual," dear reader, is offered as a guide for the regular care and feeding of your marriage. Simply follow the schedule below for a well-maintained relationship.

Regular Marriage Maintenance

Do the following as indicated.

Every Day . . .

1. Pray. Ask God to help you become the lover he would be to your spouse.

2. Ask yourself, "What can I do to make my spouse's life a little easier today?" Then do it.

3. Find small ways to demonstrate affection. Catch your mate being good. Be generous with kisses, hugs, compliments, and calls from the office.

4. Take some time to talk with your spouse. Catch up on the news. Solve today's problems. Address issues with the children. Discuss plans for the future.

Every Week . . .

1. Attend Mass together at least once a week. Make sure your kids come with you.

2. Are you and your mate getting fifteen hours a week together to talk, work together, and rekindle the romance? What changes do you need to make in your schedule to make sure you get your fifteen hours next week?

3. Review your *Twenty-five Ways to Make Love Stay — Every Day* list. Are you keeping up? What new loving actions should you add?

Every Month . . .

1. Assuming your children are developmentally ready or physically healthy enough, leave them at home so that the two of you can go out as

a couple at least once per month. If you can't go out, make time for "couple time" at home. Set the kids up with a video, or even have the sitter come to your house while you and your mate enjoy a piece of pie and grown-up conversation over candlelight in the dining room.

Every Three Months . . .

1. Review problem solving in Chapter 8. How are you doing? What skills do you still need to develop and/or practice? How, specifically, will you develop those skills?

Every Six Months . . .

1. Ask your mate how you could be an even better spouse to her. Receive any criticism graciously, give criticism kindly, and act on the discussion.

2. Read a book together on some aspect of marriage and/or family life.

Once a Year . . .

1. Go on a retreat together. Do a marriage encounter weekend or some other marriage enrichment program. Or spend a whole day in a favorite park or other place with your spouse and children, playing, praying, and discerning what God has in store for you and your family in the coming year.

Following these recommendations will help you assure the continued growth and health of your marriage.

Emergency Maintenance

Sometimes certain problems occur that require your taking your marriage into the "repair shop." Yes, it can be expensive; and yes, it is always a pain; but keeping a marriage in good working order sometimes requires some professional assistance. How can you tell when it's time for a checkup?

Counseling is automatically indicated if . . .

✔ Your arguments are becoming physical.

✔ Many of your arguments occur while one or the other of you is drunk or high. Or, many of your arguments are over drinking and/or drug use.

✔ You are fantasizing about having an affair.

✔ You are spending more and more time with a friend of the opposite sex who you feel understands you better than your mate (even if your intentions are pure).

✔ You or your mate seems to be avoiding the other.

✔ When you look at your mate, you get a sinking feeling in your gut, or become angry and/or irritable for no good reason.

Not every issue is cause for counseling, but some other issues may warrant immediate attention or special interventions. Take the following quiz to see if you are due for a marital tune-up. Mark each statement T or F.

___ My mate and I keep having the same arguments over and over.

___ I often feel picked on by my mate.

___ I often feel disappointed in or let down by my mate.

___ I wonder if my spouse really loves me.

___ I feel that my mate is a controlling person.

___ I think our arguments get out of control.

___ I wonder if I married the right person.

___ I intentionally avoid spending time with my mate.

___ I feel that my mate doesn't understand me.

___ I often think negatively about my mate.

SCORING

0-1 • No special maintenance required. Follow regular maintenance schedule as described above.

2-4 • I recommend taking a marriage enrichment course (see Appendix 3). Also, read some books on marriage and family issues and review some of the exercises in this work, especially *Twenty-five Ways to Make Love Stay — Every Day* (Chapter 4).

5+ • I would recommend considering some counseling. Don't wait until the cancer is inoperable. Get help now while things aren't too bad. See Appendices 2 and 3 for referral resources.

Appendix 2
Pastoral Solutions

(This appendix is gleaned from material in *Building a Civilization of Love in the Third Millennium,* available from the Pastoral Solutions Institute, 234 St. Joseph Dr., Steubenville, OH 43952; telephone 740-266-6461. Except for minor changes to ensure stylistic consistency, the text remains basically the same as in the original.)

Mission: The Pastoral Solutions Institute seeks to give married couples, pastors, family-life ministers, and other helping professionals cutting-edge information on marriage preparation, marriage enrichment, parenting, and pastoral counseling. The Institute supports families, pastors, and parishes in the following ways.

A. Services to Married Couples and Parishes

1. RETREATS AND TRIPS

Join us in Steubenville or on vacations and/or retreats around the world. Relax your bodies, refresh your spirits, and renew your marriages as you learn how to supercharge your marital intimacy, communication, and spirituality in an atmosphere of fun and fellowship. Meet and worship with others who, like yourself, take their Christian marriages and family lives seriously. Here are some sample topics.

The Secrets of Exceptional Christian Marriage • Whether you are engaged, or have been married fifty years, you will discover how to turn your relationship into a *powerful partnership* that fulfills you and your mate's identities in Christ. Experience the blessing that comes from learning *firsthand* how to discern God's plan for your life, truly understand your mate, develop a deep marital spirituality, discover loving problem-solving skills, and experience a passionately spiritual sexuality that pagans can only dream about.

Raising^Perfect Kids: Christian Parenting for the Third Millennium
(Almost)
• We are called to raise perfect kids. That is, kids who are perfect — in love. Learn the loving, effective, practical techniques and parenting attitudes that build character, love, empathy, and Christian altruism in your children. This is based on solid psychological, medical, and sociological research, and equally solid Christian teaching. Turn parenting into a prayer. A must for any Christian who takes his or her parenting seriously.

Other Topics in Development • Call for information on all our seminars and retreats.

2. Parish-Based Retreats, Educational Programs, and Seminars

If you can't come to us, we can come to your parish, deanery, or diocese in one of two ways:

a. The For Better . . . Forever! Parish-Based Marriage Enrichment Program

The Pastoral Solutions Institute proudly unveils its parish-based, marriage-enrichment program. To our knowledge, nothing like it exists anywhere in the Church. Couples meet monthly to learn about and discuss such issues as married spirituality, problem solving, sexuality, and many others. Meetings follow a format that involves catechesis, case studies, and discussions with an emphasis on the practical. Step-by-step meeting outlines are included in the leader's guide. The package includes a copy of the leader's guide, workbooks, case studies, take-home marriage-enrichment exercises, opportunities for greater fellowship and parish involvement, and suggested readings.

b. We Can Meet Your Needs

The Pastoral Solutions Institute is happy to design and conduct seminars or retreats tailored to the needs of your parish, deanery, or diocese. Let us know your needs, and we'll tell you how we can help.

3. Telephone Counseling and Referrals

Yours truly — Gregory Popcak, MSW, LCSW — conducts an active caseload of short-term telephone counseling clients. He has been consulted by couples and families from Hong Kong to North Pole, Alaska (yes, there is such a town). And everywhere in between. Call 740-266-6461 to ask how he might help you either directly or with a referral to a marriage-friendly Christian counselor in your area.

B. Services to Pastors and Other Helping Professionals

1. PAX (Pastoral Assessment and Intervention Screen)

A Groundbreaking Relationship Assessment Tool • The premarital assessment tools that measure compatibility are virtually useless. Just because a couple may be "compatible" does not mean the partners are healthy or even capable of sustaining a marriage. Too often, pastors report that "compatible" means "both are crazy and/or immature in the same way."

The Pastoral Solutions Institute has developed a truly meaningful assessment tool for couples. PAX is helpful in four ways: (1) It identifies the relationship type a couple exhibits and the unique challenges couples in this type of relationship will face in the first five years. (2) It identifies at-risk couples who have similar demographics to couples whose marriages often end before ten years. (3) Following assessment, PAX recommends exercises, discussion questions, and assignments specifically designed to address the weaknesses of each marital type. (4) It can be used with engaged couples as a preparation tool or with married couples to help them focus their pastoral counseling efforts.

We do not feel we are overstating that PAX is the pastoral marriage assessment tool of the next millennium. Call for more information.

2. Sharpen Your Helping Skills

The Pastoral Solutions Institute offers a series of two-to-three-day training seminars for pastors, family life ministers, and other helping professionals. Currently, we are offering the following.

Building First-and-Forever Marriages: Assessing and Intervening with At-Risk Engaged Couples • Focuses on developing a premarital program that will actually make a difference in your parish. How do you identify at-risk couples? How can you guide all of your couples toward both a greater understanding of Christian marriage and deeper intimacy through the years? The program shows you how to build a true support system for every engaged couple who comes to you.

Keeping Couples Together: Christian Solution-Focused Counseling for Pastors • Simple, cutting-edge counseling techniques for pastors on the front lines of keeping couples together. This model of therapy has been statistically demonstrated to be effective within four to six sessions. Practical and powerful interventions any pastor can use. Seminar attendees will learn to use a six-session outline that includes important questions, suggested activities, and other information to help any pastor keep his couples together. Even if you have no counseling training, this seminar will help you make a difference!

Other Seminars in Development • Call for information.

3. Technical Support

Any pastor who attends our seminars is eligible for free professional consultations on difficult marriage and family cases. We are dedicated to helping you support your parish families when they need you most.

We're on a Mission

The Pastoral Solutions Institute wants to play an active role in helping couples, families, and pastors build a true civilization of love in the third millennium. Call today and tell us your needs.

Appendix 3
Where to Turn: Resources for Couples

A Challenge

When you were in high school or college, did you learn everything you needed to know to be successful in your present work or role? Of course not. We never stop learning about things that are truly important to us. What is more important than your marriage? We read business books and seek additional job training all the time. But when was the last time you took a "training course" to learn how to be a more sensitive, loving, understanding, generous, communicative, *Christ-like* spouse? Even if it was yesterday, pick up the phone and call one of the following organizations today. Don't wait until your marriage *needs* serious help. Act now so that it never will.

Your Diocesan Family Life Office • Call the Family Life office of your diocesan chancery to learn about marriage and family enrichment programs, NFP (natural family planning) classes, recommended counselors, and a host of other resources *in your area.* These folks are working hard to help you get the most out of your Christian marriage and family life. Contact them, whatever your needs are, to discover what rich blessings they have to offer you.

Marriage Encounter • Marriage Encounter's history and reputation speak for themselves. I have known couples who have attended over a hundred Marriage Encounter weekends and each time said they learned something new about themselves and each other. What are you doing this weekend? Call your Family Life office for dates and contact people in your area.

Retrouvailles • This French word (pronounced REH-troo-vie) means "rediscover." Essentially, this is Marriage Encounter for couples who need a little more help. Utilizing more intensive seminars and training, plus optional, one-day, once-a-month follow-ups for at least six months, *Retrouvailles* provides both wonderful training and an exceptional support system for couples who are struggling to remain faithful to their vows. Call your Family Life office for dates and people to contact in your area.

PAIRS (or Practical Application of Intimate Relationship Skills) • More skills-based than Marriage Encounter or Retrouvailles, this is also a wonderful resource for couples who are serious about growing in intimacy, understanding, and love. PAIRS is not specifically Christian in its outlook, but some counseling professionals consider it to be more effective than Marriage Encounter in teaching couples important relationship skills. I recommend doing both — often. Call 888-PAIRS-4U.

Couple-to-Couple League • Training and newsletters supporting NFP. Interested in learning more about NFP (or perhaps becoming a teaching couple)? Call 513-471-2000.

Pastoral Solutions Institute • Offering retreats, seminars, and training seminars at our place or yours. Dedicated to serving the needs of Catholic families (see Appendix 2). Call 740-266-6461 for information.

Franciscan University of Steubenville Summer Conference Series • Dedicated to spiritual renewal and evangelization, the Franciscan University of Steubenville hosts a series of very well produced, very well attended summer conferences for Catholic laypeople, as well as priests and deacons. Of special interest to *For Better . . . Forever!* readers are both the Catholic Men's Conference and the Young Adult Conference hosted ever year. Of course these are but two of a host of exceptional events aimed at challenging your mind and refreshing your spirit. Call the university conference office at 740-283-3771 for information on events and locations.

Apostolate for Family Consecration (Catholic Familyland) • On the campus of a former seminary in eastern Ohio, this beautiful multi-acre facility is a center for both family catechesis and family fun. Every year, Catholic Familyland hosts conferences, seminars, and retreats aimed at increasing the Catholic family's love of the faith and each other. There is something for everyone. Adults will benefit from the talks presented by cardinals, bishops, and other Catholic luminaries, and the children will learn and enjoy participating in clown ministry, concerts, pony rides, and water slides. Camping and swimming are also available for the whole family. Call 1-800-FOR-MARY for information on events and other services.

Équipes de Notre Dame (Teams of Our Lady) • Founded in post-World War II France, this international organization helps married couples learn to "pray their marriages." Through regular small-group meetings and simple prayer exercises, married couples support one another in fulfilling the spiritual mission of their marriage. Contact your diocesan Family Life office for information on a local chapter.

Holy Family Institute • "Secular institutes" are opportunities for lay Catholics to take vows of poverty, chastity, and obedience. Members of secular institutes live in their own homes and work wherever they like, but they lead consecrated lives. The Holy Family Institute is currently the only secular institute offering this special status to married couples. Members of the Holy Family Institute belong to the Pauline Order of priests and religious, who are dedicated to evangelization through the media. Call Father Tom Fogarty at St. Paul Monastery, 330-533-5503.

Promise Keepers • Any organization that teaches men to be more generous servants to their wives and children is all right by me. I *would* say this to Catholic men who attend the more evangelical Protestant Promise Keepers. If you want to rededicate yourself to the Lord and become the Catholic husband the Church called you to be in the first place, that's fine. *But,* please remember that you are already "saved" by your baptism and participation in the sacraments. If anyone asks you, "Are you saved, brother?" simply respond, "Not only is Jesus Christ my personal Lord and Savior, but his flesh is one with my flesh and his precious blood courses through my veins. How 'bout you?" Your questioner may just convert on the spot (as well he should). Otherwise, enjoy yourself, and when you come home, lead your fellow *Catholic* men on to greater service. Call 800-888-7595.

Bibliography

Beck, A. *Love Is Never Enough: How Couples Can Overcome Misunderstandings, Resolve Conflicts, and Solve Relationship Problems Through Cognitive Therapy.* New York: HarperCollins, 1989.

Bower, K. "Why Good Catholics Make Better Lovers," *New Covenant,* April 1997.

Cameron-Bandler, L. *Solutions: Practical and Effective Antidotes for Sexual and Relationship Problems,* rev. ed. San Rafael, Calif.: FuturePace, 1989.

Catechism of the Catholic Church. The United States Catholic Conference, Inc.
— Libreria Editrice Vaticana, 1994.

Escrivá de Balaguer, J. *Passionately Loving the World.* Princeton, N.J.: Scepter Publications, Inc., 1975.

Flannery, A., ed. *Vatican Council II: The Conciliar and Post-Conciliar Documents, No. 1.* Collegeville, Minn.: Liturgical Press, 1987.

Gottman, J. *Why Marriages Succeed or Fail. And How You Can Make Yours Last.* New York: Simon and Schuster, 1995.

Hogan, R.; LeVoir, J. *Covenant of Love: Pope John Paul II on Sexuality, Marriage, and Family in the Modern World.* San Francisco: Ignatius Press, 1992.

Lawler, R.; Boyle, J.; May, W. *Catholic Sexual Ethics: A Summary, Explanation, and Defense (Second Edition).* Huntington, Ind.: Our Sunday Visitor, Inc., 1998.

Lederer, W.; Jackson, D. *The Mirages of Marriage.* New York: W. W. Norton and Co., 1990.

Lewis, C. S. *Mere Christianity.* New York: Simon and Schuster, 1943.

_____. *The Great Divorce.* New York: Macmillan, 1946.

_____. *The Magician's Nephew.* New York: Harper Trophy, 1955.

_____. *The Four Loves.* New York: Harcourt Brace, 1960.

_____. *The Screwtape Letters.* New York: Macmillan, 1964.

Lovric, M. *Love Letters: An Anthology of Passion.* New York: Shooting Star Press, 1995.

Madanes, C. "Brief Therapy for Managed Care" (seminar, November 1997). The Family Therapy Center of Maryland, Pittsburgh.

May, W. *Marriage: The Rock on Which the Family Is Built.* San Francisco: Ignatius Press, 1995.

Pope John Paul II. *Original Unity of Man and Woman: Catechesis on the Book of Genesis.* Boston: Daughters of St. Paul, 1981.

_____. "Laborem Exercens: On Human Work," *L'Osservatore Romano* (English ed.), September 21, 1981.

_____. *Familiaris Consortio.* Boston: St. Paul Editions, 1981.

_____. *Letter to Families.* Boston: Pauline Books and Media, 1994.

Pope Paul VI. *Humanae Vitae*. Trans. Marc Calegari. San Francisco: Ignatius Press, 1983.

Reiser, P. *Babyhood*. New York: William Morrow and Co., 1997.

Sandmaier, M. "Love for the Long Haul," *Family Therapy Networker,* September-October 1997.

Schwartz, P. *Peer Marriage*. New York: The Free Press, 1994.

Shaw, R. *Our Sunday Visitor's Encyclopedia of Catholic Doctrine*. Huntington, Ind.: Our Sunday Visitor, Inc., 1997.

Smalley, G. *Hidden Keys of a Loving, Lasting Marriage: A Valuable Guide to Knowing, Understanding, and Loving Each Other*. Grand Rapids, Mich.: Zondervan Publishing House, 1993.

Sullivan, H. *Conceptions of Modern Psychiatry*. New York: W. W. Norton and Co., 1966.

Wallerstein, J.; Blakeslee, S. *The Good Marriage: How and Why Love Lasts*. New York: Warner Books, Inc., 1996.

Way of the Cross, The. Baltimore: Barton-Cotton, Inc., 1965.

Weiner-Davis, M. *Divorce Busting: A Revolutionary and Rapid Program for "Staying Together."* New York: Summit Books, 1992.

Wuerl, D.; Lawler, R.; Lawler, T. *The Teaching of Christ. A Catholic Catechism for Adults,* 3rd ed. Huntington , Ind.: Our Sunday Visitor, Inc., 1991. (Note: The fourth edition, published in 1995, is available from Our Sunday Visitor.)

Index

❖ ❖ ❖

Note: For several reasons and other considerations, this index does not conform to conventional styles. For instance, some entries are lumped together, as in the case of the entries "abuse" and "abusive"; "divorce," "divorced," and "divorces"; and similar instances. Another example of this index's peculiar style would be the combining of most entries whether they are nouns or verbs, singular or plural forms, parts of book titles, and the like. Other arbitrary modifications are self-explanatory.

A

Avoidant, 175, 188
avoiding conflict, 52, 87

B

C

D

depression, 49, 52, 97, 126, 127

dignity, 20, 25, 33, 84, 85, 114, 125, 140, 146, 166, 167, 170, 177, 189, 190, 194, 205, 208, 209, 217

divorce; divorced; divorces, 15, 16, 17, 29, 54, 55, 62, 68, 77, 78, 113, 125, 126, 127, 131, 143, 148, 155, 190, 191, 198, 237, 238

domination, 85

dreams, 21, 22, 36, 40, 49, 50, 51, 55, 61, 98, 101, 110, 122, 124, 125, 126, 129, 130, 141, 145, 152, 178, 185, 186, 204, 209

drug users, 92

E

economic security, 51

ecstasy, 103, 148, 202

egalitarianism, 76, 84, 85, 86, 95

ego integrity, 131, 132

emotional-temperature scale, 186, 187, 188, 189, 196, 197

equality, 59, 60, 65, 79, 81, 84, 86, 91

erotic; eroticism, 200, 204, 205, 206, 207, 210, 212

estrangement, 23, 24, 48, 49, 62, 72, 123

eternal life, 203

eternity, 20, 27, 74, 203, 211, 213, 222

Eucharist, 202, 221

Eve, 22, 23, 24, 26, 177, 178, 203, 211, 213

Exceptional; Exceptional Marriages; Exceptional Seven Percent, 15, 16, 61, 70, 72, 74, 76, 77, 78, 87, 88, 89, 90, 91, 92, 93, 96, 107, 112, 113, 123, 142, 149, 174, 177, 210, 229, 233, 234

F

fair fighting — *see under* fighting

faith, 11, 17, 21, 35, 50, 60, 69, 73, 200, 201, 204, 216, 217, 222, 234

family life, 16, 54, 70, 84, 93, 115, 204, 226, 231, 233, 234

fatherhood, 29, 211

femininity, 24, 26, 85

feminists, 50, 200

G

H

I

J

N

O

ℙ

S

T

U

V

W

Our Sunday Visitor...
Your Source for Discovering the Riches of the Catholic Faith

Our Sunday Visitor has an extensive line of materials for young children, teens, and adults. Our books, Bibles, booklets, CD-ROMs, audios, and videos are available in bookstores worldwide.

To receive a FREE full-line catalog or for more information, call **Our Sunday Visitor** at **1-800-348-2440**. Or write, **Our Sunday Visitor /** 200 Noll Plaza / Huntington, IN 46750.

Please send me: __ A catalog
Please send me materials on:
    __ Apologetics and catechetics   __ Reference works
    __ Prayer books   __ Heritage and the saints
    __ The family   __ The parish

Name_____

Address_____Apt._____

City_____State ____Zip_____

Telephone (   ) _____

                                                         A93BBABP

Please send a friend: __ A catalog
Please send a friend materials on:
    __ Apologetics and catechetics   __ Reference works
    __ Prayer books   __ Heritage and the saints
    __ The family   __ The parish

Name_____

Address_____Apt._____

City_____State ____Zip_____

Telephone (   ) _____

                                                         A93BBABP

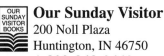

Our Sunday Visitor
200 Noll Plaza
Huntington, IN 46750
1-800-348-2440
osvbooks@osv.com

Your Source for Discovering the Riches of the Catholic Faith